Get the Picture

Get the

Random House
New York

A Personal History of
Photojournalism

Picture

John G. Morris

Front pages of *The Washington Post* (pp. 214–18):
Library of Congress/Courtesy, *The Washington Post*.

Library of Congress Cataloging-in-Publication Data
Morris, John G. (John Godfrey)
   Get the picture: a personal history of photojournalism/
John G. Morris.
     p.   cm.
   Includes index.
   ISBN 0-679-45258-3 (alk. paper)
   1. Morris, John G. (John Godfrey)   2. News photographers—United
States—Biography.   3. News photographers—History.
4. Photojournalism—History.   I. Title.
TR140.M595M67   1998
070.4'9'092—dc21
[B]   97-316

Random House website address: www.randomhouse.com
Printed in the United States of America on acid-free paper
9 8 7 6 5 4 3 2
First Edition

Frontispiece: David E. Scherman dressed for war, London, 1942.
Lee Miller/© Lee Miller Archives

Book design by Tanya M. Pérez-Rock

To Dèle and Midge;
to our children, Holly,
John, Chris, Kirk, and Oliver;
and to T'ana, without whom
there would be no book

Contents

Get the Picture

Omaha Beach, June 6, 1944: one of the eleven D-Day images by Robert Capa that survived *Life's* London darkroom accident. Fifty years later the soldier was identified as Edward Regan of Atlanta, Georgia. *Copyright © 1998 Estate of Robert Capa*

Tuesday Was a Good
D-Day for *Life*

Something woke me early on the morning of Tuesday, June 6, 1944. I drew the blackout curtain and saw that it was just another dull, gray day, colder than an English spring had any right to be. The streets were empty, and I was alone in the flat I shared with Frank Scherschel on Upper Wimpole Street in London's West End. He had departed—vanished, actually, without saying a word—several days earlier for his battle station, a camouflaged airfield from which he would fly reconnaissance over the English Channel to photograph the largest armada ever assembled. My job was to stay behind, to edit those and other photos for *Life* as picture editor of the London bureau.

I dressed as usual in olive drab, turned on the radio, made tea and read the papers, which of course had nothing to report. Then, at 8:32 London time, the bulletin came over the BBC: "Under command of General Eisenhower, Allied naval forces, supported by strong Allied air forces, began landing Allied armies this morning on the northern coast of France." "This is it," I whispered to myself, uttering the very words that Joe Liebling of *The New Yorker* later called "the great cliché of the Second World War." I hurried to the *Time/Life* office in Soho, even though there wouldn't be much for me to do—for many hours, as it turned out.

I had been waiting eight months for this day. There had been a false alarm on Saturday, when a young telegrapher in the Associated Press London bureau, practicing to get up her speed, had put out an erroneous bulletin: URGENT PRESS ASSOCIATED NYK FLASH EISENHOWER'S HQ ANNOUNCED ALLIED LANDINGS IN FRANCE. It had been corrected within a minute—"Bust that flash"—but it had sent a wave of panic through both Allied and German headquarters. Now it was for real. Tuesday was a good D-Day for *Life.* Our job was to furnish action pictures for the next issue, dated June 19, which would close on Saturday in New York, and appear the following week. Wirephotos, of poor quality and limited selection, would not do; besides, they would be available to newspapers through the pool. Our only hope to meet the deadline was to send original prints and negatives, as many as possible, in a pouch that would leave Grosvenor Square by motorcycle courier at precisely 9:00 A.M. London time on Thursday. The courier would take it to a twin-engine plane standing by at an airdrome near London. At Prestwick, Scotland, the base for transatlantic flights, the pouch would be transferred to a larger plane. After one or two fuel stops, it would arrive in Washington, D.C., and our pictures would be hand-carried to New York on Saturday.

I had rehearsed my part in every detail, from the moment the raw film arrived in London to the transfer of prints and negatives to the courier who would take them to the States—with a stop at the censor's office in between. Clearing the censors at the Ministry of Information was by now a familiar routine. Their office was on the ground floor of the University of London's tall central building, which backed onto Bedford Square. Available twenty-four hours a day, the censors were cooperative, as censors go, permitting us to sit alongside them as they worked. Our photographers knew to avoid the faces of Allied dead, shoulder patches that revealed unit designations, and "secret" weapons (although by now most were known to the enemy)—so the work was for the most part pro forma. But it was tedious in the extreme, since every single print had to be stamped, after which the censor bundled all the acceptable material into an envelope and sealed it, using a special tape imprinted with the words PASSED FOR PUBLICATION. Without the tape, it could not leave the country.

Getting the packet by car to the courier at Grosvenor Square, about a mile from the ministry, looked simple on the map, but the most direct way, down Oxford Street, was often jammed with double-decker buses, so I devised a parallel route on a series of side streets: Hollen to Noel to Great Marlborough to Hanover to Brook (I can remember every turn five decades later). This put me onto the wrong side of Grosvenor Square, but the final fifty yards could be covered on foot—while running at top speed. I left the little two-door Austin sedan Time Inc. had given me to its own fate. It was not uncommon for joyriders to take it out for a spin when I worked late, but that was no problem. A call to Scotland Yard was all that was necessary. The car would invariably be found as soon as the thief ran out of what little petrol was in the tank.

For the Normandy invasion, there were twelve photographers accredited for the wire services and six for *Life*. Only four press photographers were supposed to land with the first wave of American infantry on D-Day itself, and we managed to get two of the spots, for Bob Landry and Robert Capa. Both were veterans—Capa would be on the fifth front of his third major war. Although often unlucky at cards and horses, Capa nevertheless used a gambling metaphor to describe his situation on D-Day in his 1947 memoir-novel, *Slightly Out of Focus:* "The war correspondent has his stake—his life—in his own hands, and he can put it on this horse or that horse, or he can put it back in his pocket at the very last minute. . . . I am a gambler. I decided to go in with Company E in the first wave."

Bob Landry also felt obliged to accept this dubious privilege. The other *Life* assignments sorted themselves out. Frank Scherschel stuck with his buddies in the Air Force. David Scherman chose the Navy. George Rodger accompanied the British forces, under General Bernard Montgomery. Ralph Morse's assignment was General George Patton's Third Army, but since it would not hit the beachhead until later, he boarded a landing ship whose job it was to pick up casualties—of which there would be plenty.

Who would get the first picture? Bad weather prevented good general views from either air (Scherschel) or sea (Scherman). Rodger, landing with the

Life's D-Day photographers posed in London's Grosvenor Square a week or so before the invasion of Normandy. *Top row, left to right:* Bob Landry, George Rodger, Frank Scherschel, Robert Capa. *Bottom:* Ralph Morse and David E. Scherman flank me (*center*), their editor. Life *Magazine* © *Time Inc.*

British on an undefended beach, "walked ashore in a blaze of anti-climax," as he put it in typically modest understatement. All day Tuesday we waited, and no pictures. It was rumored that one Signal Corps photographer had been killed in the first hours, but it turned out that he had "only" lost a leg. Late on Tuesday night Bert Brandt of Acme Newspictures, having scarcely gotten his feet wet, returned to London with a *first picture!*, but not a terribly exciting one, of a momentarily unopposed landing on the French coast, shot from the bow of his landing craft. Landry's film—and his shoes—somehow got lost. A disaster. I had been told that AP would have the fourth first-wave spot, but not one of their six photographers landed that day. So it was entirely up to Capa to capture the action, and *where was he?* Hour after hour went by. We were now waiting in the gloom of Wednesday, June 7, keeping busy by packaging the "background pictures," all of relatively little interest, that now flooded in from official sources. The darkroom staff—all five of them—had been standing by idly since Tuesday morning, their anxiety about the pressure they would be under growing steadily by the hour. This nervousness would soon result in an epic blunder.

At about 6:30 Wednesday evening, the call came in from a Channel port: Capa's film was on the way. "You should get it in an hour or two," a voice crackled over the line before fading into static. I shared this information with pool editor E. K. Butler of AP, a feisty little martinet whose nickname was "Colonel." He snapped back, "All I want is *pictures*, not promises!" Around nine, a panting messenger arrived with Capa's little package: four rolls of 35-millimeter film plus half a dozen rolls of 120 film (2¼ by 2¼ inches) that he had taken in England and on the Channel crossing. A scrawled note said that the action was all in the 35-millimeter, that things had been very rough, that he had come back to England unintentionally with wounded being evacuated, and that he was on his way back to Normandy.

Braddy, our lab chief, gave the film to young Dennis Banks to develop. Photographer Hans Wild looked at it wet and called up to me to say that the 35-millimeter, though grainy, looked "fabulous!" I replied, "We need *contacts*— rush, rush, *rush!*" Again I phoned Butler through the AP switchboard, but he could only bellow, "When do I get *pictures?*" Brandt's wirephoto of troops landing apparently unopposed had scarcely satisfied the West's desperate need to believe in the actuality of invasion.

A few minutes later Dennis came bounding up the stairs and into my office, sobbing. "They're ruined! Ruined! Capa's films are all *ruined!*" Incredulous, I rushed down to the darkroom with him, where he explained that he had hung the films, as usual, in the wooden locker that served as a drying cabinet, heated by a coil on the floor. Because of my order to rush, he had closed the doors. Without ventilation the emulsion had melted.

I held up the four rolls, one at a time.

Three were hopeless; nothing to see. But on the fourth roll there were eleven frames with distinct images. They were probably representative of the entire 35-millimeter take, but their grainy imperfection—perhaps enhanced by the lab accident—contributed to making them among the most dramatic battlefield photos ever taken. The sequence began as Capa waded through the surf with the infantry, past antitank obstacles that soon became tombstones as men fell left and right. This was it, all right. D-Day would forever be known by these pictures.

One more ordeal lay ahead. We now had only a few hours to get our picture packet through the censors, and in addition to Capa's we had hundreds of other photos, the best from Dave Scherman of matters just before the landing. The British and Canadians had covered invasion preparations for days, as had the U.S. Army Signal Corps and the Navy and Air Force photographers. Nobody really cared now about such pictures, but we dutifully sent them on.

At 3:30 on Thursday morning, pictures in hand—including Capa's precious eleven—I drove my Austin through deserted streets to the Ministry of Information, where I had to wait my turn. Ours was the largest picture shipment of the week, and I almost wished I could throw all but the Capa shots overboard in the interest of time. Finally, about 8:30, the censor finished putting his stamp on all the pictures. I stuffed the big envelope, and then it happened. The censor's specially imprinted tape stuck fast to its roll. It simply would not peel off. We tried another roll. Same result. This went on for minutes that seemed hours, and I had to deliver the packet to the courier, a mile away, by nine o'clock—our only chance to make the deadline after eight months!

I left the ministry at about 8:45 and drove like a maniac through the scattered morning traffic, down the little side streets, reaching the edge of Grosvenor Square at 8:59. I ran the last fifty yards and found the courier, in the basement of the Service of Supply headquarters, about to padlock his sack. "Hold it!" I shouted, and he did.

Just after *Life*'s Saturday-night close, the editors cabled, TODAY WAS ONE OF THE GREAT PICTURE DAYS IN LIFE'S OFFICE, WHEN BOB CAPA'S BEACHLANDING AND OTHER SHOTS ARRIVED. I could only think of the pictures *lost*. How was I going to face Capa?

I am a journalist but not a reporter and not a photographer. I am a picture editor. I have worked with photographers, some of them famous, others unknown, for more than fifty years. I have sent them out on assignment, sometimes with a few casual suggestions, other times with detailed instructions, but always the challenge is the same: *Get the picture.* I've accompanied photographers on countless stories; I've carried their equipment and held their lights, pointed them in the right direction if they needed pointing. I've seconded their alibis when things went badly and celebrated with them when

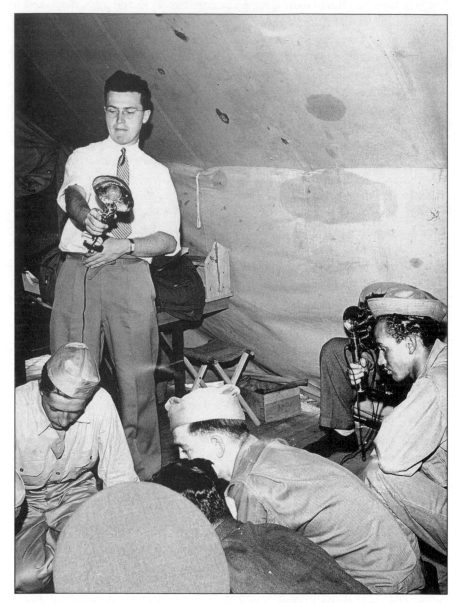

Holding the side flash—one of the many duties of the professional picture editor. Johnny Florea (*far right*) is handling the camera for a *Life* magazine story that never saw print. Consoling photographers whose work has been cut is another duty. *John G. Morris Collection*

things went well. I have bought and sold their pictures for what must total millions of dollars. I have hired scores of photographers, and, sadly, I've had to fire a few. I've testified for them in court, nursed them through injury and illness, saved them from eviction, fed them, buried them. I have accompanied unwed photographers to the marriage license bureau as their witness. Now I am married to one.

Photographers are the most adventurous of journalists. They have to be. Unlike a reporter, who can piece together a story from a certain distance, a photographer must get to the scene of the action, whatever danger or discomfort that implies. A long lens may bring his subject closer, but nothing must stand between him and reality. He must absolutely be in the right place at the right time. No rewrite desk will save him. He must show it as it is. His editor chooses among those pictures to tell it as it was—or was it? Right or wrong, the picture is the last word.

Thus the serious photojournalist becomes a professional voyeur. Often he hates himself for it. In 1936, Bob Capa made a picture of a Spanish Republican soldier, caught in the moment of death. It is one of the most controversial images of the twentieth century. Capa came to hate it, for reasons I will examine later. Don McCullin, the great English photographer who has covered conflict on four continents, says simply, "I try to eradicate the past." He is speaking of how he must deal with what he has seen, because, in fact, he has done his best to preserve the past. And Eddie Adams, whose Pulitzer Prize–winning 1968 photograph of the execution of a Vietcong prisoner by Saigon's chief of police is a kind of ghastly updating of Capa's image, says only, in his trademark staccato, "I don't wanna talk about it."

The picture editor is the voyeurs' voyeur, the person who sees what the photographers themselves seen but in the bloodless realm of contact sheets, proof prints, yellow boxes of slides, and now pixels on the screen. Picture editors find the representative picture, *the* image, that will be seen by others, perhaps around the world. They are the unwitting (or witting, as the case may be) tastemakers, the unappointed guardians of morality, the talent brokers, the accomplices to celebrity. Most important—or disturbing—they are the fixers of "reality" and of "history."

This book deals with professional picture people, but it concerns all of us who consume images. It is a book about a life lived with pictures and with the men and women who took them. Inevitably, it is also my highly personal perception of our times.

My mentor Robert Maynard Hutchins, president of the University of Chicago. He disdained the notion of a school of journalism and argued that the best journalistic education came from working in the field. I took his advice. MYRON DAVIS/Life *Magazine* © *Time Inc.*

Henry R. Luce, who with Briton Hadden founded Time Inc., was a "word man," more comfortable with editing *Time* or *Fortune* than *Life*. He nevertheless liked to browse through pictures, to the dismay of his *Life* colleagues. PETER STACKPOLE/Life *Magazine* © *Time Inc.*

2

My *Life* Begins

On a blustery March day in 1938, I appeared at the reception desk of Time Inc., high in the Chrysler Building on East Forty-second Street in New York. I was twenty-one, a recent graduate of the University of Chicago. My sister had advised me to buy a hat for the occasion, but I felt self-conscious enough as it was. Also, I didn't have an appointment. "I'm John Morris," I announced to the lone receptionist, "and I've come to see Mr. Luce." Henry Robinson Luce, founder of *Time, Fortune,* and *Life,* was the most sought-after magazine editor and publisher in America. I had a better chance of getting in to see President Roosevelt and might have been shown the exit for such brashness. Instead, I was sent to Personnel on the strength of a letter of introduction to Luce from his Yale schoolmate and my mentor Robert Maynard Hutchins, president of the University of Chicago.

Hutchins had been appointed in 1929, at the astonishing age of thirty. He had already served as dean of the Yale Law School—an appointment that had begun only two years after his own graduation from the law school. In 1929, as Hutchins began his twenty-one-year reign at the university, I entered "U-High," the university's "laboratory" high school. In the fall of 1932, at fifteen, I became one of the first six U-High seniors to experimentally enroll in college courses. It was then that I first thought of journalism as a career. The university had no school of journalism, and Hutchins wasn't about to create one. "Journalism as such has no intellectual content in its own right," Hutchins had written. "I estimate that eighty-five percent of the curriculum in schools of journalism is an inadequate imitation of the program in liberal arts and that the balance is technical training in the practices of journalism, which is an inadequate imitation of the training that could be acquired by working on a newspaper." I decided to get my own technical training by working on *The Daily Maroon*, the university's estimable student paper.

I'd set my sights higher, however. Luce's publishing empire had caught my imagination. *Time*'s brash style was widely admired; *Fortune* was the handsomest of all American magazines; and when, in November of my senior year (1936), Luce launched the weekly picture magazine *Life*, I knew there was no other place I wanted to work but Time Inc. How to attract their attention? With three coconspirators, I decided to launch "a radically different college publication," its news section modeled on *Time*, a monthly survey in the manner of *Fortune*, and "photographs of the candid camera type," like those in *Life*. *Pulse*, as we called it, paid neither its staff nor its contributors, but an exception was made for photographers, who received one dollar for each picture used that had been taken on assignment—plus an extra twenty-eight cents for a flashbulb, if one was absolutely necessary. These rates were sufficient, in those times, to attract the best student photographers. Of the five whose work appeared regularly in *Pulse*, four went on to become distinguished professionals: Paul Berg became a staff photographer for the *St. Louis Post-Dispatch*, John Cor-

A clever photoengraving salesman talked me into this cover design for the monthly I edited at the University of Chicago. Too late did I realize that each issue would require two triangular photos. To promote circulation, I told the printer to stop halfway through the run, overprint SECOND PRINTING, and go back on press. PAUL WAGNER/Pulse/*John G. Morris Collection*

coran for *Science Illustrated*, Myron Davis for *Life*, and David Eisendrath for the *Chicago Times* and New York's short-lived *PM*. The fifth, Paul Wagner, succeeded only in becoming a college president—of Florida's distinguished Rollins College.

In September 1937, as we closed *Pulse*'s first issue, I got an unexpected break. *Fortune*, on orders that probably came from Luce himself, decided to do a story on the University of Chicago and its brilliant young president. Bernard Hoffman, a Chicago-based *Life* staff photographer, was assigned to take the photographs, and I got the job of assisting him—for twenty-five dollars for one week's work. To me it was a fortune.

Bernie Hoffman turned out to be a pixie from the Bronx. He had started as an office boy at *Time*, where he had played practical jokes on the writers and made such a nuisance of himself that he had been transferred to the Time Inc. lab. Here he had begun to take the overflow photo assignments, first for *Time*, then for *Life*. A transfer to the Chicago bureau had followed—on the basis of merit this time, not because of some ill-received prank. Hoffman was the first professional photojournalist I ever met. He taught me how to avoid a few hazards of the trade—especially how not to trigger scorching-hot flashbulbs when setting up lights. One night Bernie and his wife, Inez, invited my girlfriend, Mary Adèle Crosby, and me to their apartment to meet William Vandivert, the second *Life* staffer to be posted to Chicago—and soon to be the first one transferred overseas, to London. Bill and Bernie were complete opposites: Bill was tall, quick, and college-educated; Bernie was short, slow, and self-taught. Vandivert would be one of the first journalists to explore the ruins of Adolf Hitler's underground bunker; Hoffman would be one of the first to reach the ruins of Hiroshima. Vandivert would also become one of the founders of Magnum Photos, the international photographers' cooperative whose fate and fortunes would later determine my own. By chance, the last words Vandivert would hear, on his deathbed in 1989, were in a letter I had written to tell him how much we had missed him at Magnum's fortieth-anniversary exhibition.

Bernie and Bill impressed me as utterly, lovably mad. They talked shop incessantly, gossiping about their colleagues and complaining bitterly about researchers in New York who didn't know Mississippi from Missouri and editors who invariably chose the wrong picture. Even at what was supposed to be a purely social gathering, they brought out their equipment—elaborately rigging up lights in the Hoffman living room and testing exposures and lenses. They also conferred about how to make the most of an expense account. Vandivert recalled a story about Wallace Kirkland, who, upon being assigned to a story in the Arctic, had immediately run out and brashly charged to *Life* an expensive fur coat. Bernie let out a low whistle. "That's class," he muttered admiringly. My resolve to become a staff writer quickly evaporated as I listened to all of the fun and games of the world of photojournalism. Without realizing it, I was joining a society, neither secret nor select, to which I would be bound for life.

But how to start? My trip to New York had resulted in a brush-off. I had graduated from the university as one of ten "marshals," the highest honor annually bestowed on male graduates. Robert Hutchins had winked at me when he handed me my diploma—to me it was the equivalent of getting an honorary degree. After editing the college newspaper and magazine as a Big Man on Campus, I was just as unemployed as millions of other Americans in the summer of 1938. I closed my final issue of *Pulse* and found part-time work in the university's public relations office. Just as that was about to end, a letter arrived from Time Inc. (now located in Rockefeller Center), inviting me to become an "office boy" at twenty dollars a week. The decision was painless. On November 6, I boarded *The General*, the Pennsylvania Railroad's second best overnight train to New York (on a prospective salary of twenty dollars a week one wouldn't ride the extra-fare *Broadway Limited*). After splurging $1.25 on the table d'hôte dinner in the diner, I retired to my lower berth, wrote a short love letter to Mary Adèle on train stationery and asked the porter to mail it in Pittsburgh. My next communication to Dèle, as she was known, was a Western Union telegram sent from New York the following afternoon: START WORK TOMORROW MORNING IN MAIL ROOM. SAW HENRY LUCE.

If you can't start at the top, the next best thing, perhaps, is to start at the bottom. Then there's nowhere to go but up. The bottom, at Time Inc. in 1938, was the mail room, located on the twenty-eighth floor of the Time & Life Building, which looked down on Rockefeller Plaza. A windowless room approximately twenty feet square, it had all the charm of a large closet, as well as eight human occupants: Herbert Brower, the paternal Irish supervisor, and seven office "boys," all in their late teens or early twenties. I was one of the three "CBOBs," or College Boy Office Boys. The other four, presumably high school graduates, were making a career of the mailroom. It was up to me to push my way out and up—or perish. There was no training program.

Time Inc. occupied the top seven floors of the thirty-three-story building. Luce and his personal staff occupied half of the top floor plus a penthouse whose other half was occupied by *Architectural Forum*. When Luce came to work, the brown-shirted Rockefeller Center elevator operators whisked him instantly to the top, stopping for no one. The thirty-second floor housed the company's circulation executives and *Life*'s advertising and promotion people. The three editorial departments followed in descending order: *Life* on 31, *Fortune* on 30, *Time* on 29. *Time*'s businesspeople took 28; various corporate offices occupied 27.

Along with the telephone and telegraph operators, the mailroom staff provided the vital communications links for the 827 New York-based Time Inc. employees (several hundred circulation clerks worked out of Chicago). Each floor had its own force of two to four CBOBs. The company employed outside messenger services for routine errands, but we insiders were entrusted with *confidential* matters of *great* importance. I was dispatched to Abercrombie and Fitch to return an unwanted gift for Mr. Luce (a paisley umbrella); I purchased Tenderleaf tea bags for *Life*'s general manager; I went to a Madison Avenue bank to make a deposit for the company. The bank teller asked me to please inform Time Inc.'s treasurer that the account was still a million dollars overdrawn. (I think he was joking.)

My first break came in early December, when Mr. Brower, learning that I was a touch typist, offered me the post of relief telegraph operator in the Time Inc. wire room. This meant relieving the regular "girl" not only at lunch but also all day Saturday. It was an easy assignment; the only hard part was having to send interminable *Time* copy corrections to the printer in Chicago, in off-hours when no teletype operators were on duty. The wire room was part of the editorial nerve center of *Time.* I could look right through the open door into the corner office of the managing editor. When Luce himself was present one could feel the added tension on the entire twenty-ninth floor. I had many opportunities to size up the *Time* writers as they hung around. Luce's hires were a various lot, but remarkable men: James Agee, Roger Butterfield, Robert Cantwell, Whittaker Chambers, John Hersey, John S. Martin, Leon Svirsky, and Charles Wertenbaker, among others. Oddly enough, they were drawn to *Time* despite the fact that their work appeared anonymously.

Time's circulation had leveled off at around 700,000, but *Life*'s was mushrooming into the millions. It would soon pass those of *Collier's* and *The Saturday Evening Post.* Advertisers were flocking to the magazine. It went into the black for the first time in January 1939, as I celebrated my third month as a CBOB. Increased ad pages meant a corresponding (though more restrained) increase in editorial pages, and that meant that additions would have to be made to the staff. Unfortunately, most of the CBOBs shared my ambition. It wasn't going to be easy.

Wilson Hicks, Daniel Longwell, and John Shaw Billings were the "trinity" who ran *Life* magazine: executive editor Longwell had enough story ideas to fill two or three magazines; Hicks, also executive editor, had the job of winnowing them down and assigning photographers; managing editor Billings decided which stories would run. Life *Magazine © Time Inc.*

3

The Thirty-first Floor

A t *Life*, pictures, not words, came first, and I began to pay attention to the story suggestions and schedules that routinely passed through our hands in the mailroom. I snooped diligently, learning how to pitch a story idea, and began bombarding the editors with my own. None was accepted, but my persistence finally got me moved out of the mailroom and up to *Life* editorial on 31—into the realm of John Shaw Billings, Daniel Longwell, and Wilson Hicks, our triumvirate, our troika, our Trinity (depending on the day and their mood). Another young editor, Edward K. Thompson, was being groomed for their ranks. He would in fact become *Life*'s managing editor of the longest duration, the most popular editorial executive in the history of the company—everyone loved Ed—and in my judgment the most capable. Thompson came from the grassiest of the grass roots, the prairies of North Dakota. At the *Milwaukee Journal,* where he had been the picture editor, he had been the stringer for both *Time* and *Life;* Hicks had brought him to New York as his principal assistant early in 1937. Ed really knew pictures. Alfred Eisenstaedt once said to me, "Ed could read a picture from a negative, upside down, in the hypo."

Billings was managing editor for the first eight years of *Life*. One never forgot who was boss when Billings was around. The very personification of Power, he sat in judgment on the stories proposed for each issue, deliberately keeping aloof from the travail of producing them. Thus he felt free to throw out a story that might have required weeks of work, and cost thousands of dollars, in favor of a story shot in one afternoon. His cultural tastes were strictly middlebrow, and he mooned over Shirley Temple—he reserved seats at Radio City Music Hall for every picture starring the child starlet.

One did not speak to Billings—always "*Mr.* Billings"—unless spoken to. His chauffeured Packard delivered him to the Forty-ninth Street entrance of the Time & Life Building at 10:00 A.M. and picked him up promptly at 6:00 P.M. He seldom left his office except to go to the men's room. His big worktable was connected by intercom to all his key subordinates. One buzz, and a writer would come flying down the hall.

Next to Billings in the hierarchy, occupying an adjacent office on the thirty-first floor, came Longwell, one of two executive editors. He was responsible for Ideas, of which he had far too many. Longwell had begun his career in the Luce empire in 1934, hired away from the publisher Doubleday Doran to develop picture features for *Time.* His first coup was a candid series revealing the casual things President Franklin D. Roosevelt did at his desk while signing a trade agreement—reading a letter, whispering to his secretary, lighting a cigarette, smoking. Thomas D. McAvoy of Washington's *Daily News* had captured it all with a Leica while the regular White House photographers were making the traditional, posed "just one more"s with their nine-pound Speed Graphics. They kidded McAvoy about shooting "in the dark"—that is, without a flash, using only available light—but they all ate their hats when *Time* ran three pages. The layout created a sensation. Stephen Early, the president's press secretary, was not amused, and thereafter FDR made a point of avoiding McAvoy.

Longwell next picked up some pictures made by Peter Stackpole, a young Oakland, California, freelancer, who caught ex-President Herbert Hoover snoozing at Charter Day ceremonies at Berkeley. With Margaret Bourke-White, McAvoy and Stackpole would become the first of *Life*'s staff photographers—joining Alfred Eisenstaedt, who had been recommended to Longwell by Kurt Korff, the former editor of *Berliner Illustrirte Zeitung* (whose publishers stubbornly spelled *Illustrierte* without its first "e"). Korff was a major influence on Longwell. He had fled Hitler with Kurt Safranski, *BIZ*'s picture editor, and had been hired as a supposedly "secret" Time Inc. consultant. The two aspired to top positions at *Life* but were considered too Teutonic—"secret" consulting was the closest they could get to the centers of power. Korff recommended the creation of a "star system" of photographers, pointing out that ego gratification was as important as salary and could take some pressure off salary—a point taken very much to heart by management. The star system had another key advantage: star photographers promoted the magazine with their own celebrity.

Life needed a professional picture editor, and in March 1937 it found him at Associated Press. Wilson Hicks had been in charge of feature pictures at AP. He was given the same title as Longwell, just to keep the two of them—and everyone else—on their toes. Hicks was a small-town guy surrounded by city slickers, a family man in a world of womanizers, an inheritor of work rather than wealth. He had been at *The Kansas City Star,* then moved over to AP, where he had been lucky enough to get himself stuck on the New York photo desk when nobody quite knew what a photo desk was. The AP Wirephoto network had begun operation in January 1935, with receivers in twenty-five cities. The costly new service was still meeting opposition from conservative newspaper publishers when, on August 17, the AP bureau in Seattle flashed word that round-the-world flier Wiley Post had crashed at Point Barrow, Alaska, also killing his passenger, the great homespun humorist Will Rogers. Hicks, on the AP photo desk in New York, worked around the clock to get pictures flown to San Francisco, the closest transmission point. They had been taken with an amateur's folding Kodak by two AP "stringers" in Point Barrow—one a medical missionary, the other a storekeeper. It was one of AP's first big picture scoops.

There was great camaraderie on the thirty-first floor. We lunched together and drank together. Rockefeller Center was surrounded by good, cheap restaurants. One could get excellent Italian spaghetti at the Red Devil for thirty-five cents à la carte—fifty-five for a complete lunch. The Champlain offered quite good French cuisine at sixty-five cents. If one went out with Earl Brown, a Harvard graduate, there were only certain restaurants where one was welcome— Brown was Time Inc.'s first African-American hire. For drinks after hours, nothing could beat the Three G's, across the street from our Forty-eighth Street entrance. It nurtured many an alcoholic.

Each day climaxed at about 5:30, when one of us would run—often frantically—to Grand Central Station with the pouch of pictures and copy for the *Twentieth Century Limited*'s 6:00 P.M. red-carpet departure to Chicago. (Airplanes were then too unreliable.) In a jam, one could talk the elevator operator into dropping to the lobby nonstop, Luce-style. The trick would then be to run with the lights on a diagonal course from the Time & Life Building's Forty-eighth Street entrance to Grand Central, at Forty-third and Vanderbilt (this, I realize, is when I must have figured out my strategy for getting to Grosvenor Square a few years later). Taxis were no help. If you missed the train, it was said, you need not bother to return to work the next day. The following morning, as the *Century* arrived at Chicago's La Salle Street Station promptly at nine, a messenger from R. R. Donnelley would be waiting to whisk the pouch to the printer's gigantic presses.

My next big break came at the end of July 1939, as a substitute researcher in *Life*'s two-man sports department. The researchers in all departments except sports were then women—the chauvinism of the times. My first task was to persuade tennis champion Alice Marble, who had just won Wimbledon, to demonstrate her strokes for the stroboscopic lights of stop-action photographer extraordinaire Gjon Mili. Thus my first substantial assignment as a *Life* staffer took me to one of the unmarked shrines of twentieth-century photog-

The most exacting task of a CBOB (College Boy Office Boy) at Time Inc. was to run with *Life* copy and layouts for the 6:00 P.M. departure of New York Central's crack train, the *Twentieth Century Limited.* Airplanes were then too unreliable to get copy on time to the Chicago printer, R. R. Donnelley & Sons. Life *Magazine* © *Time Inc.*

raphy: the former Chinese nightclub on the second floor of 6 East Twenty-third Street that had become Mili's studio. There was no hint, at street level, of what lay above, just a bell marked MILI. Alice and I ascended the amazingly steep staircase, clutching the banister. Mili loomed at the top. He greeted us quietly and made it clear that we would get right down to business, walking us to the center of the vast floor—a studio fifty-five feet square and thirty-three feet high. It had been transformed on this occasion into a miniature tennis court, complete with net. "Miss Marble"—his voice, so soft on the landing, now boomed around us as he moved toward his equipment—"all you have to do is hit the ball the way you normally would. Pretend that I'm your opponent. Let's start with a serve." Since Mili in no way resembled a Marble opponent, the make-believe did not come easily. Nevertheless, after a few tries, Marble got into the spirit of the enterprise and whacked the ball straight at his camera. "Harder!" he shouted, seemingly unconcerned about the well-being of his equipment—or himself. At this she came close to annihilating Mili. The pictures—each smashing instant frozen cold—ran in the August 28, 1939, issue of *Life,* with Marble jumping the net for an "opener" (my own modest contribution to the scenario).

Born in Albania and raised in Romania, Gjon (pronounced "John") Mili emigrated to the United States in 1923. After studying at MIT, he took a job at Westinghouse but stayed in touch with an MIT professor, Harold Edgerton, who was developing the first "stroboscope," a set of lights that could match the speed of a moving object, thus making it appear to stand still. By 1937, Edgerton was making stop-action photos at one hundred-thousandth of a second—capturing the splash of a drop of milk, the trajectory of a bullet, the impact as a foot kicks a football. Edgerton challenged Mili to put the stroboscope to journalistic use, and Mili set up a makeshift studio in an abandoned church in Montclair, New Jersey. After experimenting for several months, he quit Westinghouse and took his work to *Life*, then less than a year old. The response was positive: *Life* gave Mili six assignments in 1938.

Mili possessed outrageous charm. His friend Jean-Paul Sartre described him as a man "without resentment: he likes everything: eating, drinking, dancing. Harlem he knows better than any white man; New York he knows better than anyone." Mili's friends were not only photographers but painters, sculptors, journalists, dancers, and playwrights. Henri Cartier-Bresson, one of the most devoted, called Mili's studio "the Athens of New York for so many of us." Once a year Mili revived the spirit of his Chinese dance hall and gave an all-night party, with seemingly inexhaustible supplies of food and drink. The dancing went on until dawn. Volunteers saw to the food preparation (photographer Eliot Elisofon cooked fantastic spareribs). Music and entertainment were provided by friends such as Duke Ellington and Zero Mostel. Gjon himself, dressed in corduroys and a plaid shirt, topped with a black felt fedora, led the dancing. I never managed to stay until the end, but I'm told that when it was all over, Gjon would quietly leave with one of the succession of women who kept him company over the years.

Ever restless and inventive, Mili photographed a wide range of subjects, from Pablo Picasso "drawing in light" to the 1945 founding of the United Nations in San Francisco and the 1961 trial of Adolf Eichmann in Israel. The great tragedy of Mili's extraordinary career was also one of the worst disasters in the history of the New York City Fire Department. One night in 1966, the Twenty-third Street studio caught fire. The studio floor fell into the basement, killing twelve firemen. Gjon arrived on the scene in the early morning. He pleaded with the fire marshals to let him enter the smoldering building. Fearful of another collapse, they gave him only a few minutes. He managed to walk out with many precious negatives, but the shock was the first of a series of accidents that slowed him down in later life but did not stop him. In 1978, at seventy-four, he made an exquisite photographic study of George Balanchine's New York City Ballet performing *The Nutcracker.*

Closing sports stories introduced me to the *Life* "system." At *Life*, it was the pictures that determined the length of the story, measured in pages and half pages. Photostats of the pictures, sized exactly as they would appear in the magazine, were rubber-cemented onto stiff layout sheets, each representing either one page or a two-page spread. Blocks of dummy type, also exact size, were pasted in to show the writer exactly how many lines, of how many characters each, were needed to accompany the picture layouts. For this purpose, writers were provided with special copy paper, ruled horizontally to provide a maximum of twenty agate-typed lines per page and vertically to allow for ninety characters (maximum) per line. The writer worked from a photostat of the original layout sent to the printer in Chicago.

I must have been impressed with the system, because I saved for posterity my checking copy for the very first *Life* story I helped close—on August 3, 1939, for the issue dated August 14. The subject was the Women's National Swimming Championships in Des Moines, Iowa. The photographs were by Fritz Henle, one of the talented refugees working at the time through the Black Star agency. The copy was written by sports editor John Field. My job as researcher demanded checking, for factual accuracy, every single word in the story, putting a black pencil dot over each ordinary word and a red dot over proper names. This was a practice begun at *Time*, and the researcher, not the writer, was held accountable for any errors; *Life*'s writers were notorious for disregarding the facts. Thus the writer-researcher relationship tended to be adversarial.

To maintain quality, overproduction was required of every editor. A small *Life* department such as Sports would be expected to offer executive editor Dan Longwell, every Monday, two or three complete new picture stories for the issue closing the following Saturday. The pictures had to be *great*. Even so, only one sports story would be likely to make the book. Even that was not guaranteed. Some other back-of-the-book department—Science or Movies or Modern Living—might get that space. Only two departments—The Week's Events (Foreign and Newsfront, that is, domestic news) and Articles (normally profiles called "Close-ups")—were guaranteed space. Other "departments" were in fact formulas for picture stories that could be supplied by any department: "Speaking of Pictures," "Picture of the Week," "The Photographic Essay," "LIFE Goes to a Party."

I didn't have to spend long at *Life* to face the facts: we were entertainers as much as journalists. Photographers worked from "scripts," and stories were "acts." The world's celebrities were our unpaid—and often reluctant—actors. Irreverence was all. The choices we made might be considered amoral, but deadlines couldn't wait on morality. We had to "fill the book" each week. It didn't matter whether we led off with a chorus girl or a cardinal, but there had to be a good mix because the magazine had to sell. It *did* matter whether the pictures had "impact." It was hard to define just what that meant, but Gjon Mili came close when he said that a good picture requires "a brief collusion between foresight and chance. . . . It need not invite reflection so much as create a shock which alerts the viewer to the strangeness of the passage." One would never hear such eloquence from the top editors at *Life*. They were a generally inarticulate lot, expressing approval and disapproval in splutters and grunts. One got used to it; one learned to grunt.

Life's writers were literary tailors, more in the business of measuring words than writing them. And they were often poor picture editors. Some tended to be obsessive about the "facts" of the picture. Others were simply too inhibited, or perhaps too intellectual, to find the right image or follow the narrative through a set of contacts. Luce himself was not considered a good picture editor, though he loved to take part, much to the distress of all in his proximity.

Life recognized no external competition when it came to pictures. Newspapers were faster but lacked coherent display space and quality reproduction. When *Life* republished the best newspaper photos, readers often thought they were seeing them for the first time. By the day's magazine standards, *Life* worked very fast. One could shoot and close a story on Saturday and see it on newsstands across the country the following week. *Look* appeared only every other week, and it closed four to six weeks in advance.

After the Mili assignment, my next challenge was a story on horse racing, with Alfred Eisenstaedt. Wilson Hicks asked me if I had ever seen a horse race. I hadn't and thought about lying, certain that honesty would cost me the assignment. Instead, I told the truth, and Hicks surprised me by immediately giving me the story, with the rationale that I would bring a "fresh point of view" to it. With fifty dollars in company cash in my pocket I took a Thursday-night train upstate to Saratoga Springs. It was the height of the August season. I was supposed to get things lined up on Friday; Eisenstaedt would join me Saturday for two or three days of intensive shooting. I had no idea what to expect. Eisenstaedt, then forty, had the wide-eyed naïveté of a child. I knew that he was considered a prima donna by the other *Life* photographers, but this could easily be explained by his exceptional record. The very first photographer hired by Luce for the *Life* staff, Eisenstaedt was a Berliner who had served in the German Army in World War I and had been wounded in Flanders. His family's small fortune had disappeared in the postwar inflation. He had turned to selling belts and buttons but continued pursuing his hobby, photography. He was inspired by Dr. Erich Salomon, whose candid photographs of world statesmen, made with an Ermanox camera on small glass plates, were making photographic history in Germany's illustrated magazines.

On December 3, 1929, Eisenstaedt quit belts and buttons and became a photographer for Pacific and Atlantic, the Berlin affiliate of Associated Press. Six days later, he was off to Stockholm on his first assignment, to photograph Thomas Mann receiving the Nobel Prize. After that he photographed George Bernard Shaw in London, Benito Mussolini greeting Hitler in Venice, the

League of Nations in Geneva. He shot the early movie stars—Marlene Dietrich, Charles Chaplin, Anna May Wong, Gloria Swanson—and musicians—Wilhelm Furtwängler, Sergei Rachmaninoff, Arturo Toscanini, Igor Stravinsky, Vladimir Horowitz, Yehudi Menuhin, Jascha Heifetz, Richard Strauss. He photographed society in Saint-Moritz, the prostitutes of Les Halles, Haile Selassie's ragged troops in Ethiopia. He crossed the Atlantic, from Friedrichshafen to Rio de Janeiro, in the dirigible *Graf Zeppelin.* In 1935, Eisenstaedt immigrated to the United States, arriving on the *Ile de France* with Leon Daniel, who had headed Pacific and Atlantic. Together they formed a new agency called Pix. Eisenstaedt's *Life* contract required that his pictures be credited to Pix and that his paychecks go there. It wasn't until twenty years later that Eisenstaedt realized he had been defrauded by Daniel; he had been getting only about half the money due him. A big spender Eisenstaedt was not. I found it difficult to relax with him, even for a moment. He hated beer and wine, and he had given up his two daily cigarettes earlier that year. He and his young South African wife, who was always by his side, did like to indulge in chocolate sodas, however. Years later, "Eisie" would become everybody's favorite photographer, a clowning prankster, the man who reminded Sophia Loren (whom he adored) of her obstetrician. I can only say that she was fortunate not to have met him in 1939. I wrote to Dèle from my Saratoga hotel room, "If we get what the editors want it will be a miracle."

There was no miracle. Eisenstaedt turned in 120 pictures, all perfectly workable images of the races—the horses in full gallop, the frenzied fans and bettors at the finish, and a few "artful" shots, including one of Eisie and me (or, rather, of our shadows) standing on a platform—but the pictures did not knock either one of us out. Still, I dutifully captioned them all and wrote five closely typed pages of research on "George Bull and the Saratoga Association." To no one's surprise Wilson Hicks was unimpressed, and the story never ran. I was disappointed, but Eisenstaedt was philosophical, never a man to brood over small failures or remonstrate with the editors. He just went off on another assignment. In time, I would learn to do the same.

Alfred Eisenstaedt's photograph of our shadows from a platform at Saratoga Springs, New York, where we had been sent by *Life* to cover the horse races. This was one of the more interesting pictures in the take; the story never ran. ALFRED EISENSTAEDT/Life *Magazine* © *Time Inc.*

Foreseeing American intervention in World War II, Henry Luce instructed his editors to "cultivate the martial spirit." Executive editor Longwell came up with this special issue on the U.S. Navy. The lead story was a mock battle at sea. The final spread showed a battleship firing its 16-inch guns, over the headline BOOM! Longwell's fun-loving colleagues prepared one special copy with the headline BOO! and left it on his desk. W. EUGENE SMITH/Life *Magazine © Time Inc.*

4

"To Suffer or to Fight"

On Sunday, September 3, 1939, Great Britain and France declared war on Germany, as required by their pact with Poland, which Hitler had just invaded. The onset of World War II finally brought America out of the Depression; it also marked the ascension of *Life*. As Henry Luce once commented, "Though we did not plan *Life* as a war magazine, it turned out that way." War also gave me job security. Soon I was working so hard on war news that I scarcely had time to think of the implications. My job was to analyze the daily, always conflicting, communiqués of the belligerents, in order to map the German advance into Poland and the situation on the western front (it wasn't immediately apparent that nothing would happen there until the following spring). Then I was put to work charting the war at sea. Fortunately, I was not indispensable, and I was permitted to take a long-planned trip to Chicago, to get married. The next month, following her first visit to a New York obstetrician, Dèle told me she was pregnant. Mary Heather Morris was born at Sloan Hospital for Women on June 23, 1940. The day before, at Compiègne, in the very railroad car where Germany had surrendered to France in 1918, France had capitulated to Germany. Hitler's conquest of western Europe was virtually complete.

Life listed only nine staff photographers when I joined it in 1939—Carl Mydans, Hansel Mieth, John Phillips, Hoffman, Vandivert, McAvoy, Stackpole, Eisenstaedt, and, of course, Margaret Bourke-White—but somehow, despite its tiny staff, the magazine managed to give the appearance of never missing a world event. Besides being the first alphabetically, Bourke-White was also first in public reputation. Luce had noticed the work of the twenty-five-year-old

Cleveland industrial photographer in 1929 and had invited her to New York. He offered her a contract to work half-time for his new magazine, *Fortune*, for $10,000 a year. For *Fortune*'s first issue, she and Luce went to Indiana to do a story on "The Unseen Half of South Bend." She permitted Luce to carry her cameras, a privilege she granted many a man but which I, luckily, escaped—unlike most *Life* photographers, Bourke-White traveled heavy. Peggy, or Maggie, as she was generally called, knew how to make good use of her abundant sex appeal. In 1930 she made her first trip abroad. Assigned by *Fortune* to photograph German industry, Bourke-White decided to also proceed, on her own, to the USSR, where Western photographers had not been welcome. "Nothing attracts me like a closed door," she said as she proceeded to open them on this and subsequent trips to the Soviet Union.

Luce's magazines, ever fearful of communism, were slow to recognize the threats of Nazism and fascism. Reporting for *Fortune* on Germany's furtive rearmament in contravention of the Treaty of Versailles, Bourke-White photographed troops training with mock tanks and wooden guns. *Fortune* concluded, in January 1933, that the German Army "is as yet no threat to the peace of Europe." It was the month Hitler took power.

It is significant that, aside from a brief visit by Bourke-White to Barcelona in 1938, *Life* sent no staff photographer to cover the Spanish Civil War. *Life* made up for it, however, by often publishing the pictures of a Paris-based Hungarian freelancer who made no fewer than ten trips to Spain, from the war's outbreak in the summer of 1936 to its tragic end in January 1939. In September 1936, this man, Robert Capa, shot the picture of a lifetime, one of the most important images in the history of photography: a Spanish Loyalist soldier, charging down a hillside, is caught in the moment of death. It was only one of a series on the front at Córdoba, published that year in the French magazine *Vu*. A year later, *Life* ran it as the frontispiece for a story, "Death in Spain: The Civil War Has Taken 500,000 Lives in One Year." London's *Picture Post* hailed Capa as the "Greatest War Photographer in the World." His professional triumph was marred by personal tragedy, however. In 1937, Gerda Taro, his German girlfriend and a photojournalist of the first rank, *the* love of a life of many loves, was killed when a tank collided with the car in which she was riding during the Battle of Brunete. Later that year, Capa dedicated his book on the war, *Death in the Making*, "For Gerda Taro, who spent one year at the Spanish front, and who stayed on."

Robert Capa was born Endre Ernő Friedmann on the Pest bank of the Danube in Budapest, on October 22, 1913. He was the second son of a Hungarian couple who ran a successful dressmaking salon. Hungary went through trying times following World War I, shifting first to the left and then to the right. By the time Endre finished gymnasium, the country was under the fas-

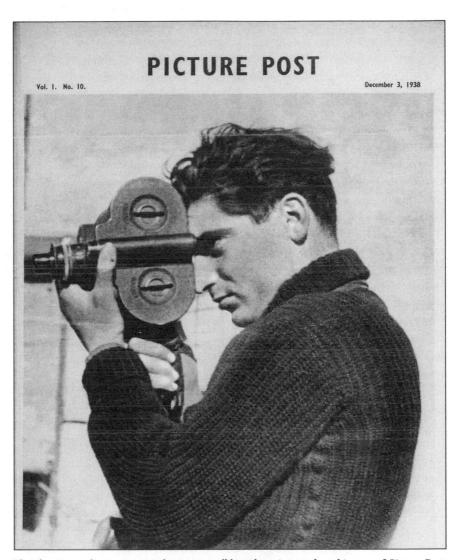

The photojournalist as romantic hero may well have been invented on this page of *Picture Post*, which also decreed Robert Capa "the greatest war photographer in the world," a distinction that would weigh heavily upon him in the years to come. (He is, in fact, wielding a movie camera in this photograph.) Picture Post, *London/Hulton Getty Picture Library*

cist regime of Admiral Miklós Horthy. There was little opportunity in Hungary for a bright young Jew, especially one who looked to the left. In 1931, Endre, whom the family called "Bandi," left for Berlin, one step ahead of the police. There he drifted into photography (a vocation that seems to come naturally to Hungarians), getting a job in the darkroom of the Dephot photo agency, run by his fellow countryman Simon Gutmann. Capa soon began taking pictures.

Hitler's rise to power in 1933 made it advisable for Capa to move again. He arrived in Paris in September. It quickly became his city, a fitting capital for a man without a country. Endre became André. He would have starved had it not been for help from other exiles, among them the great Hungarian photographer André Kertész and Fritz Goro, a German exile who would become *Life*'s star science photographer. In 1934, André Friedmann met Gerda Pohorylles, a stunning native of Stuttgart and a political refugee herself. She was working for Maria Eisner, the Milanese founder of Alliance Photo, a picture agency. Gerda introduced André to Maria as "Robert Capa, a famous international photographer." Maria saw through the ruse but played along, offering to sell André's pictures as those of "Capa." Perhaps inspired by her lover, Gerda (whose given name in Germany had actually been Gerta) also took a nom de guerre: "Gerda Taro: photographer." Soon Capa and Taro were both working in Spain, sometimes together, sometimes—as on that last, fatal day—separately.

Thanks to Capa's strong images, *Life* took an almost sympathetic view of the Spanish Loyalists, who were fighting for survival against Franco, Hitler, and Mussolini. Not until Neville Chamberlain surrendered the Czech Sudetenland at Munich in November 1938 did *Time* wake up to the simple fact of Hitler's voracity. The change was dramatized by Luce's decision to edit the magazine himself for a week and to send *Time*'s foreign news editor, Laird Goldsborough, on a "long-overdue sabbatical." I remember the sigh of relief that went up on the twenty-ninth floor when the openly pro-Mussolini and discreetly anti-Semitic Goldsborough was sent packing. He would in fact never return to edit foreign news and became a kind of company ghost, drifting the halls until his suicide in 1950—out the window of the office he rented in the Time & Life Building.

Luce's fresh stand against fascism was heartening, but our Sinophile boss, born in 1898 to missionaries in Tengchow, was much more interested in Nationalist China's struggle against Japan than he was in Republican Spain's fight against Franco. Yet China was an area almost unknown to *Life* staff photographers until 1941, when Carl Mydans went to Chungking to work with *Time* correspondent Theodore White. Until then, *Life* had relied on the pictures of the wire services and freelancers, among them Edgar Snow, the American journalist who first reported on the Chinese Communists in the Yenan caves. The best pictures from the Japanese side came from Yonosuke Natori, a Japanese photojournalist whose pictures reached *Life* through the Black Star agency, as did those on the Nationalist side from the Swiss photographer Walter Bosshard. But the most memorable reportage from that side, surprisingly—since he was also covering Spain that year—came from Robert Capa. With precious little financial support from *Life*, Capa went to China in January 1938 with Dutch moviemaker Joris Ivens. Overcoming such obstacles as acute dysentery and the intrusive Chinese bureaucracy, Capa made notable stories on the battle over Taierhchwang and on the Japanese air raids on Hankow—possibly the first-ever war photographs published in color.

World War II was not going well for our side (everyone knew which side we were on even though America was officially neutral). Poland had lasted less than a month (*Life* never even managed to get a photographer there). In the first four months of the war, German U-boats sank more than 110 Allied vessels, including the passenger liner *Athenia*, the British aircraft carriers *Ark Royal* and *Courageous*, and the battleship *Royal Oak*. I assisted John Garrett Underhill, *Life*'s brilliant one-eyed military expert, in charting the sinkings.

In December 1939, I was dispatched to Ellis Island in New York harbor to cover a "POW" story with a twenty-year-old photographer named W. Eugene Smith. Gene hailed from Wichita, Kansas, and I liked him from the day I met him, although somehow the early stories we worked on together never made it into the magazine—including our report from Ellis Island on the "*Columbus* internees," the crew of a Hamburg-based passenger liner that had been scuttled by its crew following its interception by a British destroyer. Gene's widowed mother, Nettie, was not with us that day—a notable detail, given how much time this haunted, proud, and possessive woman spent trailing her son. Gene was already a semiprofessional photographer, covering sports for the Wichita newspapers when his father, a grain dealer ruined by drought and depression, shot himself in the spring of 1936. Gene was summoned from school and gave his own blood in a vain effort to save his father. That traumatic day was but one in a life filled with trauma and perhaps accounts for some of Gene's bizarre behavior in later years—and also for his artistry. Gene Smith was the most humane and sympathetic of photographers, as attested by any number of his pictures, but especially "Tomoko in Her Bath," one of the century's defining images (page 275).

The western front was quiet, but on November 30, 1939, Soviet troops attacked Finland. *Life* sent Carl Mydans to cover the heroic Finnish defense. His wife, Shelley, a *Life* researcher, stayed in Stockholm to handle communications while he took a northbound train to Haparanda and then proceeded on foot into Finland and the thick of the action. Three months later, the Finns were overwhelmed by superior Soviet forces, but not before *Life* had published Mydans's photos in a sickeningly jubilant picture spread of Russian dead lying in the snow, with such captions as "Red Dead" and "Wolf Food." Mydans was embarrassed by this use of his pictures—he knew the gallant Finns were actually losing. Censorship prevented him from revealing the true picture—he had plenty of shots of an equally large number of Finnish dead.

Things would soon get much worse for the Allies. On April 9, 1940, the Germans invaded Norway, simultaneously occupying Denmark against passive resistance. On May 10, they blitzed into Holland and Belgium, and then went on into France. Throughout the campaign, as in Poland, *Life* had no staff photographer with the advancing Germans. All of *Life*'s German-born photographers were now in New York. Henry Luce once remarked, in a jest close to the truth, that Adolf Hitler had aided the founding of *Life* by driving so many talented Jewish photojournalists out of Europe. All Luce had to do was "sit in New York and wait for them to land." When they arrived, they usually went straight to Pix or Black Star, the two principal picture agencies that had been founded by refugees. In addition to Eisenstaedt, Pix got George Karger, Hans Knopf, Nina Leen, and Eric Schaal; Black Star took in Ralph Crane, Herbert Gehr, Fritz Goro, Fritz Henle, and Walter Sanders. Robert Capa was briefly affiliated with both agencies.

Among the thousands of refugees who fled Paris was a Latvian-born portrait photographer named Philippe Halsman (who would also join Black Star). His wife and daughter had gone to the States ahead of him. Philippe eventually reached Marseilles, where the American consul told him that the Latvian immigration quota of eighteen people per year was filled for the next seven years. Thanks to the intervention of Albert Einstein, with whom Philippe had exchanged letters years before, Halsman's name was added to the list of European writers and artists who received visas through Eleanor Roosevelt's Emergency Rescue Committee. Then unknown to *Life*, Halsman would become one of the magazine's star contributors, making more than one hundred covers. His portrait of Einstein was used for a U.S. postage stamp.

Life's London office was teeming with photographers, more than could be effectively employed at the time. In addition to staffers Vandivert, Mydans, and Bourke-White, pictures were coming in from Bill Brandt, Cecil Beaton, James Jarché of *Weekly Illustrated*, Hans Wild, and George Rodger. There was also Algerian-born John Phillips, *Life*'s first foreign staff photographer, who had begun his tenure at the magazine covering subjects such as the Dublin Horse Show and the lord chief justice's garden party. When it came to journalism, John had the timing of a Rolex. In March 1938 he arrived in Vienna just ahead of Hitler's abrupt *Anschluss;* Phillips and his film barely escaped the SS. In the following six months Phillips joined Bourke-White to produce a twelve-page *Life* essay on Czechoslovakia, and he photographed the Warsaw ghetto and Poland's preparations for war, plus the Romanian royal family. On September

15, back in London, he photographed Neville Chamberlain as, clutching an umbrella, the British prime minister boarded a British Airways plane for Munich, where he would cede the Czech Sudetenland to Hitler. Phillips went straight to the disputed area, getting out at the last minute as German troops rolled in.

In America, the great debate was on between the interventionists and the isolationists. I was caught between my own deeply held pacifist beliefs and a boss who was among the most ardent of the former. In 1938, two months after Munich, Henry Luce's *Life* ran a fourteen-page picture story (in effect an editorial) calling upon America to rearm. Luce advised his colleagues to prepare for Armageddon. On May 10, 1940, Luce and his wife, Clare, had almost been caught by the rapid German advance in Belgium. Luce cabled home from Brussels, I DEEPLY WISH ALL PRIGGISH, PIOUS PACIFISTS COULD BE HERE TODAY. IN THE BEAUTIFUL CALM SUNLIGHT, RARELY BROKEN BY SIREN'S SCREAM, THERE ARE ONLY TWO REALITIES—TO SUFFER OR TO FIGHT. Two months later, Luce sent a confidential memo to his top executives, headed "WAR," in which he summed up their "journalistic duty": "1) To continue to sound the Danger signal in all its aspects. . . . 2) To cultivate the Martial Spirit. . . . 3) To show that America is worth fighting for—since, incredible though it may seem, there appear to be those who doubt it. 4) To be hawk-eyed in our observation of Preparedness and to be savage and ferocious in our criticism of all delay and bungling."

This was pretty typical of Luce's often overheated prose style. It was just as well I wasn't higher up the totem pole at the time the memo circulated. I was quietly maintaining my own position, looking to the example of my mentor Robert Maynard Hutchins—Luce's primary intellectual opponent—who simply felt that the United States was morally unprepared to demonstrate democracy to the world. In a radio address, Hutchins advised caution: "If we go to war, we shall not know what we are fighting for. If we stay out of war until we do, we may have the stamina to win and the knowledge to use the victory for the welfare of mankind." I was deeply moved and fired off a wire to Chicago: REGRET THAT I DO NOT SPEAK FOR LIFE BUT SPEAKING FOR MYSELF ALONE MAY I SAY THAT I'M WITH YOU ALL THE WAY. Hutchins responded by letter, writing, tongue in cheek, "I look forward to your assuming control of *Life* magazine at an early date."

I had registered for the draft in October 1940 as a conscientious objector (although I was not a member of a recognized "pacifistic religious sect," as the law required), qualifying this choice by saying that I would fight if the country was attacked (an unimaginable possibility at the time). In any case, my request for c.o. status was ignored because I had already been deferred as a husband and father.

A poker game at the Halsman Studio, New York, in the early 1950s. Gjon Mili is sitting in the white chair. *Clockwise from him:* Dmitri Kessel, Robert Capa, Pepi Martis, Philippe Halsman, and Cornell Capa. *Photo and copyright* © *by* YVONNE HALSMAN

5

The "Picture Men"

One day in May 1940, chief researcher Rachel Albertson called me into her office. I had been working as a researcher for nine months already, without making the masthead, and I figured something was wrong. So I was astonished when she offered me the most envied job on the floor: research assistant to Alexander King, Time Inc.'s only certified genius. He bore the somewhat nebulous title of editorial associate, and he was paid a handsome $250 a week to perform no particular duties except act as agent provocateur for fresh ideas and as office gadfly. Sharp-tongued in several languages, King openly ridiculed Hicks and Longwell. He had been hired by Luce himself on the basis of a severe critique he had written of *Life*. He also had the support of Clare Luce—he had once saved a play of hers from critical disaster.

Born in Vienna in 1899 as Alexander König, Alex King had been raised on the mean streets of New York's Lower East Side, but he was far from culturally impoverished. An accomplished commercial artist, he illustrated dozens of classics for the Limited Editions Club and in 1932 founded *Americana*, "A Magazine of Pictorial Satire," with such contributors as José Clemente Orozco, Peggy Bacon, George Grosz, and Miguel Covarrubias. Despite the Depression, it lasted two years.

A determined nonconformist, King wore only green suits, blue shirts, and pink ties—he had dozens of each. He had only one functioning kidney and was often in severe pain. Consequently, he became a morphine addict. Whenever he asked me to close the door of our shared office, I knew it was time for his next fix. I grew accustomed to the sight of my boss injecting himself. "Ah, yes, much better," he would sigh. I knew little of Alex's personal life except that he had a girlfriend, one Margie Bell, a ballerina who had been the model for Disney's Snow White. Later they married.

King was sought out by photographers who lacked either the nerve or the inclination to see Wilson Hicks. Thus I first met André Kertész, another Hungarian genius. When he visited us, Kertész complained, in a mixture of French, English, and Hungarian, about the way he was being treated at Condé Nast, where he was repeatedly given *House & Garden* assignments, which he despised.

Lewis Hine, the documentary photographer who almost single-handedly won child labor reform, came to see us, out of work and desperate for it, at age sixty-six. He found work at *Fortune* but was too much of a nonconformist for *Life*. Ninety-seven-year-old William Henry Jackson, the photographer credited with the creation of Yellowstone National Park (he was the first to document its wonders), came by just to pay his respects to the brilliant Alex King. James Van Der Zee visited from his Harlem studio to pitch an unusual series of photographs on weddings and funerals.

One day Alex announced, "John, it's time I got myself fired." He was seriously in debt, thanks to drugs, alimony, and a weakness for charge accounts at record stores. A new job awaited—Alexander Ince wanted to make him the editor of a revived *Stage* magazine. Resigning wouldn't do, for it would mean forgoing $5,000 in severance pay. So King forged Mr. Billings's signature, knowing that he would be caught. In no time at all, Alex was operating out of Sardi's.

I had worked for the man for only two and a half months, and I was sorry to see him go, even though it fell to me to clear out his office—a two-week ordeal that required sifting through the various "treasures" Alex had collected from would-be *Life* contributors. There were family albums, daguerreotypes, sporting prints, fossils; an alligator with a bulb in its mouth and a contraption that Alex insisted was "the world's first vacuum cleaner." All had to go. The *Stage* venture didn't last long, and King went steadily downhill, becoming a regular visitor to the Federal Narcotics Hospital in Lexington, Kentucky. Eventually he pulled himself together, however, and finally found the line of work for which he seemed destined—he became a star on Jack Paar's television show and wrote five books of best-selling memoirs in as many years.

Just before Christmas 1940, the Time Inc. house organ, *f.y.i.*, carried a two-line item: "John Morris, who has been doing *Life* research for the past year, is now assistant to Wilson Hicks." I had known something was up when Hicks paused briefly one day to interrogate me as we were passing each other outside the men's room. Germ-phobic Hicks had emerged clutching a paper towel and now held it delicately by its edges. "Ever work on a newspaper, John?" he asked, depositing the towel in the trash. He seemed amused when I responded, without missing a beat or blinking an eye, "Yes, *The Daily Maroon*." (In truth, the University of Chicago's student newspaper was one of the better papers in the Chicago area.) I must have passed the test, because the next day Hicks offered me the job.

Except for Abe Rosenthal of *The New York Times*, Wilson Hicks was the most controversial boss I've ever had. Of *Life*'s two executive editors, he was the one who had to make the tough decisions: which stories to cover, around the world, and which *not* to, which was more often the case. It was no wonder he was generally disliked. Nobody loves a naysayer. In going to work for Wilson, I crossed a divide. I was now fully caught up in the daily battle between the "word men" and the "picture men." I tended to side with the photographers, and my reward was acceptance into the extended families that photographers habitually create.

One of the first was Robert Capa's. He arrived in New York in October 1939, and right away we became friends. My clearest early memory of him is of his antics at the Rockefeller Center skating rink, where we *Life*rs occasionally spent lunch hour. Capa was not much of a skater, so his (transparent) strategy was to latch onto the prettiest girl in sight and let her do the work. They made it once around the rink and then spilled, spectacularly, right in front of some delighted Time Inc. bigwigs lunching rinkside.

It was not long before Capa took me home to the brownstone on West Eighty-ninth Street where his mother, Julia, lived, along with his brother Cornell and Cornell's wife, Edith—"Edie." Julia was a good cook and a somewhat obvious actress who enjoyed attention. She had acquired the nickname "Mother Goose" because she had adopted so many children—all the friends that Cornell and Bob were in the habit of bringing home. Cornell worked in the lab at Pix, then Capa's agency. It had become a meeting point for the "Red Bagel" gang from the Bronx, a motley crew of aspiring photographers—Yale Joel, Ralph Morse, Phil Schultz, and Eileen Darby (who was admitted to this distinctly New York gang even though she actually hailed from Oregon). There was also a young man who worked in his father's shirt business; they called him "Munkacsi" (after the talented Hungarian who had revolutionized fashion photography) so he wouldn't feel out of place. When you added up all the girlfriends and boyfriends and their friends, it was usually a party of twenty-seven, a number that did not daunt Julia in the slightest.

The second family that adopted the Morrises was much smaller. It consisted of Hansel Mieth, the first woman photographer hired by *Life* after Bourke-White, and Otto Hagel. Hansel and Otto had the ruddy faces of peasants. They had been childhood sweethearts in Fellbach, a suburb of Stuttgart, Germany, where they had been born four weeks apart in 1909. Otto was the son of a roofer and became a clockmaker's apprentice. Hansel was a shopkeeper's daughter, and went to work for a dressmaker. The clever pair saw no future in

Robert Capa (*left*) was the delight and despair of his mother, Julia, whom he called "Mother Goose" because she took in so many of his friends. It fell to younger brother Cornell Capa (*right*) to maintain the family tradition following Bob's untimely death.
© EILEEN DARBY

Fellbach, so they rode off together on a motorbike, making a little money as street musicians. For three months, they took refuge in a Yugoslavian monastery, where Hansel—until then known as Johanna—passed undetected as a boy (the monks must have been *very* distracted). In 1928, Otto decided to try his luck in America and signed on to a freighter. He jumped ship in Baltimore and rode the rails to San Francisco. By December 1930, Hansel had saved enough to buy steamship passage to San Francisco through the Panama Canal. But when she landed in New York, Otto demanded, by phone from San Francisco, that she cash in the rest of the ticket and hurry overland to him. She bought a $55 jalopy and started out, without benefit of a driver's license. When the lovers were finally reunited, in front of Otto's San Francisco rooming house, Otto announced triumphantly to Hansel, "I told the landlady you're my wife." Confused by his still-raw English, made more garbled by his excitement at seeing her, Hansel thought Otto was confessing that the landlady was his wife. She hit him so hard that she knocked out a tooth. This misunderstanding could have been avoided, of course, if Otto had addressed Hansel in their native tongue, but he was a determined anti-Nazi and wanted to become Americanized as fast as possible. Otto and Hansel, my Grimms fairy-tale couple, were to become my closest lifelong friends. We first met in 1940 in New York, where Hansel was working for *Life* and Otto for *Life* and *Fortune*.

Another *Life* family Dèle and I adored was that of Dmitri ("Mitya") Kessel. His wife, Lillian, was a kindergarten teacher, and his sister, Manya, ran a custom lab on Forty-sixth Street. As a Ukrainian teenager in World War I, Dmitri had been trained to fight for the tsar but had wound up, in 1919, as a Red Army cavalry officer, fighting the Poles. After many close calls, Kessel had immigrated to New York in 1923. There he found work in the garment district

My Grimms fairy-tale couple:
Hansel Mieth and Otto Hagel share a
placid moment at the light box.
PETER STACKPOLE/Life *Magazine*
© *Time Inc.*

and took pictures on weekends. He showed his portfolio to *Fortune* in 1936 and was rewarded with an assignment on Simmons mattresses. It was published, and the following year he was working for *Life.* He specialized in big photographic productions: the Sistine Chapel; the wedding of the shah of Iran. I never got to go on a job with Dmitri, but I did go fishing with him at Saranac Lake in the Adirondacks, his favorite place. Once he was summoned straight from Saranac to go to Rome for the funeral of Pope Pius XII. The Kessels' Fifty-seventh Street apartment was a kind of clubhouse for my little family in its growing years.

To become a *Life* photographer, it was not necessary to have a college education, let alone come from an Ivy League school. Several photographers had never even graduated from high school. It was necessary to speak English, but not grammatically; an accent even helped. It didn't hurt to be Jewish—this in a company notorious for its WASP snobbishness. Hicks was interested only in the quality of the pictures. He gave Gordon Parks, a black photographer, his first big *Life* break—a $500 guarantee on a very dangerous, but ultimately successful, story on a Harlem gang leader. Parks's next important assignment was covering Paris fashions; on the ship over to Europe, Parks received a cable from Hicks offering him a staff job.

Life photographers came from all sorts of places and professions. Dmitri Kessel had worked for a New York furrier; George Karger had been a German banker. Fritz Goro was a German intellectual who spoke the language of scientists. Andreas Feininger, born in France of American parents—his father was the painter Lyonel Feininger—studied architecture before turning to photography. Philippe Halsman was trained as an engineer and designed his own camera.

There was no easy way to get hired as a *Life* photographer. An ambitious young photographer could grow old and despondent waiting to get in to see Hicks. The trick was to get Hicks's attention. Myron Davis, my childhood friend and *Pulse* photographer, was recommended to Hicks by the impish Bernie Hoffman on the grounds that Myron had performed as a "ballerina" in an all-male student musical. This got Hicks's attention, all right, and Myron was hired on the basis of his portfolio, but word of the ballet number leaked to the staff. A few weeks later Robert Capa, in Chicago on temporary assignment, met Myron in the darkroom and suggested a pas de deux. Capa was on the floor before he knew it. Hoffman had neglected to tell Hicks that Myron had also been a member of the University of Chicago's wrestling team.

Often it fell to me to interview newcomers, which is how I came to meet a young Kansas City native named David Douglas Duncan. His talent was so obvious that I rushed him in to see Hicks. Hicks held Duncan's story on the Yucatán "on approval," but it never ran. Duncan had an easier time in 1946, when Hicks hired him instantly upon his discharge from the Marines, where Duncan had distinguished himself for his combat coverage. Hicks did not always wait for photographers to come to him. He offered a staff job to New Zealander George Silk on the basis of one great picture—of a Papuan native leading a barefoot Australian infantryman, his eyes bound in bandages, away from battle in New Guinea. Already a fine photographer, Silk became a great one. Later he turned his talent for action photography to sports and created some classic sports images.

Life's photographers had no desks, on the principle that they had no business sitting around the office, anyway. Instead, they had lockers in the *Life* lab on West Forty-eighth Street, a drab building that also housed a pharmacy. Only Margaret Bourke-White had an office there *and* a secretary. The *Life* lab had in fact begun as Bourke-White's personal one, specified in her *Life* contract. The contract also gave her a printer and two assistants. Bourke-White was a notorious overshooter, working mostly with large (4-by-5-inch film) cameras and film packs. She demanded, and her printer saw to it that she got, excellent 11-by-14-inch enlargements, from full negatives. She did not, however, object when the editors cropped her pictures. *Life*'s other photographers, seeing these superb prints, were emboldened to demand the same quality for themselves. What was unfortunate was that they tended to try to imitate Bourke-White's large-format technique, often "compromising" by shooting the square 120 format (2¼ by 2¼ inches) when lightweight 35-millimeter cameras were better adapted to reportage.

Myron Davis, one of *Life's* youngest staff photographers, shows how to get a little elevation for a long shot. After covering wartime Washington and Franklin Roosevelt's White House, Davis was sent by *Life* to the South Pacific, where he photographed several invasions commanded by General MacArthur. *Time Inc. Archives*

George Silk was offered a staff job at *Life* on the basis of this picture. GEORGE SILK/*War Memorial Museum, Canberra, Australia*

In 1940, fed up with a six-month dry spell, Bourke-White quit *Life* to join Time Inc.'s highest-ranking defector, Ralph Ingersoll, on his experimental newspaper *PM*. A former *New Yorker* managing editor, Ingersoll had helped Luce through an early *Fortune* crisis and then became publisher of *Time* and the company's de facto number three (after Luce and Roy Larsen). Ingersoll quit in April 1939 and, with money from Marshall Field, launched *PM*, an afternoon New York tabloid whose revolutionary aim was to survive without advertising. *PM* gave play to many a great photographer, including Weegee. But it was too good to last. Ingersoll went off to war, and Bourke-White soon tired of the limitations of tabloid space and newsprint reproduction and returned to *Life. PM* folded after the war.

Wilson Hicks had more to be concerned about than the handling of a staff of temperamental photographers. The picture business had few fixed rules, and

Life's practices tended to create standards for the industry. Hicks set page rates for the use of pictures—fifty dollars a page in the early days. He established day rates for freelancers working on assignment—twenty-five dollars and up. He offered "retainers" to favored photographers (e.g., Kessel and Mili)—usually a guarantee of ten days' work a month, with payment by day rate, or by page rate for the pictures actually used if that came to more.

This was Hicks's world, and there was much to learn. One week I presented Hicks with an exclusive picture, shot by architect R. H. Shreve, of two American bombers poised to take off for Britain from Gander, Newfoundland—then a secret operation. Shreve had given it to me on condition that it be cleared by the British embassy. Hicks ignored this caveat and proceeded to offer it for "Picture of the Week," to close on Saturday, my day off. I grew suspicious when, by Friday afternoon, no effort had been made to clear the picture, so I placed an ultimatum on Hicks's desk on Friday night: if the picture was not cleared before going to press, I would not report for work on Monday. Late Saturday morning an indignant Hicks called me at home: "John, how could you think that we would not clear that picture? Bart Sheridan [Hicks's other assistant] is on his way to Washington this minute to do it."

I had reason to be wary. I knew of an earlier incident, in 1940, when Charles Chaplin had obtained a court injunction against *Life*, stopping the publication of a film clip from *The Great Dictator,* which was being kept under wraps by Chaplin and his studio, United Artists. Hicks had tried to shift the blame to *Life*'s Hollywood correspondent, Richard Pollard, who had been ordered by Hicks to use "any means necessary" to obtain a still. Pollard had paid fifty dollars to a film cutter for a tiny piece of negative and had made it clear to Hicks how he had obtained it; the magazine went to press on a Saturday night, with Chaplin as Hitler ("Adenoid Hynkel" in the film) as "Picture of the Week." Chaplin went to court on Monday. Hicks was on the phone to Pollard: "That picture was stolen. You're in trouble." Pollard protested, "But I told you it was stolen! You still wanted it!" A revised edition of *Life* had to be printed and shipped.

That spring, I received a raise—to forty dollars a week, allowing the Morrises to move to a larger apartment. The Monday after the weekend move I reported to work, only to be told by Ed Thompson, "Congratulations, you're being transferred to the Coast. How soon can you move?" There was a small party to celebrate my departure. At *Life* almost any excuse was good for an office party. As it ended, Thompson's assistant, Helen Robinson, reached into her desk and pulled out a little envelope, a "going-away present" but also a kind of warning: "Hollywood's a rough town." Cautiously, I opened the envelope. It was the film clip stolen from Charlie Chaplin.

July 1941: Los Angeles, where the air was clear and distinctly fresh—and California's car culture well established. JOHN G. MORRIS

6

Hollywood Bureau

We arrived at Los Angeles's Union Station on July 17, 1941, a Thursday, in a style to which we were definitely *not* accustomed. At the time, there was no way one could go nonstop from coast to coast—certainly not by plane. Time Inc. had booked us a bedroom on the overnight *Commodore Vanderbilt* from New York to Chicago. We spent the weekend there to show off one-year-old Heather to our families. It was the first time the two grandmothers had seen her. It would also turn out to be the last.

The *Super Chief* departed Chicago's Union Station at dinnertime on Tuesday. My mother had offered to make sandwiches. Dèle reassured her that my fifteen-dollar Time Inc. per diem would enable us to eat in the diner. Not only that—Heather, whom we had nicknamed "Tuppy," through an overdose of A. A. Milne ("Now then! Tuppence for a fresh-caught mackerel!"), would have a full bed of her own. We were aboard America's most glamorous train, on the Santa Fe "Trail of the Stars," as the advertising campaign described it. The *Hollywood Reporter* dutifully recorded each day, under "Chicago to L.A." and "L.A. to Chicago," the names of movie people making the thirty-eight-hour journey. From "Chicago to New York," and vice versa, celebrities traveled overnight on the *Twentieth Century Limited*. It was virtually required of them to stop for lunch at the Pump Room of the Ambassador East Hotel, the hangout of Chicago's gossip columnists.

We sliced southwest through the Illinois cornfields, crossing the Mississippi during dinner. By midnight we had also crossed the Missouri River, near Liberty, where my father had been born just after the Civil War. His father had come by covered wagon from Kentucky. It never ceases to amaze me how much history two generations can encompass. It's also surprising how little we retain of it, without pictures.

Kansas was clicking past when we awakened the next morning. All day long we sped across the plain: Emporia, Hutchinson, Great Bend, Dodge City. I was reminded that railroads do not go straight. Like rivers, they generally take the easiest way. By dusk, we were cutting across the southeastern corner of Colorado to enter New Mexico through Raton Pass. It was dark when we reached the Rio Grande at Albuquerque; we stopped for half an hour to refuel, while grim-faced Navajo and Hopi sold souvenirs. I had never before seen the Southwest and was disappointed to discover that we would bypass Santa Fe, North America's oldest capital.

A cheery Dick Pollard greeted us at Los Angeles's Union Station. We piled into his Ford convertible for the fifteen-mile trip to Beverly Hills, following Sunset Boulevard all the way. Was *this* Hollywood? At first it looked for all the world like Queens—used-car lots, bungalows, filling stations—except for the fact that there was not a pedestrian in sight. California's car culture was well established. To our astonishment, people even *ate* in their cars. I saw my first drive-ins and carhops. Even if a bit drab, everything looked clean, and the air was fresh. The sky was blue, with only a slight haze. Smog would not arrive until 1943, with the county's transformation from a primarily agricultural one to a primarily industrial one.

At the Beverly Hills post office we crossed the Pacific Electric tracks (since removed in favor of freeways) to the business district. Pollard parked diagonally on Canon Drive, in front of the *Beverly Hills Citizen,* and we climbed to the *Time/Life* office on the second floor. It was anything but glamorous: a front room shared by two *Time* correspondents and a secretary, a back room consisting mainly of Pollard's desk, piled high with messages, and, in the corner, his laundry.

Life had enormous prestige and power in Hollywood, to the point of occasional embarrassment. Designation of a film as *Life*'s "Movie of the Week" almost guaranteed a big box office. Celebrities, or their agents, would go to elaborate lengths to attract *Life* to a party in the hope that it would become the subject of the weekly feature "LIFE Goes to a Party." A cancellation of the entire event might follow if *Life* declined. Press agents fawned all over Pollard. He returned calls from those he respected or those who amused him. Once Pollard got himself into trouble by not paying enough attention to his own idea. George Glass of United Artists had phoned to say he was "desperate" over a picture called *New Wine* that the critics were sure to "murder." How to distract them? Pollard suggested giving its relatively unknown star, Eleanor Counts, a champagne shower in something skimpy. Glass did and released the picture to the wire services. That Saturday, Pollard received an irate wire from New York:

USING AP PHOTO OF ELEANOR COUNTS CHAMPAGNE SHOWER AS "PICTURE OF THE WEEK."
WHY DIDN'T YOU COVER?

"Harlots and starlets" is how bachelor Pollard described the aspiring actresses who spent much of their time trying to get his attention. Those were the days of the Star System, with many actresses under contract to the studios. A *Life* story could lift a young woman out of obscurity and into the limelight overnight. Carole Landis (who had only recently been Frances Lillian Mary Ridste), a buxom cavewoman in Hal Roach's *One Million B.C.*, succeeded in catching Pollard's eye. When Peter Stackpole's pictures of her appeared in *Life*, her pay went from $75 a week to $750. Landis called Pollard to ask what she could do to repay him. Dick thought for a moment and then answered, "I've always wanted a Swiss army knife." When I last had lunch with Pollard in Santa Barbara, only months before his death in early 1994, I asked if he had ever taken an actress up on one of those offers. "Not intentionally" was his deadpan reply.

Photographers loved to work with Pollard. He was unobtrusive, and he was helpful in small but important ways. One day, a Columbia Pictures press agent named Magda Maskel suggested photographing Rita Hayworth in a black lace nightgown that Maskel's mother had made. Pollard and photographer Bob Landry met Maskel at Hayworth's apartment. She knelt on a bed in the nightie, looking provocative, and Landry snapped away. Good, but *something else* might be done. Pollard spoke up: "Rita, take a deep breath." That was it. The perfect frame. Not only did Landry's photo become one of the most popular of all World War II pinups, it brought Hayworth a new husband. When Orson Welles saw it in *Life*, he determined to marry her. It may now seem odd, but *Life* did not immediately recognize the usefulness of "girl covers" in selling magazines. *Life* was six months old before the first such cover appeared—a chaste long shot of Jean Harlow, fully clothed, walking away from the camera. Six months later, *Life* ran its first mildly sexy cover, Peter Stackpole's portrait of "The Prettiest Girl in Paradise." The Paradise was a New York nightclub.

In *Life*'s thirty-six years as a weekly, thirty-three *Life* photographers covered the movies, most of them working from the Los Angeles office (it moved about four hundred yards out of Beverly Hills onto the Sunset Boulevard "Strip" two months after I arrived). Of them all, Peter Stackpole most deserves the credit for creating *Life*'s candid approach to movie reporting. Stackpole claims to have inherited an appreciation of the female form from his father, sculptor Ralph Stackpole, a friend of the Mexican muralist Diego Rivera. The elder Stackpole had wanted his son to be a painter but had made the mistake of giving him a Leica. Peter had taken it to school and made candid pictures in class, shooting up through the inkwell of his desk. He went to work as a freelancer for the Oakland newspapers and photographed a snoozing ex-President Hoover during

At the request of *Life*'s Hollywood correspondent, Dick Pollard, Columbia Pictures press agent Magda Maskel lent her own sexy nightwear to Rita Hayworth. "Rita, take a deep breath," Pollard commanded. Rita complied, producing one of World War II's pinup classics. BOB LANDRY/Life *Magazine* © *Time Inc.*

Charter Day ceremonies; his editors at the *Oakland Tribune* refused to run the picture for fear of offending the paper's owners, the family of Republican senator William Knowland. *Time*, however, paid Stackpole a handsome hundred dollars for the shot. Peter used the money to buy film so that he could photograph the construction of the Golden Gate and Bay bridges. He showed such nerve in climbing the girders that the contractors gave him a pass and a movie camera to record their own exploits. Peter, like many of his photographer brethren, had a talent for charming his way into situations where most people would be refused entry.

Stackpole's work attracted the attention of San Francisco's famous Group f/64 (among them Ansel Adams, Imogen Cunningham, Willard Van Dyke, and

Before there was a *Life* magazine, Peter Stackpole attracted the attention of *Time* with candid pictures of former president Herbert Hoover dozing on a commencement platform. Stackpole submitted his spectacular pictures of the building of San Francisco's Bay bridges for *Life*'s first issue, only to get beaten out for the cover by Margaret Bourke-White's pictures of the Fort Peck Dam in Montana. Peter became one of *Life*'s first four staffers, later specializing in Hollywood pulchritude. I suppose that he managed to take this picture on the Golden Gate Bridge with a self-timer. PETER STACKPOLE/Life *Magazine © Time Inc.*

Edward Weston). Named for the lens aperture that gives dramatic depth of focus, the group came to stand for "straight" photography—no poses or artificial lighting for Group f/64. Cunningham sent some of Peter's bridge pictures to Frank Crowninshield, who published them in *Vanity Fair*. Peter began shooting assignments for the Time Inc. San Francisco bureau and was invited to New York just before *Life* began publication. He had hoped that one of his Golden Gate Bridge pictures would make *Life*'s first cover, but Bourke-White's Fort Peck Dam was chosen, to go with her lead story (at *Life*, the photographer was considered the "author") on the rough frontier life of the Montana dam workers. The captions, unsigned, were by poet Archibald MacLeish. Luce labeled this the first "Photo Essay," then a form of photojournalism new to America. Stackpole's Golden Gate Bridge made *Life*'s cover six months later.

Despite his aerial derring-do and recognition by Group f/64, Stackpole's real interest lay in recording female pulchritude; he was a natural for the Hollywood bureau, and while there he shot the great days of the stars: the eight-year-old Shirley Temple, Elizabeth Taylor at twelve, Mickey Rooney as Andy Hardy, Judy Garland in *The Wizard of Oz*. He photographed Ingrid Bergman, Joan Crawford, Bette Davis, Marlene Dietrich, Greer Garson. He captured Vivien Leigh, Ginger Rogers, and Joan Fontaine fondling their Oscars. And the men: Gary Cooper, Clark Gable, Cary Grant, Jimmy Stewart, Bing Crosby, Bob Hope, Frank Sinatra. Occasionally Stackpole came too close to the stars; once he became embroiled in a statutory rape case against Errol Flynn. Stackpole was warned by Humphrey Bogart that Flynn's attorneys might try to finger Stackpole as the culprit. The case was dismissed.

In this heady, weird place, I was having the time of my life. From my home in Westwood, near the UCLA campus, I could cruise down Sunset Boulevard to make the rounds of the studios. Their back lots were a living museum of movie history. There was the Welsh village of *How Green Was My Valley*, just filmed by John Ford. I saw the Atlanta of *Gone With the Wind*. I visited the location for Alexander Korda's *Jungle Book* in Sherwood Forest (its actual California name) and went out onto the desert to watch Errol Flynn as the doomed General George Custer in *They Died with Their Boots On*. The previous day, a poorly timed "U.S. Cavalry" charge had collided with the "Indians," leaving one stuntman dead. Such fatalities were not unusual.

From time to time, we came through with offbeat *Life* exclusives. One such gave me the opportunity to demonstrate just how thoroughly confused one could become trying to keep track of Hollywood's abundant blondes. With Bob Landry and Steve Brooks, a Paramount press agent, I spent an arduous afternoon interviewing Veronica Lake about her extraordinary hair—how she washed it, combed it, kept from setting it ablaze—only to fail to recognize her the next day when I was at lunch with Brooks at the Paramount commissary. Lake sauntered by with her hair pinned up and smiled in our direction. "Who's that?" I asked Steve. "Yeah, right," he said, grinning as he watched her sway into the crowd. "No, I'm serious, I'd really like to know," I said. "Idiot!" he snorted. "You only spent the afternoon with her yesterday!"

Perhaps the greatest domestic tragedy of World War II was the evacuation of U.S. citizens of Japanese descent from the West Coast to detention camps beyond the Sierras, often breaking up homes on a few days' notice. ELIOT ELISOFON/Life *Magazine © Time Inc.*

7

The "Day of Wrath"

Los ANGELES, December 7, 1941: It was a quiet, lazy Sunday morning, with the temperature going into the eighties. The big event in Westwood was to be a celebration of my twenty-fifth birthday; Dèle was in the kitchen, baking a cake. Jim Brown and Bob Herschel, childhood pals of mine who had become our "boarders," were out in the street, passing a football back and forth. I was about to join them when the news came over the radio that the Japanese had bombed Pearl Harbor. The war we had been dreading was here at last. Instinctively, we knew that it would profoundly affect us all, but we were too shocked to think about it at that moment.

I called the office and reached a breathless Sidney James, the *Time/Life* bureau chief. He told me to get a photographer and head down to the Japanese-American section called "Little Tokyo," near the Civic Center. I wasted no time. I called Johnny Florea, a young photographer we had been trying out, and agreed on a rendezvous. Then I raced downtown on Beverly Boulevard, running red lights, even going up and around on the sidewalk at one clogged intersection. I wasn't going to be late for my first war. Little Tokyo was quiet. Police patrols had been doubled, and MPs were also patrolling the streets. The residents were staying indoors, listening to the news. A cop griped to us, "We gotta protect the Japanese against the Americans, not the other way around." We kept roaming the downtown streets, finding little that photographically told the story except for shots of people reading the extra editions of the Los Angeles papers that appeared shortly after two o'clock. In four-inch block letters, the *Los Angeles Times* screamed: WAR!

At about 5:00 A.M.—it was now Monday—we headed back to the bureau, where Sid James was putting together a massive file from the entire staff, to be wired to New York for the *Time* closing that night. *Life* had closed on Saturday as usual, with an unfortunate "Junior Miss" fashion picture on the cover. It couldn't be changed. Presses did stop, however, for a new lead: "War: Japan Launches Reckless Attack on U.S." The lack of images of the event itself was maddening. Bob Landry had just sailed from Pearl Harbor with a naval task force, but there was no telling when he would be heard from. The editors were compelled to use pictures previously taken in Hawaii by staff photographer William Shrout, giving them melodramatic captions: "Civilians saw the sky darken with American fighters engaging Jap squadrons and Flying Fortresses (like this) head out to sea." Sheer nonsense, of course. Truth became one of the war's first casualties. None of us imagined how truly disastrous that surprise attack had been.

The events of my twenty-fifth birthday thus made meaningless my claim to conscientious objection. I had said I would fight if the country was attacked—which seemed inconceivable. I had been a qualified pacifist; contrary to my better instincts, I soon became an active propagandist. The Pearl Harbor attack brought Henry Luce a great sense of relief. His drive to inspire American intervention was over. In a typically fervent *Life* editorial he wrote, "We have come to the end, now, of as pusillanimous an epoch as there ever was in the history of a great people: the twenty years of American history between 1921 and 1941. . . . The epoch that is closing was much less tragic than it was shameful. . . . This is the day of wrath. It is also the day of hope. . . . For this hour America was made." He wrote as well to Franklin Roosevelt: "The dearest wish of all of us is to tell the story of absolute victory under your leadership."

The Los Angeles bureau went to war almost merrily. Our leader was the dynamic, unflappable Sid James, who often took assignments directly from Luce. Luce had made a mysterious visit to the bureau just before Pearl Harbor, slipping into our untidy offices unannounced and almost incognito—one unlucky *Time* correspondent had mistaken him for a press agent, greeting Luce with the note of mild irritation typical of such encounters. Luce was in town to coach James through secret negotiations for the purchase of the Los Angeles *Daily News*, an afternoon tabloid. Pearl Harbor brought an end to that deal and to business as usual for everyone.

Sid James was the exception among Time Inc.'s top brass. He had never gone to college, let alone to an Ivy League school. He had worked his way up in newspapers, starting as a Saint Louis police reporter. He had learned the trade by covering, as he put it in his 1994 memoir, *Press Pass*, "shotgun assassinations on busy street corners, family quarrels that ended tragically, armed robberies . . . muggings, stabbings, drownings, suicides and auto accidents." Far from being hardened by such savagery, Sid never lost his sense of compassion; he was a great boss.

Our little bureau was forced into rapid expansion. Pollard entered the Army Signal Corps, one step ahead of the draft. Helen Morgan replaced him on movies. We clearly needed more photographers, and we found them in a seemingly unlikely place: Fremont High. This Los Angeles public school, whose alumni I took to calling "Group FHS" as an echo of San Francisco's Group f/64, owed its success to the inspiration of one devoted schoolteacher, Clarence A. Bach. I have no idea how he taught, but his results were impressive. Our association with FHS began when Dick Pollard, needing an extra photographer for a sudden *Life* assignment, remembered a talented *Los Angeles Times* photographer whom he had seen covering a Pomona College track meet. It was George Strock, a recent Fremont graduate. Not only did Strock begin getting *Life* assignments, he introduced a second Fremonter, Bob Landry, who introduced a third, Johnny Florea, who introduced a fourth, Mark Kauffman, who introduced a fifth, John Dominis, who introduced a sixth, Jack Wilkes, who introduced a seventh, Hank Walker. A few Fremont alumni got away to other magazines, but I have the same high regard for the members of the Fremont High Society that I do for the members of the Royal Photographic Society.

Strock became a *Life* staffer. He was sent to Europe briefly to cover the Vichy French and then to the Pacific. One day in early 1942, we had a call from New York. Strock had failed to report on time for a convoy that was due to sail from San Francisco. He had left New York by train several days earlier. Strock was overly fond of alcohol, so we first checked his favorite L.A. bars. No luck. We had given up the search when news arrived that he had somehow made his convoy. A day or so after the convoy's departure, an executive of the Union Pacific Railroad received a letter of commendation for a bartender on the *City of San Francisco*. It was signed George Strock, War Correspondent.

Fremont's most successful alumnus was Bob Landry, who made five *Life* covers in his first year. But his professional triumphs had a personal cost. Bob was out of town a lot, and after one of those long trips, his wife, Peggy, demanded a divorce. She wanted to marry Dick Pollard—and did. But there were no hard feelings. In fact, Bob attended the Pollards' engagement party.

Like Landry, Johnny Florea had worked for the Hearst newspapers before coming to *Life*. Florea, despite a certain resemblance to Jackie Gleason, had little to joke about during his early days at *Life*. Nothing he photographed seemed to make the magazine. In 1942, his luck changed, with thirty published stories to his credit. After covering the war in the Pacific and in Europe, Johnny returned to Hollywood, where he specialized in elaborate photographic dramatizations.

In February, we received further reinforcements in the person of Eliot Elisofon, who arrived overland from New York, his Buick station wagon crammed with top-of-the-line equipment. A green-eyed Peter Stackpole witnessed the unloading one Saturday morning and then disappeared. He returned grinning two hours later, having purchased a brand-new Linhof camera. Eliot was already something of a legend when he arrived. Born of Russian immigrant parents who lived just off the Bowery, he had put himself through Fordham University, majoring in philosophy. He was self-educated in the arts, and he had found his genius in photography. Eliot was one of Alex King's discoveries and made the magazine regularly.

One cool February evening, Dèle and I were listening to one of Franklin Roosevelt's "fireside chats" when air-raid sirens sounded, for real, followed by a partial city blackout. I called Sid James at home. He had already learned the bare facts: a Japanese submarine had fired shells into an oil storage depot north of Santa Barbara. I agreed to leave for the scene immediately, picking up Elisofon, who lived around the corner.

There were no freeways in those days. Driving up the coast road, we were soon stopped by civil defense guards, whom we feared far more than the Japanese. After a brief hassle, they permitted us to drive on through the blackout with parking lights, all the way to Santa Barbara. We arrived at the scene just before daybreak and, at a roadside diner near Goleta, found the press: twenty or thirty reporters and photographers plus cameramen from the five newsreels. Sentries patrolled a fence that blocked access to the "battlefield." We were all told to wait for an escort, who was on his way from G-2, Southern California Defense Command, headquartered in Pasadena.

Soon after sunrise, frustrated and bored, I walked over to the fence and chatted up one of the sentries. "Wanna see somethin'?" he asked. He reached into his tunic and pulled out a jagged shell fragment slightly larger than my hand. I immediately offered him five dollars. "For five bucks you can only borrow it." I gave him the five, demanding that the deal be considered exclusive, and hid the fragment under my coat. Elisofon was deep in conversation with the other photographers, explaining the virtues of one of his pricey lenses. I stepped on his foot and said, "Let's go up the road." As soon as we were out of sight, I pulled out the shell. He photographed it in my hand, over a strand of barbed wire. That picture became the frontispiece of the following week's *Life*.

Eventually, the G-2 officer came to give us a tour of the damage, which was slight. Disappointed, the press corps rapidly departed to meet deadlines in L.A., which permitted Eliot and me—our deadline still several days off—to get another exclusive. In the diner, I had heard talk of a shell that had gone "way up in the hills." We drove high up into the coast range until we came to a sentry at a farmer's gate. We waved and called out, "The colonel sent us," and drove right by. Finally we arrived in a meadow. There sat a solitary soldier, guarding the neat hole left by a five-inch shell from the Japanese submarine. It had failed to explode and was, so he claimed, already on its way to Aberdeen Proving

Ground for ballistics tests. Eliot composed a vertical that served as a virtual map of the "engagement": the soldier looking out to sea, the Channel Islands in the distance. The submarine must have come right past them. The "Battle of Santa Barbara" may not have made the history books, but how long had it been since the continental United States had been under enemy fire? The site is now commemorated by a plaque that stands on the golf course of the Sandpiper Country Club between the clubhouse and the first tee.

Elisofon's most dramatic Hollywood wartime production was a work of fiction, a "picturization" called "Have You Heard?" The basic message was "Loose lips sink ships," a project suggested to *Life* by the White House. What we needed for the story was a master of suspense. Who better for the job than Alfred Hitchcock? We pitched him our proposal, and he and his wife invited Sid James, Eliot, and me for lunch at their home in Bel Air. Hitchcock hustled about fixing us cocktails from a well-equipped rolling bar. It took two such lunches to work out the script. It was fun to watch a genius at work. Seating himself at the head

Not long after Pearl Harbor, the White House proposed that *Life* dramatize the dangers of "loose talk." Los Angeles bureau chief Sid James and I enlisted director Alfred Hitchcock, who was delighted to concoct a fictional story line: first a false rumor, then a true one, reaches Axis ears. For the next-to-last scene we chose a bar in Santa Monica where a spy (*right*) overhears talk of a departing troopship. Recalling that Hitchcock always played a cameo role in his productions, I cast him—to his delight—as a bartender (*center*). I can now truthfully say that I have directed the great director. He didn't need much coaching. ELIOT ELISOFON/Life *Magazine* © *Time Inc.*

of the table like a chairman of the board, he asked, in that measured, deep velvet voice, "Well, gentlemen, where shall we begin? What's the most unlikely place for a rumor to start?" A soft, slightly wicked smile crept across his face. "How about a church?"

Thus our story commenced at Hollywood's First Methodist Church. The "Sunday service" was actually a midweek choir practice, with half the choir filling in as the congregation. Hitchcock insisted that we first lay a false trail: The minister says a prayer for "our soldier boys who must leave our shores." A woman seated in the third pew wearing an elaborate hat interprets this as news. She is next seen on a bus, speculating out loud as to where "the boys" are going. A man with a mustache in the seat behind her overhears this and embroiders the story as he passes it along in a steam bath, from which it travels to a restaurant, a gas station, a dentist's office, and so on, until it finally reaches a haberdasher, who says, "I never listen to rumors. You shouldn't spread such talk." But the next day an Army officer enters the haberdashery to order tropical-weight shirts, which he must have by the following Tuesday. The haberdasher guesses that a troopship is departing and speculates aloud about its destination. This news finally reaches the ear of a spy in a bar in Santa Monica. He communicates it to the crewmen of a German submarine that lurks off Malibu. The troopship is torpedoed. As we prepared to shoot the semifinal scene, I thought of something. Hitchcock loved to walk on in his films. Why not cast him as a Santa Monica bartender, an apron around his plump belly? He was delighted, and I set him up behind the bar.

The Santa Barbara shelling led *Life* for March 9, 1942: "Japanese Carry War to California Coast." Four weeks later, the lead was "Coast Japs Are Interned in Mountain Camp." It was another report by the team of Elisofon and Morris. We had driven in the first Army convoy of Japanese Americans from Los Angeles to Manzanar, a "reception center" in the High Sierra. They were the vanguard of 120,000 Japanese and Japanese-American residents of the Pacific coast who were interned shortly after Pearl Harbor, in one of the sorriest episodes in the history of American civil rights. Of course, there was never any serious domestic security threat. Intercepted Japanese cables revealed no role assigned to Japanese Americans in sabotage or espionage. But the FBI rounded up 343 Japanese aliens in Los Angeles alone in the first ten days after Pearl Harbor, acting on tips supplied, ironically, largely by American-born Japanese (*nisei*) themselves. In Hawaii, by contrast, the 158,000 resident Japanese were not incarcerated; they were needed too badly for the war effort. Economic self-interest—let's just call it greed—was the determining factor in the creation of an artificial crisis in California. Local farmers saw an opportunity to get rid of their hardworking competitors in the Japanese-American community—and

One night in February 1942, during one of Franklin Roosevelt's radio "fireside chats," a Japanese submarine fired half a dozen shells at an oil storage depot just north of Santa Barbara, California. With *Life* photographer Eliot Elisofon and most of the Los Angeles press corps, I arrived at the scene at daybreak, only to find the area cordoned off. I chatted up one of the sentries, who reached under his tunic and revealed this jagged shell fragment. For five dollars I borrowed it—exclusively—and held it for the picture that led the magazine. ELIOT ELISOFON/Life *Magazine © Time Inc.*

immediately replaced them with low-paid Mexicans. A spokesman for California's Grower-Shipper Vegetable Association was quoted in *The Saturday Evening Post:* "We're charged with wanting to get rid of the Japs for selfish reasons. We do."

Teamed with Florea, I visited the Japanese fishing colony on Terminal Island in Los Angeles harbor. We saw Japanese families, facing eviction, panicked into selling their possessions for almost nothing—an electric refrigerator would go for three dollars. This desperately sad scene went almost totally unreported in the California press, which was dominated by the Hearst newspapers and the then-reactionary *Los Angeles Times.* If there was any threat, it was from Americans seeking vengeance on the Japanese. The attack on Hawaii had understandably provoked intense hatred. In the second issue after Pearl Harbor, *Life* ran a tasteless story headed "How to Tell Japs from Chinese." Three weeks later, in a cover story on "Pacific Coast Defense," a *Life* photo showed a Santa Monica woman demonstrating "How to kill a Jap" in hand-to-hand combat. "Many of the women are convinced they personally will have to fight Japs," the caption continued. I was appalled but took some small consolation in the fact that *Life* was generally more restrained than the press as a whole, especially the tabloids.

On February 19, President Roosevelt issued Executive Order 9066, enabling the Army to designate "military areas" from which all "undesirable" persons could be removed. A few days later, the areas were defined as a strip 80 to 100 miles deep along the coast. At sunrise on March 22, Elisofon and I joined the 140-car convoy of some five hundred Japanese, carrying all the possessions they could, as it formed near Pasadena's Rose Bowl. All day long the pathetic procession moved on, punctuated every ten cars by an Army jeep. We crossed the coast range into the desert of sagebrush and Joshua trees, past dry alkali lakes and through red-rock canyons, following the line of the Los Angeles aqueduct. Finally, at 6:30, as the sun set behind the snowy Sierras, we reached Manzanar, a camp of prefabricated tar-paper-clad barracks that had been hastily assembled—and still lacked plumbing. It was to be the home of ten thousand innocent people for an average of two and a half years.

It was the first time I had seen an American president cave in to the pressure of venal fellow politicians and a jingoistic press. Unfortunately, it was not to be the last. *Life,* to its credit, ran a fairly factual account of the situation, even referring to the "reception center" as a "concentration camp." That, I must admit, was an exaggeration. It would be three years before the world fully realized what concentration camps were all about.

Dèle, and Mavis Elisofon, accompanied us on the trip to Manzanar. I did not want to let Dèle out of my sight. Just a fortnight before, we had lost our child, our Heather, the "Tuppy" whom we had gently bound to her seat with napkins as a makeshift high chair so that she could breakfast with us in the diner of the Santa Fe *Super Chief.* Pearl Harbor had come, ironically, at the happiest time of our lives. It was followed by the absolute worst. Heather was a buoyant, bright, and healthy child who shared the love that filled our home. I worked long hours, but Dèle and Tuppy were inseparable. At night we could hear the roar of warplanes being tested at Douglas in Santa Monica, but the war had still not really touched the three of us—we would be four in June.

When the Elisofons arrived, we found them an apartment nearby. They held a housewarming on the night of March 7, 1942, and we walked over the hill to attend. Jim Brown was at our home that evening, baby-sitting until he went off to work the midnight shift at Northrop. Dèle and I met him on the front porch. We checked on Heather, who was sleeping peacefully, and then went to sleep in the next room. We heard nothing during the night. I went to Tuppy's crib first thing the next morning, and she seemed . . . lifeless. My scream brought Dèle running. We called the doctor immediately, but we knew it was no use. Tuppy had strangled in the very zipper jacket designed to protect her from such accidents. An inquest followed, and of course we were exonerated, but I cannot imagine to this day how it could have happened. I still cannot talk about it.

Now we felt the war closing in on us. The defense industry became our running story. Morale was high; there was work for everyone. *Life* surveyed the entire industrial scene in a photo-essay entitled "The West at War," with a cover of an aircraft assembly-line mechanic working in pith helmet, shorts, and tool belt. We shot at Lockheed (where P-38 fighters were made), Douglas (A-20 attack bombers and transports), North American (B-25 bombers and P-51 fighters), Northrop (Vengeance dive-bombers), Consolidated (B-24 bombers and flying boats), and Ryan (trainers). We went to shipyards, munitions plants, and the new Kaiser steel mill. We photographed union meetings and showed the presidents of the "rival" aircraft companies lunching together to swap information and parts. Cooperation among competitors was the order of the day.

California was an armed training camp. Bases of all kinds were scattered from Chula Vista, at the Mexican border, to Crescent City, near the Oregon line. Elisofon and I covered the first desert maneuvers of General George S. Patton's First Armored Division, near Indio. The troops did not know it, but they were being trained for the invasion of North Africa, eight months in the future. Patton was far from reluctant when it came to publicity. Elisofon, whom Patton called "Helzapoppin!," had shot a color cover of Patton at Fort Benning, Georgia, in his red-white-blue-and-yellow-striped command tank, for a special "Defense Issue" of *Life.*

Eliot and I, riding in a jeep with Gladwin Hill of *The New York Times,* soon spotted Patton's tank, now in drab desert camouflage, way out in front. We raced up and pulled alongside. The hatch flew open, and Patton emerged. I yelled, "General, what's going on here?" "How the hell would I know?" "Old Blood-and-Guts" barked back at me. "Tank warfare is a helluva lot like spaghetti! You can't push it from behind! A general has to be up front pulling it!" An hour later, we found him at lunch, sitting picnic-style in the sand with his aide, Captain Richard Jensen. An African-American orderly was serving them. Jensen would later be killed in North Africa, almost before Patton's eyes. It was said that Patton cried then, and I can well believe it, for there was a very tender father-and-son relationship between the two men. Patton was gracious, offering us coffee while we chatted—though he did most of the talking—comparing modern tank war with battles of the past. I would see Patton once more, at a briefing in Normandy. After all that careening around in a tank, Patton would die, ironically, following an auto accident.

On June 16, 1942, Dèle gave birth to a whopping, screaming, eight-pound, nine-ounce girl at Cedars of Lebanon Hospital in Hollywood. We named her Mary Holly Morris. The timing could not have been better—just the distraction we needed from our so-recent loss and the grim march of war. A few weeks later, a small package arrived from Tiffany's. We had received a similar one only two years before, for Heather. It was a silver porringer, inscribed "For Mary Holly Morris from HENRY R. LUCE and Her Father's Friends in Time, Inc."

Wilson Hicks decided that he could "use me" back in New York that summer. The atmosphere in Rockefeller Center was tense. One by one, my male friends were disappearing from civilian life. America was becoming a society of women, children, the elderly, and the "deferred." I was still one of those last, classified 3-A for fatherhood but not counting upon it to last. The Allies were reeling in retreat. After Pearl Harbor, the Japanese had overwhelmed the Philippines and many islands of Micronesia and Melanesia, plus Hong Kong and most of Southeast Asia. Having conquered western Europe, the Germans had reached Stalingrad and Leningrad; in North Africa, they threatened even the Suez Canal. The full extent of our losses was hidden by censorship. Graphic pictures of the catastrophe at Pearl Harbor were not released for an entire year.

In February 1943, Hicks sent me to relieve Ray Mackland, *Life*'s Washington, D.C., editor, for a month. Washington was the Allied command center for the entire world and bursting at the seams. A visitor could never be sure of a bed in this boomtown. On occasion I slept in a hotel manager's office. The administration was furiously writing contracts to build "the arsenal of democracy." Across the Potomac, a huge five-sided, five-story building that would be called the Pentagon was under construction.

It was Mackland's task—and mine, in his absence—to deal with the censors. Naturally, *Life*'s editors sought to cover the war realistically, without interference. In 1938, *Life* justified a photo-essay by Robert Capa on the Spanish Civil

War thus: "Dead men have indeed died in vain if live men refuse to look at them." But when it came to American dead, the censors banned such pictures, as they had in World War I. In January 1943, covering the savage battle for New Guinea's Buna Beach, George Strock made a picture of the bodies of three Americans awash in the sands. Not until September did *Life* manage to argue it through the censors, publishing it with an editorial that concluded, "Why print this picture, anyway, of three American boys dead upon an alien shore? Is it to hurt people? To be morbid? Those are not the reasons. The reason is that words are never enough."

Having had a taste of it, I envied Mackland his Washington assignment, but I wanted to get even closer to the action. I could see that there was going to be a need for a comparable post in London, where the buildup for a second front was already under way. I volunteered to go.

LIFE

Vol. 16, No. 20

May 15, 1944

THE MEN FROM THE UNITED STATES, CARRYING BAYONETED SPRINGFIELD RIFLES, GET GOING ACROSS ENGLAND UNDER THE FLAGS OF THEIR COUNTRY AND THEIR REGIMENT

AMERICAN INVADERS MASS IN ENGLAND

It became obvious upon my arrival in London in October 1944 that the long-touted invasion of Western Europe was months away. We concentrated on stories of the buildup for it. In February, photographer Frank Scherschel and I flew by military transport to Belfast to see what was going on in Northern Ireland. The next day we photographed this parade of the 101st Airborne Division, but we were permitted neither to identify the division nor to tell where the picture was taken. Hence the erroneous headline. FRANK SCHERSCHEL/Life *Magazine © Time Inc.*

8

The Longest Wait

On September 20, 1943, Dèle and Holly saw me off at Grand Central Terminal, on the first leg of a trip to Saint John (New Brunswick), Liverpool, and London. I was traveling with John Scott of *Time*. Another Morris—then nicknamed "Fidget" because of his in utero rambunctiousness—was on the way. It was a tough departure, but there were no tears; we were determined not to cry. After an uneventful voyage aboard the 3,500-ton Norwegian freighter *Mosdale*—detouring almost to the Azores to avoid the U-boats that had been reported in our path—we reached Liverpool and took a train to London. Scott and I checked into the Savoy Hotel (nothing but the best for Time Inc.ers) and taxied to the office of Time and Life Ltd. on Dean Street in shabby, ethnic Soho. We had virtually guaranteed our welcome by bringing silk stockings, cigarettes, lemons, eggs, and whiskey to the thirty-five or so employees.

The front offices were occupied by *Time* correspondents, under bureau chief Walter Graebner. There were two payrolls. The Americans were paid in dollars from back home. The Londoners included an Indian Marxist (fired after he refused British army service), an Irishman who had been *The March of Time*'s soundman, a former Spanish Loyalist general, and a lovely young Englishwoman who handled the "soft" feature stories. My fellow countrymen were Mary Welsh of Thief River Falls, Minnesota, and the Chicago *Daily News;* Wilmott Ragsdale, late of *The Wall Street Journal;* William Walton from a downstate Illinois daily, AP, and *Time* Foreign News. It would have taken a soothsayer to predict that Mary would become Mrs. Ernest Hemingway; Ragsdale a bridge tender and journalism professor; and Walton a landscape painter and confidant of President and Mrs. John F. Kennedy.

I'd never met anyone like Lee Miller. Before she was *Vogue*'s war correspondent she had been a model for the magazine; Edward Steichen photographed her at the suggestion of Condé Nast himself. She was also the modernists' muse. Every part of her was celebrated: her lips hover over a Man Ray landscape; it is her eye that swings on his surreal metronome; the shape of her breast inspired a champagne glass. ABOVE: DAVID E. SCHERMAN © *Lee Miller Archives*; OPPOSITE: © *1998 Man Ray Trust/ADAGP/Paris*

Virtually everyone else seemed to work for *Life*. That was to be my domain. Wilson Hicks had given me the title of London picture editor, saying, "Never forget, John, *you're* in charge. It's *your* neck if we don't get those pictures on the big day." He was speaking of D-Day, of course. Just to keep me alert, however, Time Inc. was up to its old tricks—creating a turf war within the office by deliberately assigning two people to the same job, giving them different titles, and leaving them to slug it out. Sherry Mangan arrived on the scene a month later. He had written for *Time* and *Fortune* but had no *Life* experience. Mangan had been told by Dan Longwell, *Life's* *other* executive editor, that *he* would be in charge in London, with the title of *Life* London manager. We both would work under Walter Graebner, the overall bureau chief. I saw trouble ahead.

By the time Mangan appeared, I had the *Life* team running smoothly. There was little for Sherry to do, so he decided to make work for all of us by *managing*. He was notorious for his methodical lists. Once, in a sleepy, dead-end conference called by Graebner to discuss story ideas, I happened to glance at the top of Sherry's yellow pad. He had neatly printed the words STORY SUGGESTIONS and, under this, NO SUGGESTIONS. It didn't matter. Our pictures were hitting the magazine regularly. When I arrived, there were just three staff photographers, and they couldn't have been more different. Longest in residence was the German-born Hans Wild, whose beliefs as a conscientious objector only spurred him on in covering the 1940 Blitz and the 1942 "spite bombing." Wild had started at *Life* as London darkroom manager. Photographer Dave Scherman was the wisecracking spark plug of the London staff. He had gone to work for *Life's* Promotion Department upon graduating from Dartmouth College; his further education came from reading *The New Yorker*, whose humorist S. J. Perelman he adored and attempted to emulate. Sent to London in the fall of 1941, Scherman developed what *Life* called "a new accent to picture coverage of war" by dramatizing, in lush photo-essays, the values the Allies were fighting for—hearth and home, romance and heroics, and good old English literature. It was Scherman, with *Vogue* photographer Lee Miller, who first took me to the White Tower restaurant on Percy Street in Soho, a virtual annex of Time Inc. Its Greek Cypriot proprietor, John Stais, specialized in finding the foods, such as corn on the cob and fresh strawberries in sour cream, that only expense accounts could afford.

I had never before met anyone even remotely like Lee Miller. Born in 1907 in Poughkeepsie, New York, Lee had delighted in getting herself expelled from one school after another. In desperation, her father, an industrial plant superintendent, had sent her off to Paris at eighteen with two chaperones. She had immediately ditched them and had soon found her place among the artists and intellectuals of the Lost Generation in its waning days. The plastic and cinematic arts were exploding, under the influence of the Cubists and Surrealists.

Lee became their darling. Picasso painted her; Jean Cocteau cast her as an armless statue in his film *The Blood of a Poet;* and she was for three years the American expatriate photographer Man Ray's model and lover. He taught Lee photography, but it was she who invented his famous "solarizations" when she accidentally snapped on the light in his darkroom, overexposing the black background of a portrait.

When I met her in October 1943, Lee was married to an Egyptian businessman but was living with Dave Scherman in the Hampstead home of Roland Penrose. Penrose, a distinguished artist, was then off in Italy, serving as a captain in the British Army Camouflage Corps. Eventually he would marry Lee, father her son, Antony, and receive a knighthood for founding London's Institute of Contemporary Arts. Thus the rebellious girl from Poughkeepsie died, in 1977, as Lady Penrose, wife of the illustrious Sir Roland. The title tickled her.

While they did their best to make me feel at home in London, inviting me to the house on Hampstead Heath for both Thanksgiving and Christmas, Lee and Dave did not solve my housing problem (my days at the Savoy were obviously numbered). Frank Scherschel, *Life*'s third London-based photographer, came to the rescue. Frank had a flat on the third floor of a house on Upper Wimpole Street. In peacetime a dentist had made his office there. His chair remained affixed to the second floor, but he and his practice had fled to the countryside for the duration.

The defensive Battle of Britain was over. The offensive Battle of Europe was joined. Scherschel had come to London two months ahead of me, assigned to cover the U.S. Eighth Air Force, which now flew with the Royal Air Force in massive air attacks on the Continent. In September, Frank flew a mission to Stuttgart in which thirty-five B-17 bombers were lost to flak and fighter attacks; his plane barely made it back across the Channel, crash-landing in Kent.

I soon realized that my housemate had a lot to teach me. Born in Chicago of immigrant parents, Frank had supported himself since the age of fourteen, never finishing high school but becoming one of the star photographers of the *Milwaukee Journal* in the days of flash-powder photography. Despite the old-fashioned start, Scherschel was always on the cutting edge of the new technology. In the thirties, *Journal* photographers, led by Scherschel and Edward R. "Eddie" Farber, adapted Harold Edgerton's MIT strobe technology to press cameras, even forming a company, Strobo Research, to market strobe units. Edward K. Thompson was the *Journal*'s picture editor before he joined *Life* in 1937. He hired his old crew to work freelance for *Life* and in 1942 invited Scherschel to join the staff. After four months in the North Atlantic covering supply convoys during the Leningrad blockade, including a very dangerous run to Murmansk, Frank survived eight months of war in the Pacific and celebrated Christmas on Guadalcanal.

In London, Frank had become deeply attached to a lovely dark-haired English girl named Patricia, who gave him the emotional support he needed to face his hazardous assignments. Our little household was made complete by the delightful presence of the downstairs butler, Lloyd, and his wife. Lloyd was the authentic English butler. His figure and voice were imposing: he had been a professional toastmaster at state banquets. Lloyd never lost his cool. In the worst raids, he would call upstairs, "Gentlemen, would you care for a cup of tea?" Meaning: Would we care to take shelter in the cellar kitchen?

On the morning of December 7, Lloyd called from downstairs to say that there was a telegram for Mr. Morris. I was anxious about the impending birth of Fidget and thought, Maybe this is it. I opened the envelope with trembling fingers. It said only HAPPY BIRTHDAY TO YOU—such a letdown I almost cried. But on December 16, just before lunch, one of the office staff rushed to me with a cable in an envelope. I tore it open and read: FLASH IT'S A BOY PERIOD DELE SAYS QUOTE JOHN DALE ARRIVED DECEMBER FIFTEEN WEIGHS SEVEN POUNDS SEVEN OUNCES EVERYTHING UNDER CONTROL STOP ALL MY LOVE UNQUOTE CONGRATULATIONS REGARDS WILSON HICKS.

Bob Landry had arrived from the States in November. There was wariness on both sides after our time together on Sunset Boulevard. Unlike Scherman and Wild, who took routine work for granted, Landry wasn't interested in simple around-town assignments, preferring to rest rather determinedly on his impressive laurels—he had been the only press photographer with the Pacific fleet at the time of Pearl Harbor. Landry followed this scoop of a lifetime with coverage of the British Eighth Army's desert engagements with Erwin Rommel, then shot an essay on South Africa, covered the invasion of Sicily, and made no less than four *Life* covers. He installed himself at the Dorchester Hotel on Park Lane, sharing a suite with Walter Graebner; he also shared Graebner's excellent sources, which in my mind justified such luxury. Landry was a genius of the creative expense account. A Time Inc. bookkeeper once noticed that during a period when Landry was charging five dollars a day for taxis, he had been stationed on an aircraft carrier. Challenged, Landry snorted, "You should've seen the size of this thing."

One of Graebner's contacts set up Landry for an exclusive photo of the RAF's air chief marshal, Sir Arthur Harris, poring over the "Blue Book" of bomb damage assessments, in the supersecret London headquarters of Bomber Command. The *Life* headline read THE BRAIN BEHIND THE DEATH OF BERLIN LOOKS AT HIS WORK FROM AFAR. I soon learned what would happen if we attempted to take a closer look. A set of photographs arrived one day in the diplomatic pouch from Stockholm. They showed, in gruesome detail, the human devastation that Allied bombs were causing in Berlin: stacks of bodies awaiting burial, hospital wards jammed with wounded children. I made up a packet for New York and headed over to the Ministry of Information to pay my respects to my friends the censors, knowing full well how slim were my chances of getting these pictures on the plane to New York. When it was my turn, I fixed a perfectly neutral expression on my face and set the packet before the British censor on duty. He smiled thinly, opened the packet, and carefully examined each photo, taking his time and occasionally backtracking. After he'd gone through the entire packet he looked up at me, smiled again, and said, in the clipped, nasal voice preferred by censors, "These photographs are very interesting. You may have them back after the war." It was the last I ever saw of them.

Such run-ins were becoming dull routine, part of the daily grind of wartime London, but they also provided good material to swap over cocktails in the evening. The nights were always full of fun and intrigue. From time to time I attended a "whiskey pour" at the Dorchester, where one Pamela Churchill reigned. She was the mother of the prime minister's grandson, Winston, and was now estranged from her husband, Randolph. It was here that Pamela first got together with Averell Harriman, Roosevelt's top envoy to London and Moscow; thirty years later she would marry him, but now was the time for flings. A state of siege may be the best excuse for casual sex. "The war had made England promiscuous," Charles Wertenbaker pronounced in his 1954 novel of a thinly disguised Time Inc. and its London bureau, *The Death of Kings*. Another denizen of the Dorchester, Wert had joined us early in 1944 to become *Time/Life*'s chief of correspondents. Intersecting triangles were a theme for Wert in fiction and in life—eventually he would marry *Time* correspondent Lael Tucker, who had gone to London as the wife of another correspondent, Stephen Laird.

Working the day shift at Grosvenor Square and the night shift at the Dorchester and other venues left me exhausted. Thus in late January, when Scherschel suggested a trip to Belfast to look into some stories and perhaps have a little fun, I quickly agreed. It was rumored that Northern Ireland had become a staging area for parts of the American Third Army, under General Patton. We obtained orders to fly there in a DC-3 of Troop Carrier Command and checked in at the Red Cross Officers' Club in downtown Belfast.

The next morning, we pestered a sour-faced Army public relations officer for a lift into the countryside. "Well, okay," he muttered, "but I'm not promising anything." As the verdant landscape rolled by, I worried that he wasn't kidding, but before long we turned onto a narrow asphalt road, passed row upon row of tents, and finally emerged onto a huge drill field. There, marching in review for their commander, Major General Maxwell D. Taylor, were several thousand men of the 101st Airborne Division. We jumped out and Frank started shooting. We were, of course, forbidden to identify either the division or its location; in fact, when Scherschel's picture later ran as a *Life* lead, the head-line read: "American invaders mass in England."

We felt so good about our scoop that we decided to go to the other Ireland—Eire—for the weekend. We changed into civilian clothes, enjoying the war cor-respondent's greatest privilege. Leaving our uniforms and films behind in Belfast, we boarded the train for Dublin. It seemed absurd to be able to abandon World War II so easily, simply by taking a train to a neutral country, where the German embassy and Japanese consulate remained open for business, their flags flying.

On the flight from Belfast back to London, while distractedly reading a pre-cious copy of James Joyce's *Dubliners,* I suddenly came to terms with a thought that had been nagging at me for months: I would have to seize control of the *Life* picture staff; the idea that Sherry Mangan and I would be battling over of-fice turf through D-Day was simply ludicrous. I went to Walter Graebner and explained that no good could come to one small staff with two heads, especially in view of the critical times ahead. Graebner, who seemed as exhausted by these old Time Inc. antics as I was, readily agreed but was careful to explain that the order had to come from New York. Mercifully, it took only a weekend for the answer to come back, and, amazingly, logic prevailed: Mangan would return to *Time* as a correspondent; Morris would run the *Life* picture operation.

Frank Scherschel continued his hazardous coverage of the Eighth Air Force, flying a number of missions with B-26 bombers to top secret targets just across the Channel. Once I accompanied him to a B-26 base and learned the secret: the Germans were preparing sites for rocket launches against England, and the Allies were systematically trying to knock them out, whenever and wherever they could find them.

One simply had to stop thinking about the cruelty now commonplace on both sides, although I had been astonished by the casual teatime confession of a young American bombardier: upon returning from a mission over northern France one day, he had simply jettisoned his last bomb on a group of cyclists on a country road. Were they German soldiers? "Mightabeen." Could you see them clearly? "Naw."

A weird sense of the theatrical—or, rather, the cinematic—began to take over as more and more characters from my Hollywood tour began showing up. First to arrive was Herbert Bregstein, who had covered the movie colony for Walter Annenberg's Triangle Publications; he took up residence with us at Upper Wimpole Street. Strutting onto the scene was Samuel Goldwyn's own press agent, J. B. L. "Jock" Lawrence, now an army officer (he would finish the war as a full colonel and would be awarded the Légion d'Honneur). Despite his mili-tary trappings, Jock was a publicist to the bone; he defied the censors, much to

my obvious delight, and authorized Bob Landry to photograph the unprecedented buildup of munitions and supplies for the invasion. Landry, at last
handed an assignment he considered worthy of his talents, rose to the occasion. His picture essay ran as the lead, headlined: PRE-INVASION: U.S. ARMY PILES GI-
GANTIC WAR STORES IN BRITAIN FOR USE AGAINST GERMANS. This was indeed a
stunning display. "The island is slowly sinking under its weight," Graebner
wrote in the accompanying text.

With such photographic coups as these, we were not thrilled to have to share
our material, but we had joined in a wartime pool with the three wirephoto
agencies—Associated Press, Acme (owned by Scripps-Howard, which later
merged it with United Press), and International News Photos, the Hearst organization (later acquired by United Press to create United Press International).
The advantage for *Life* was in gaining equal access to major news events, despite being a weekly. The disadvantage was that we had to "make available" our
best "hard-news" pictures for distribution over the wires. Just how we did that
was often a matter of dispute. The three wire services thoroughly distrusted
one another, but they were united in their distrust of *Life* and disdain for its ex-
travagant ways. However, they loved to sell us pictures, and *Life* was *the* showcase.

In Fleet Street at that time, news pictures were sold not as a "service" but in-
dividually. Speed was of the essence, and big money often awaited the first
agency with an exclusive. It was not uncommon for a messenger to run out of
the darkroom with a wet print, hoping it would dry before it hit the editor's
desk.

My own invasion team was growing. Robert Capa arrived from Italy in late February. Capa had done eight successive stories on the Allies' Italian campaign,
until it bogged down at Monte Cassino. George Rodger soon followed from Italy.
Rodger had joined the *Life* staff in 1940, during the Battle of Britain, and covered the war on three continents. More adventurer than journalist, George had
a lifetime's flirtation with bad luck, attaining the recognition he deserved only
in the last months before he died, in 1995, at eighty-seven. His early years had
been right out of Conrad. The son of a Cheshire businessman, George had left
school to work his way around the world on tramp steamers, winding up in
America at the start of the Depression, where he made his way doing odd jobs.
When he returned to England penniless in 1936, the BBC hired him, "much to
my amazement," as a portraitist for its magazine, *The Listener.* We had met
briefly in *Life*'s New York office in 1942, when *Life* published a wartime odyssey
he had shot. The story proclaims: "75,000 MILES: George Rodger has gone to
more sweat and pain to get a few pictures than any other LIFE photographer"—
the photographer-hero cult in high gear at *Life.* But Time Inc. blundered by

trotting out George for a promotional gambit. While addressing a gathering of the magazine's advertisers, George opined that the RAF's Lancaster bombers were more effective than the U.S.'s Flying Fortresses. A Boeing executive was in the audience, and that was *that* for George's career as a *Life* pitchman; he was just as happy. George was not well suited to be a corporation man, and indeed he was the perfect partner for a scheme that Capa had in mind. He and Capa met in Italy in 1944, and it was there, in a quiet moment on the Italian front, that Capa told George of his postwar dream of a picture agency where photographers would be their own bosses. It sounded sensible to George, and three years later he would join Capa as one of the founders of Magnum Photos.

On April 6, Ralph Morse arrived from New York, full of such energy that it was almost depressing; we London office old-timers were now hunkered down, in *waiting* mode, and fresh faces tended to jangle the nerves. In truth, though, I was delighted to have him on board. Over horse-meat steaks at Dean Street's one French restaurant, Ralph and I guardedly discussed his invasion assignment: I wanted him to cover nothing less than General Patton's Third Army, which was scheduled to follow the First Army into action. Despite his youth, at twenty-five Ralph was already a seasoned pro. He had proved himself at the savage battle for Guadalcanal, where he had made one of the most macabre images ever published by *Life:* a Japanese soldier's skull propped up on a tank as a trophy of war. Later, Ralph almost lost his life, and did lose his film, when a U.S. cruiser sank under him.

So: Capa, Scherschel, Landry, Scherman, Morse, Rodger—at last, I thought, my team is complete. London was now the center of the biggest armed camp ever assembled, and the numbers were increasing with each passing day. My former boss Edward K. Thompson, now a lieutenant colonel, showed up on leave from his top secret job on General Walter B. "Beedle" Smith's staff, and then there was Sergeant David "Chim" Seymour, whom I had remembered from New York as a somewhat mysterious friend of Capa. Gradually, I learned his story. The son of a distinguished Warsaw publisher of books in Hebrew, his nickname came from the unpronounceable family name, Szymin. Chim, pronounced "Shim," had met Capa in Paris and freelanced with him in Spain. His story of Barcelona under aerial attack had been a lead in *Life*. In 1939, Chim headed to New York (in a roundabout way—sailing with Spanish refugees bound for Mexico), where he Anglicized his name and joined the army. Chim's commanders had the good sense to use his photographic talents. Employed as a "photo interpreter," Chim helped to plot invasion sites.

In this frenzied season, Capa threw a party that remains memorable even by wartime West End standards. Capa never needed much inspiration for a party, but in this case he had much to celebrate—the successful appendectomy of his girlfriend, Elaine Fisher, known as "Pinky," and the arrival in town of his old

The aftermath of an all-night party given by Bob Capa landed Ernest Hemingway in the hospital, where Bob and his girlfriend, Elaine Fisher, a.k.a. "Pinky," visited him a day or so later. I sent Bob's pictures of the visit to New York, where one made a page in *Life*. I held back one of them, however, taken when Papa got out of bed and Pinky spread wide his hospital gown (page 77). *Copyright ©* *1998 Estate of Robert Capa*

friend from Loyalist Spain and Sun Valley, Ernest Hemingway. Capa greeted him jovially as "Papa." Hemingway, then forty-four, barrel-chested and full-bearded, was accredited as a *Collier's* correspondent but irreverently sported a British battle jacket instead of the "Eisenhower jacket" that most of us correspondents wore. Capa proudly introduced his friend to the rest of us as "Ernest." Hemingway spoke, not terribly intelligibly, in pure staccato. *Life's* Colonel Ed Thompson—who would later buy exclusive first rights to *The Old Man and the Sea*—came to the party with Frank Scherschel and me, but he didn't realize who "Ernest" was until the next morning. When all the liquor was consumed—as I recall, it took us only until four in the morning to accomplish this—Papa left the party in the care of Dr. Peter Gorer, a friend of Dave Scherman's and, unfortunately for all involved, the owner of a car. Dr. Gorer promptly drove headlong into a water storage tank, sending Hemingway into the windshield and then a hospital bed. Capa and Pinky visited the old man a day or so later. With his head bandaged in a turban and his thick beard stuck out over the sheet, Hemingway resembled an Arab potentate. I sent along Capa's picture of Hemingway in bed, and it made a full page in *Life*. I didn't bother including the other shots on this roll—when Papa got up to head to the gents, Pinky playfully tugged on his hospital gown, revealing his wide rump. Capa thoughtfully recorded the moment on film, a picture that became my most amusing wartime souvenir.

A few days later, Capa secretly reported to the headquarters of the 1st Infantry Division's 16th Regiment, on a country estate near Weymouth, and was given permission to board the U.S. Coast Guard transport *Samuel Chase*. There he found officers studying a giant sponge rubber model of a French beach code-named "Omaha."

The long wait was almost over. The longest day was about to begin.

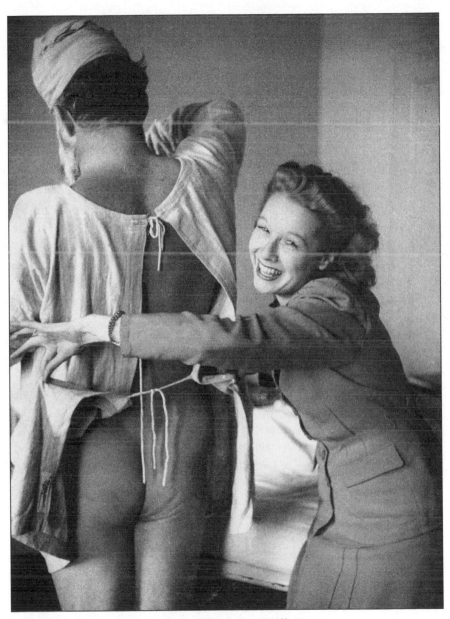

Copyright © 1998 Estate of Robert Capa/John G. Morris Collection

This young German stood in a lineup of prisoners who had been firing upon us (barely missing me) only an hour earlier during the siege of the port of Saint-Malo. When I took this picture I could only think, You poor kid. JOHN G. MORRIS

9

To the Beach

Thanks to Capa's courage and the London bureau's luck, his few pictures of D-Day occupy a prominent place in our century's visual history. Nevertheless, I am forever haunted by what we lost. Capa himself took the news of the melted emulsions well and never discussed the subject with me, but his bitter disappointment over the destruction of the other images was quietly recorded in letters home to his mother and brother. Bob Landry was another matter; he had to be restrained from taking a swing at me after he got the news that his D-Day film had vanished. It could not be accounted for from the moment it had left his hands, but I was a convenient scapegoat.

London nights now had an empty, eerie quality to them; Capa's party seemed months in the past. On June 13 I wrote to New York: "The strain of the first week has begun to wear off and we're working only 'til midnight now instead of to the early hours of the morning." What I was *not* free to say was that I had left the office after midnight with some photos by Landry and Scherschel to be wirephotoed for the pool. I walked a few blocks down Oxford Street to Selfridge's big department store. There, in the sub-sub-sub-basement, was the secret transmission point for wirephotos to all the world. I waited my turn, retrieved the prints, and came up to the street at about 4:00 A.M. A few minutes later the air-raid sirens sounded, the first time in many weeks. I kept on walking; 24 Upper Wimpole was only ten minutes away. There was a distant explosion, and then, as I reached home, the all clear. Dog-tired, I went to bed.

At eight I was awakened by the sirens, the blood crashing in my ears. Now I was alarmed. There had hardly been a daylight raid on London since 1940. Rocket batteries opened up in Hyde Park with a mighty, repetitive *whoosh*ing. Hardly a comforting noise. *What the hell was going on?* Another explosion, followed by the all clear. I made a cup of tea and distracted myself with the morning papers, but soon there was another alert, and I could hear the noise of an airplane motor, sounding a bit out of sync. More rockets. The peculiar-sounding motor cut out, followed by another explosion. Just where, it was hard to tell, but mercifully not close.

Then it came to me: V-1. I remembered the secret briefing I had attended a few months before at the A-26 bomber base. Now it was obvious that V-1 rockets—which we almost immediately dubbed "buzz bombs" or "doodlebugs," as they sounded like oversize insects—were being aimed at London. Some were obviously hitting "targets" at random. I tuned in to the BBC, which said nothing about it; just the news from Normandy and other fronts. I dressed and went to the office. Every face looked anxious. There was growing anxiety as the day went on, with alternating alerts and all clears. It seemed to me that the city of London was about to suffer a nervous breakdown. Everyone watched the sky. You could actually see the bloody things overhead, and when the motor cut out, there was a dreadfully prolonged moment of uncertainty until the bomb landed—followed by relief that it hadn't hit *you*. The rocket batteries were soon silenced—it did no good to shoot down buzz bombs over the city, since they exploded anyway.

The following morning, Churchill took to the BBC: "pilotless aircraft" were being aimed at England, the prime minister confirmed, citing this as evidence of the growing desperation of the "Nazzees." Immediately the populace calmed. It might have helped more had we learned that Hitler was himself almost killed by a V-1 on June 17. The drone went berserk in midflight, turned around, and landed atop the führer's command bunker at Margival in northern France. There were no casualties, but Hitler took off for Berchtesgaden in a funk, leaving his generals to bicker among themselves.

The V-1 presented a special photojournalistic challenge. At first we concentrated on trying to photograph the thing itself, not realizing that a stronger story lay in the anxious faces of Londoners looking up. One day a bomb fell in Tottenham Court Road, close enough to shatter the windows of our beloved White Tower restaurant—which continued to serve lunch. I went to the bomb site for a look. I could not photograph what I saw: an Army command car had been hit and the driver blown out. In the wreckage I saw—only—his head.

George Rodger was back from Normandy; I was on my way there—a quick trip as "Acting Coordinator, Press Photographers, Western Front" (a position I had invented, itching as I was to get closer to the action—and, truth to tell, Normandy now seemed a safer place than London). I was organizing my gear at the office when we heard the now-familiar noise of a buzz bomb exploding nearby. George offered to "go have a look" and came back with one of the most moving images of the war—a woman lying serenely on a stretcher as she is carried off through dust and rubble.

. . .

On July 16, I landed at low tide on Utah Beach, courtesy of the Western Naval Task Force. I was accompanied by William Johnson of *Time* and Ned Buddy, who had created for himself a function similar to mine, but for the newsreel pool. Our landing was opposed only by seagulls—an odd introduction to France (where I live today). A jeep met us and we headed into the ruined village of Sainte-Mère-Église. Twenty miles away was the port of Cherbourg, captured in battle only three weeks before, its docks destroyed. The civilian population was not in sight. Their homes and shops had virtually all been destroyed.

Sainte-Mère-Église had been the dateline for many a D-Day story. I immediately thought of Bill Walton, who had dropped in on the town by parachute at 1:00 A.M. on June 6, landing three feet off the ground in a pear tree. As Robert Capa was *Life*'s D-Day hero, Walton was *Time*'s. In the spring, Bill had taken the required three-week training to qualify as a paratrooper. On D-Day he had jumped from General James Gavin's plane. Gavin was commander of the 82nd Airborne, whose battalions suffered casualties of up to 70 percent. Walton was eventually rescued from the pear tree and spent the following three days under fire; he was awarded the Bronze Star. He was also the subject of much anxiety at 10 Downing Street—soon after D-Day, the 82nd Airborne had received a call asking after Bill. Pamela Churchill was worried about one of her favorites.

We drove south on N13, the highway that runs parallel to the sea, and made a left turn at Carentan, also in ruins, to head toward Isigny, in the direction of Omaha Beach. There we turned off on a departmental road for about two and a half miles; the road turned to gravel and led immediately to a small place called Vouilly—not much more than a château that had been taken over as the First Army press camp. It was one of the most elite press camps in history. My tentmates, at one time or another, were none other than Robert Capa, columnist Ernie Pyle, Bob Casey of the Chicago *Daily News*, H. R. Knickerbocker of the Chicago *Sun*, and Gault MacGowan of the New York *Sun*. They treated one another with affection, but I soon learned that their camaraderie meant no lessening of their competitive instincts. The wire services were always eager to scoop one another with news of some military advance, occasionally announcing the event before it happened. On my first afternoon there, I returned to camp in time to see Wes Gallagher of AP charge up to Henry T. Gorrell of UP, and shout, "Hank, you son-of-a-bitch, you know goddamned well that you took Saint-Lô six hours ahead of the U.S. Army!" Saint-Lô had fallen only the day before I got to Normandy. It had been a savage battle, involving at least eight divisions of the U.S. First Army. The town was demolished, and there were thousands of casualties (the Allies suffered casualties at the rate of one thousand a day for the first forty days after D-Day).

My plan as pool "coordinator" was to go out each day with a different photographer, to learn his problems, and to satisfy my own curiosity. On July 24, I accepted an invitation from AP photographer Bede Irvin to join him the following day in covering "some brass"—among them Lieutenant General Leslie McNair—on a visit to the Saint-Lô front. But the next morning Frank Scherschel showed up at the press camp and insisted that I accompany *him;* much to my irritation at the time, Frank had already made excuses on my behalf to Bede, who went off without me. Frank's coveting of his "coordinator" saved my life. Bede walked into the most massive air attack in frontline history: more than two thousand bombers from the U.S. Eighth Air Force and the RAF dropped five thousand tons of explosives at Saint-Lô. The first wave of planes accurately hit the German positions, but the resulting dust and smoke blew west, covering the Americans positioned nearby, and that's precisely where the second wave dropped their bombs. General McNair and Bede Irvin were among those killed, in one of the worst friendly-fire incidents of the war.

Scherschel and I got the news that night. The next day, feeling guilty, perhaps, about my narrow escape, or invulnerable, I felt compelled to take a foolish and unnecessary risk. Frank had decided to do a story on artillery spotters, and I watched enviously as he departed with one in a single-engine plane that took off from a cow pasture. He came back half an hour later with aerial photos of the front. I strapped my own camera onto my chest and demanded the next ride. We went up, and in an instant I felt removed from the war and, oddly, *safe.* I confessed later in a letter home to Dèle, "It was odd, sitting up there in the air so peacefully, and at the same time being able to see the shells, or rather the smoke of shells, bursting in the enemy lines. The war seems very impersonal in the air." Such are the surreal moments of peace available in war.

On August 4, with Bob Landry and Pete Carroll of AP, I made it to Rennes, capital of Brittany and the most strategic city to fall since Cherbourg. Its capture meant that the Breton peninsula was effectively cut off from the rest of France. Landry and I split up as soon as we reached the center of town—there was no point in my shooting the same pictures. It turned out to be an awkward moment for Rennes. The last Germans had left during the night, along with the mayor, a collaborator. At the Hôtel de Ville (town hall), a Gaullist officer whom I had known in London explained that a new *préfet,* for all of Brittany, had been installed during the night—explaining the empty champagne glasses on the mayor's desk. A new mayor was in process of being chosen in the next room. A few minutes later, I was introduced to him.

There was a lot of confusion outside. A company of French Senegalese troops, just released from German internment, was being rearmed and paraded through the square. German prisoners were being interrogated on the steps of the Théâtre Municipal. Hearing a commotion, I saw gendarmes hustling two young women, one walking her bicycle, off to jail. They were obviously being accused of collaboration, perhaps only as whores. I took a picture as a woman angrily spat at one of them. I tagged along to the gendarmerie, where they joined other collaborators in a dark cell that could have been a scene from the Terror. When I rejoined Landry a little while later, he told me that he had intervened to stop the beating of a collaborator that was about to turn into a lynching.

That night Bob Capa suggested that we take a trip to Mont-Saint-Michel, which had survived the war unscathed, its tourist facilities intact. I readily agreed. We checked into La Mère Poulard, famous for its flaming omelettes, where we were joined by our fellow Time Inc.er Bill Walton and by Ernest Hemingway, who was on duty for *Collier's*. Papa and Capa heartily celebrated the fact that they had not been killed a fews day earlier when Hemingway had insanely insisted that the two of them advance, without benefit of supporting troops, on the enemy near the village of Saint-Pois.

What Capa hadn't particularly counted on was that I saw a good story nearby, and we might have to work. The German garrison of the port of Saint-Malo, only thirty-two miles from Mont-Saint-Michel, was stubbornly refusing

Signs such as this, barring the way to the undamaged sanctuary of Mont-Saint-Michel, meant nothing to us war correspondents, who were free to go pretty much anywhere—at our own risk. Mont-Saint-Michel was worth it. *Copyright © 1998 Estate of Robert Capa*

to surrender, although surrounded by the U.S. 83d Infantry Division. I was excited by the psychological drama of the situation. Capa had little faith in my story idea but saw that he would have to indulge me. That evening a crowd of the curious was gathered at La Mère Poulard. One, a farmer who had lost his cows in the bombardment, told Capa that he would nevertheless like to "do something for the Americans." Bob quickly replied, "How about dinner?" The farmer agreed to alert his wife and to meet us the next afternoon at 5:30.

The next day we discovered that the 83d had made some progress during the night. We drove along the shore road toward Saint-Malo until finally, with another six miles to go, we took refuge in a little seaside resort hotel that was serving as an observation post. A German pillbox was holding up further advance. In the bar, which had doubtless been serving drinks to the enemy the day before, we encountered a lieutenant colonel who was the regiment's artillery commander. A West Pointer, he seemed to be having trouble making up his mind, trying to guess the Germans' intentions. Capa, who despised indecisive officers, said cynically in his heavy accent, "Why don't you *ask the Germans* what they intend to do?" The colonel fired right back at him, "*You* speak German. *You* ask them."

To my horror, Capa agreed. Someone pulled out a big white handkerchief and tied it to a pole. When Capa took the camera off his neck and gave it to me, I suddenly realized that I too had a challenge. What a story! I would cover Capa. I prepared to follow him, but Capa would not have it. "You have two children, you idiot!" While we were arguing, a machine gun began firing—fortunately—for the whole expedition then fell apart.

Capa and I lunched on wine and cheese and then settled down to wait until something was done about the pillbox. After an hour or so I became restless and curious. I went outside and began talking to a corporal, on guard at the next corner. I asked him about the pillbox. He eyed me in a peculiar way and directed me to follow him. We walked inland one block, where a backstreet ran parallel to the road by the sea. "This way," he said and ran across to the opposite side, taking cover behind a wall. As I followed, there was a single, muffled shot. I dropped down beside the corporal. "Funny, that never happened before," he said as he pointed in the direction of the pillbox—as though I now cared. He added, "When we go back, you better run for it." "You're telling me!" I replied. After a minute, he was off. I followed, and again there was a shot. One hour and a couple of drinks later I heard a small fuss outside the bar. A dozen or so prisoners had been brought in to the very corner where I had been shot at; the pillbox had at last fallen. I looked over the lineup, wondering which man had shot at me. My eyes fell on a frightened young soldier, scarcely fifteen. You poor kid, I thought, and took his picture.

Back at La Mère Poulard, the farmer showed up on time. Somehow, six of us mounted the jeep: Capa and Hemingway on the driver's right, the farmer on his left, Walton and I in back. We drove over the causeway and off into the fertile countryside. We stopped more than once on the way—everyone wanted the honor of pouring us a drink. Finally we reached our host's farmhouse; his wife looked as though she had been cooking for weeks. We finished with homemade coffee éclairs and, of course, Calvados. The farmer's daughter then sang Breton folk songs in the moonlit garden.

On the way home we had to cross a bridge over a small river called the Couesnon. What was left of the Luftwaffe had been bombing bridges at night, and they had narrowly missed this one. As we approached, feeling no pain from the night's festivity, the jeep suddenly disappeared. Walton and I found ourselves on the side of the road, Bill on his back, I on my knees. Looking around for the jeep, we saw it comfortably filling a bomb crater, right side up. Hemingway, Capa, and the driver were still snug in their seats. They howled at us: "Deserters!" As soon as we could stop laughing, we all gave a push, shoved the jeep out of the hole, and got under way. Not for long. A solitary German bomber could be heard in the distance. Papa insisted that we all get out and lie in a ditch until the danger passed. We reached our hotel a little after midnight, ordered a nightcap from the bar, and stepped outside to see the "late show." From the medieval ramparts we watched the distant flashes of fire, obscuring the stars, as the Germans counterattacked near Mortain. Then, refreshed by the night breeze off the sea, we fell into bed.

With Henri Cartier-Bresson as my guide, I made the rounds of photographers of the Resistance who had photographed Paris during the German Occupation and the Liberation. Henri had himself been actively photographing the Germans—while hiding underground after escaping from a German prison camp—and the Liberation, but whether from modesty or simply because he hadn't made prints, he did not show me his pictures of that period at the time I was buying for *Life*. This is one of those photographs. © HENRI CARTIER-BRESSON/*Magnum Photos*

10

"Paris Is Free Again!"

My four-week "vacation" at the front was over. It was time to return to active duty, to the task of running the picture desk in London. On August 14, Ned Buddy and I left the First Army press camp by jeep for Cherbourg. Ernie Pyle, as I recall, was the only correspondent who said good-bye to me. The others were too busy to notice. No wonder everyone loved Ernie. We crossed the Channel in a U.S. Coast Guard cutter just after midnight and took a morning train from Portsmouth to London—sixteen of us crammed into a first-class compartment meant for six. I returned from France naïvely optimistic about a quick end to the war. *Life* that week proclaimed a "Break-Through in France" with pictures by four of our photographers. The cover, by Bob Landry, showed the resolute face of a U.S. infantryman, his face unshaven, his helmet camouflaged, a wedding band on the fourth finger of the hand that held his rifle.

In my first London letter to Dèle I wrote, "I can't see how the German army is going to fight much beyond Paris." I was a victim of my own propaganda. Dwight Eisenhower and his commanders at Supreme Headquarters had no intention of taking Paris, if they could possibly avoid it. It was Adolf Hitler who now wanted a battle for Paris, partly in revenge for the aerial bombardment that had destroyed Berlin and a dozen other German cities. Hitler had just appointed a tough new German commander for Paris, General Dietrich von Choltitz, and had given him orders to hold Paris at all costs. If it could not be held, he demanded that it be blown up—with its priceless treasures, from the Louvre and Notre Dame to the Eiffel Tower. Eisenhower sought only the destruction of the German armies. To stop and fight for Paris would mean that the Allies would literally run out of gas. Unfortunately, this plan was made without the French. After four years of German occupation, the citizens of Paris were organizing a full-scale revolt. Their impatience was understandable; they were desperately hungry and almost without fuel, power, and transport. The Nazi swastika flew from the Eiffel Tower and from German headquarters in the Hôtel Meurice, just down the rue de Rivoli from the place de la Concorde. Every day, Parisians were humiliated by the sight of a German regiment marching down the avenue des Champs-Élysées, led by a band playing "Prussia's Glory." The city appeared to be quiet, but almost every morning men and women of the Resistance were executed by firing squad.

The Paris insurrection broke out in force on Saturday, August 19. General von Choltitz vacillated, first carrying out Hitler's orders to set explosives under the city's monuments, then delaying their explosion until it was too late and secretly asking the Allies to come quickly so that he could surrender with honor. On Friday, August 25, tanks of General Philippe Leclerc's Deuxième Division Blindée, or DDB (phonetically called the "Daydaybay"), and units of the U.S. 4th Division entered Paris even as Hitler was demanding of his chief of staff, "Jodl, is Paris burning?" It was the day the war should have ended.

All six *Life* photographers entered Paris on that great Day of Liberation. The lead story proclaimed "Paris Is Free Again!" Bob Capa and Charles Wertenbaker, the chief *Time/Life* correspondent, particularly distinguished themselves, riding into Paris in the second jeep after General Leclerc himself—evading the general's ban on all but French correspondents. George Rodger also rode with the French. He had photographed Leclerc three years before, in Chad, where Leclerc, then a colonel, had just defeated the Italians at Kufta. General Omar Bradley, realizing that the use of artillery would make of Paris another Stalingrad, had given strict orders to his commanders: "No fighting!" But the Germans were not entirely cooperative. Many garrisons held out, and the soldiers were heavily armed with machine guns and grenades. German Panzer tanks dueled with American-made Shermans. Capa soon found himself a battle to photograph, as the FFI (Forces Françaises de l'Intérieur—the Resistance) and French marines stormed the Chamber of Deputies. Ralph Morse, further down the Left Bank, photographed the capture of German prisoners under the Eiffel Tower. Dave Scherman got to the Gare Montparnasse just as General von Choltitz, having surrendered, came to take orders from General Charles de Gaulle.

That weekend in London, I had the thrill of editing the *Life* photographers' combined take, some 1,300 frames, and sent off the best, through the usual censorship at the Ministry of Information, to New York. From the MOI censors I went to SHAEF (Supreme Headquarters Allied Expeditionary Force) public relations on Grosvenor Square. I had to get to Paris but found myself at the end of the line. *Everybody* wanted to go to Paris, and the city had already been declared off limits. Only those with the most essential and urgent business could go. I settled for orders that would put me onto a twin-engine courier plane to Normandy. I landed on Tuesday morning, August 29, in a pasture about 160 miles from Paris. Hitchhiking in Army jeeps and command cars, using a Michelin map acquired during my first sojourn in France, I reached the city limits well after midnight. My Michelin map was no longer useful, and I had forgotten to bring even a tourist map of Paris, so I stayed with the convoy I had rolled in on, unsure where we were headed or when to hop out. We moved slowly through the deserted streets in the blackout. The silence was punctuated only by distant bursts of gunfire. It was 3:00 A.M. when my last lift dropped me off at the Hôtel Scribe. The Germans had used the hotel as a press center; now it was accommodating Allied correspondents, and, miraculously, it had room to spare. I checked in and enjoyed the luxury of a single room.

The next day, I found Capa and Wert in the temporary *Time/Life* office, a large room on the first floor, with a balcony from which one could yell down at the other correspondents as they came and went. Filmmakers George Stevens, Irwin Shaw, and William Saroyan had the room next door (they were supposedly at work on a Signal Corps film). Capa, Walton, and the Wertenbakers soon moved to quarters in the more select Hôtel Lancaster, on the rue de Berri. Capa took only a maid's room, but it was a good address—next to the office of the European edition of the *New York Herald Tribune*, which had been forced to stop publication on June 12, 1940. The Scribe, however, continued as press headquarters until the war ended. One could eat for virtually nothing, and the bar never seemed to run out of champagne. Artist Floyd Davis memorialized the bar in a painting that ran across two pages in *Life*, with unflattering caricatures of twenty-six war correspondents, including Hemingway, William L. Shirer, H. V. Kaltenborn, *The New Yorker*'s Janet Flanner and Joe Liebling, *Vogue*'s Lee Miller, and, of course, the *Time/Life* crowd. Lee Miller spent months at the Scribe, sharing a suite with Dave Scherman. One night she invited me up to the room for a drink; we found Scherman already in bed, reading. The next evening I saw Lee again, in the hotel lobby. With the exciting news that "Roland's here—he's just come from Italy!" she again invited me up for a drink. There, reading in the same bed, was Roland Penrose.

I was eager to prove that I could operate as well in Paris as in London. One of my problems was making contact with French photographers. Capa, reveling in the city he loved more than any in the world, came to my aid. At breakfast in the Scribe, he said, "I have a friend who will help you. He is a Parisian, a photographer, and he speaks English. He has even been to New York. His name is Henri Cartier-Bresson. He has been living underground in Paris during the Occupation, and he knows everybody, *everybody*."

I had never heard of Cartier-Bresson, although he already had an international reputation among the handful of prewar cognoscenti of photography. I was pleasantly surprised when the next morning, at the door of the Hôtel Scribe, Capa introduced me to a slight young man with blue eyes and a soft voice. He had come on his bicycle. He was very cordial, offering to help me find photos of the Occupation and the Resistance. We walked off together, his bicycle between us, to find photographers, particularly those who had risked their lives to work underground during the Occupation. Henri was one of them himself, but whether from modesty or because he did not have prints to give me, he did not even mention it. One of the first calls was on Robert Doisneau, who gave me photos of Parisians tearing up pavements to make barricades. René Zuber and Pierre Roughol supplied pictures of men and women manning them—Roughol's showed a pistol-packing, helmeted housewife with two hand grenades. Roger Berson offered a photo of a Resistance sniper perched on a rooftop, with the Sacré-Coeur in the distance.

Finally our stomachs called for lunch. Henri suggested we go to his family's apartment, at 31 rue de Lisbonne, near the Parc Monceau in the bourgeois Eighth Arrondissement. His parents were in the country; the faithful family maid served us. The household furnishings were straight from Proust. Henri apologized almost as soon as we sat down at the big oak table: "I am sorry, but we don't trade on the black market, so there is very little." Nevertheless we lunched quite adequately on cabbage with a kind of tomato sauce, dark bread, and red wine.

After lunch Henri took me to meet Brassaï, a poet and sculptor as well as photographer. Born Gyula Halász, he had taken his nom de plume from Brasso, the Transylvanian city where he had been born. I already knew his 1933 book *Paris de Nuit*, and was amused to learn that he timed his long exposures by smoking cigarettes—when his smoke was out, he closed the shutter.

A few days later, still making the rounds, I paused for a midafternoon beer in the sunshine of the terrace of the Café Select on the boulevard Montparnasse. I had not been there long when an Army command car drew up. Down jumped an unsoldierly soldier who looked very familiar indeed. It was Master Sergeant David Seymour, on his first post-Liberation visit to Paris! Chim! We had not seen each other since preinvasion London. His intelligence outfit had just moved to the outskirts of Paris. He asked immediately about his old *copains* Capa and Cartier-Bresson. Were they still alive? "Just come with me," I replied. Capa had invited me to a cocktail party that very afternoon in the apartment of Michel de Brunhoff, editor of Paris *Vogue*. There, with many toasts and embraces, Chim was reunited with Capa and Henri. Lacking only George Rodger, who had gone on to Belgium with British forces, it was a meeting of the men who would become Magnum's principal founders.

Things were going well for *Time/Life*, far better than could have been expected. Wertenbaker had rented two floors in the Guaranty Trust building, adjoining the Hôtel Crillon on the place de la Concorde, the classiest address in Paris. We had ten telephone lines, although no switchboard. My office, which had housed a German staff officer, looked down on the rue Royale and the entrance to Maxim's. I had borrowed a bicycle and was getting to know my way around central Paris. It must have been in those tours of the recently liberated city that I resolved to live there one day, and today I do.

One Monday morning we heard that Marlene Dietrich had arrived in town, to entertain the troops. A good story, I thought. I phoned her at the Ritz and she told me to stop by. At the Place Vendôme desk they said, "Miss Dietrich will be right down." A few minutes later she swept down the stairs dressed in a white satin evening gown, an ermine wrap thrown over her shoulders. Noting my confusion, she said quickly, "Oh, I have a date with Willie Wyler, but he hasn't shown up. So let's go into the bar and talk." Taking my feet out of my mouth, I stepped forward, lent my khaki-clad arm, and off we went down the long passage, lined with illuminated showcases, to the famous little bar on the rue Cambon side of the Ritz.

The bar was crowded with its usual mix of brass and bylines, with not a seat in sight. But with Dietrich on my arm—right this way—there was a table. I noted Hemingway drinking with Mary Welsh of *Time*—they had just become a couple, although he had not had the courage to inform his wife, Martha Gellhorn. In her autobiography, Mary told how Marlene had intervened to make peace after a fierce quarrel she and Papa (he called her "Pickle") had had at the Ritz. I didn't have to worry about what to say. Marlene was gay and talked to me as though I were an old friend, telling me about her arrival.

"It was too wonderful. There was absolutely nobody at Orly last night to meet me, so I came into town on the ATC bus and checked in here just after dark. To be back in Paris again! Fantastic! Paris, my love, my old home. I couldn't wait to see it again. So even though the city was blacked out, I went for a walk, all alone. I started toward the Opera, but almost at the first corner I was stopped by two GIs. They could barely see me in my USO slacks and thought I was a Red Cross girl.

" 'Say, kid,' one said, 'where's the Red Cross club around here?'

" 'Search me,' I replied. 'Where's it supposed to be?'

" 'They told us it was near the Madeleine, wherever that is.'

" 'Oh, that's easy,' I said. 'You go right down here—down the boulevard des Capucines.'

"Then the other soldier spoke up: 'Say, how'd you get to know your way around this town?'

" 'I used to live here,' I said.

" 'You don't say,' said the soldier. 'What's your name?'

" 'Marlene Dietrich.'

" 'Oh, sure,' said the soldier after a pause. 'And I'm General Eisenhower. Pleased ta meetcha.'

"You can imagine their surprise when I took them into a little café and the light showed them who I really was! We all laughed so hard, we had to have a drink to celebrate." She went on to tell how the two GIs had then taken her out on the town—or perhaps she had taken them, it was hard to tell which. Dietrich was completely at ease, talking in rapid succession about friends in Hollywood, New York, and London but mostly gushing on about "dear, dear Paris." Finally Wyler arrived, outranking me in his lieutenant colonel's uniform (he was making documentaries for the U.S. Air Force). He kissed Marlene on the cheeks and settled down beside us. My time was clearly up. Besides, I was due in London on my way back to New York. As I excused myself, Dietrich lifted her eyes. Imploringly, she said, "May I ask a favor?"

"Naturally."

"When you get to New York, will you call my husband and give him my APO number?"

I pulled a piece of scrap paper from my pocket—it was the letterhead of the German officer who had occupied my office. She wrote:

> *RUDOLPH SIEBER*
> *12 EAST 86th NEW YORK CITY BUTTERFIELD 8-4000*
> *husband of Marlene Dietrich*
> *tell him where you saw me and give him my A.P.O.*

Diagonally across the two corners she wrote:

> *cable Jean Gabin that I am in Paris.*
> *Paris is not the same without him.*

The day before I met Dietrich, I had asked for home leave. The Paris office was due to get a new picture editor, the quite capable (and French-speaking) Elmer Lower, and I did not care to hang around to engage again in Time Inc.'s ongoing experiment with two-man rule. Besides, I was desperate to see my family—and the son I had never met. I spent several weeks in London, awaiting my replacement. London was now a "service station" for the Continent. We were in the front line only when an occasional V-2 fell into the streets. The battle for Germany had to be covered, and we needed new photographers. From the D-Day team, first Landry and then Scherschel had gone home. Dave Scherman was doing features in Paris. Capa had gone to Toulouse with Wertenbaker to make contact with Spanish exiles, who were plotting Francisco Franco's overthrow. George Rodger, with the British, and Ralph Morse, with Patton's Third

Army, were left to cover the Allied offensive, and they clearly needed relief, which came with Johnny Florea and George Silk, newly arrived from the States.

At about this time, pictures reached the West that substantiated the terrible rumors that had been suppressed by Allied governments for more than two years: the Germans were methodically murdering Jews and other "undesirables" in mass killing centers. In the issue of August 28, 1944, *Life* ran the first picture story of what would come to be called the Holocaust. Headed "LUBLIN FUNERAL: Russians honor Jews whom Nazis gassed and cremated in mass," the pictures showed ovens full of the bones of men, women, and children, the shoes they left behind, the pits used as common graves.

Sadly, the story was relegated to page 34, facing an ad for Campbell's Soup: "How to make a meal out of a sandwich." *Life* was not alone in playing down the news of extermination. *The New York Times*, two years earlier, had given six inches on page 7 to a story headlined "1,000,000 JEWS SLAIN BY NAZIS, REPORT SAYS." It was not until *Life*'s own photographers–George Rodger at Belsen, Margaret Bourke-White at Buchenwald, Johnny Florea at Nordhausen—recorded such scenes at the war's end that the American public began to sense the full impact of the Holocaust. By then it was too late.

On November 20, I received orders authorizing me to proceed to the United States "by military aircraft and/or surface transportation." I chose to fly, and after a twenty-six-hour flight on piston-propelled military transports, from London to Prestwick to the Azores to Newfoundland to New York, we landed at La Guardia Field, where I found a pay phone. Shaking with excitement, I called Dèle—we had spoken only twice in fourteen months. Once home, I held her in my arms for a full fifteen minutes, with Holly and John Dale Morris II gaping from the sidelines. It was strange to acquire a son so suddenly.

At the office, Wilson Hicks grunted a hello. Otherwise the reception was warm. I had brought with me the first take of a picture story by Ralph Morse, who had begun following a wounded soldier from the moment of his arrival at a battalion aid station in Lorraine through treatment at field hospitals in France and England. Morse would follow him home. The pictures were remarkable, but Hicks at first gave them the brush-off, keeping me on the defensive. But when Morse himself arrived with more pictures, just before Christmas, Hicks joined the bandwagon, acclaiming the story as one of *Life*'s greatest.

My next assignment was the Chicago bureau, as midwestern editor (though

OVERLEAF: **This October 1944 spread in *The Illustrated London News* followed by a few weeks the single page of photographs on the Holocaust that had appeared in *Life* on August 28. Against the larger back- drop of the war, these first pictures out of the death camps drew scant attention. *Illustrated London News Picture Library***

THE MOST TERRIBLE EXAMPLE OF ORGANIS
MASS MURDER BY THE GERMANS

[Continued.]
barbed wire, never intende vide permanen modation for mates, and racks were cle as fast as the could be k Some, it is t of hunger and but the fa method of ex tion was by gas. In th concrete cells for the pur victims were so tightly t died on thei the gas was in. Fifteen after the in of the gas, t tioners entere and removed In the cent camp stands stone bui

LUBLIN'S " CAMP OF ANNIHILATION ": THE BARRACKS' INTERIOR, SHOWING REMNANTS OF ROPES USED TO HANG VICTIMS.

THE EXTERIOR OF THE TORTURE CHAMBER AT THE MAJDANEK "ANNIHILATION CAMP," SITUATED SOME TWO TO THREE MILES OUTSIDE LUBLIN.

A FEW OF THE CYLINDERS CONTAINING PO
THIS WAS THE NAZIS'

THE GAS CELLS INTO WHICH THE PRISONERS WERE PACKED SO TIGHTLY THAT THEY DIED ON THEIR FEET
AS THE POISON GAS WAS PUMPED IN.

IT is not the custom of "The Illustrated London News" to publish photographs of atrocities, but in view of the fact that the enormity of the crimes perpetrated by the Germans is so wicked that our readers, to whom such behaviour is unbelievable, may think the reports of such crimes exaggerated or due to propaganda, we consider it necessary to present them, by means of the accompanying photographs, with an irrefutable proof of the organised murder of between 600,000 and 1,000,000 helpless persons at Majdanek Camp, near Lublin. And even these pictures are carefully selected from a number, some of which are too horrible to reproduce. The Majdanek camp was called by the Germans themselves "the camp of annihilation"; built over an area of 20 square kilometres and surrounded by
[Continued above.

THE FURNACES IN WHICH THE GERMANS CREMATED THE BODIES OF THE MEN AND WOMEN
THEY HAD DELIBERATELY ASPHYXIATED BY POISON GAS.

THE OPENING IN THE ROOF OF THE GAS C
THROUGH WHICH "CYCLONE" CRYSTALS WERE

RUELTY IN THE HISTORY OF CIVILISATION.
HE MAJDANEK "CAMP OF ANNIHILATION."

orld's biggest
rium. In this
rium are five
ens, where five
were never
to go out.
d night, pillars
smoke belched
e chimneys, as
dies of the
were dragged
e gas chambers
t. Even in
st horrible of
the Germans
ethodical; a
f bodies, then
of logs, another
f bodies, an-
er of logs; and
One thousand
ndred corpses
disposed of
twenty-four
and the ashes
furnaces were
collected and
Germany as
[Continued below.

AN ENORMOUS QUANTITY OF LOCKS FROM THE PRISONERS' LUGGAGE WAS FOUND IN THE CAMP: FOREIGN CORRESPONDENTS VIEWING THESE LOCKS.

SOME OF THE PASSPORTS AND IDENTITY CARDS BELONGING TO THE VICTIMS OF NAZI BRUTALITY AT MAJDANEK CAMP.

OR THE WHOLESALE SLAUGHTER OF PRISONERS. OF EXTERMINATION.

THOUSANDS OF PAIRS OF BOOTS AND SHOES, ONCE BELONGING TO FREE MEN AND WOMEN, HERE COLLECTED FROM THE VICTIMS FOR CONSIGNMENT TO GERMANY.

OF "CYCLONE" CRYSTALS; SUCH CANS WERE BY THE SCORE IN THE MAJDANEK CAMP

Continued.]
fertiliser for Nazi kitchen gardens. This story as it stands is almost incredible in its bestiality, but German cruelty went further still at Majdanek. Prisoners who were too ill to walk into the camp—there to strip and neatly hang their clothes on pegs specially provided for the purpose before going to their death—were dragged alive to the furnaces and thrust in alongside the dead. And the man chiefly responsible for these mass murders? Herr Mussfeld was his name, the camp commandant. And yet no one man can be held responsible for these mass murders, not even Himmler; the whole German nation is involved, for it has chosen its leaders and presumably admires them. This camp, as it stands to-day, is a grim reminder of that streak of utter inhumanity which is found in every German.

THE CRYSTALS OF THE POISONOUS CHEMICAL KNOWN AS "CYCLONE." THE GERMANS USED THE WORD CYCLONE—"ZYKLON"—AS THE TRADE NAME FOR THIS GAS.

On April 12, 1945, Myron Davis
and I were prowling the Chicago Loop
for a story when we heard this woman
scream in anguish. She had just seen the
headline put on display at a newsstand
only moments earlier: FDR DEAD.
MYRON DAVIS/Life *Magazine © Time Inc.*

not for long). We were returning to the scene of my childhood, our courtship,
our marriage—and now, two blocks away from where we lived in Hyde Park,
the odd fortress that guarded the world's most carefully kept military secret.
There, under a grandstand of the University of Chicago's football field, atomic
physicists had just achieved the first self-sustaining nuclear chain reaction,
laying the theoretical groundwork for development of the atomic bomb. The
first bomb would explode in six months in Alamogordo, New Mexico.

I had no sooner agreed to the Chicago assignment than the war took a dras-
tic turn for the worse. On December 12, in the deep underground bunker of his
headquarters near Frankfurt, Hitler ordered his commanders to launch a massive counteroffensive against American positions in the Ardennes, Belgium. It
took the Allies by surprise, developing into what would become known as the
Battle of the Bulge, and would further drain America's manpower pool. For me,
the consequences were enormous. On February 13, 1945, my draft board re-
classified me as 1-A: eligible for immediate induction. Meanwhile, my *Life* colleagues were in the thick of it. Capa, covering the Battle of the Bulge, was shot
at by a GI who suspected he was German—the Germans had infiltrated our
lines with English-speaking soldiers in American uniforms. Capa would then
jump with paratroops, crossing the Rhine to photograph the "last man to die"
in Leipzig. Florea documented the grisly "Malmédy massacre," when a German
officer ordered the execution of 159 American prisoners. With Silk, he pur-

sued the retreating Wehrmacht. Florea was determined to be the first photographer to "piss in the Rhine" and, taking his stand near Cologne, threatened to kill Silk if he invaded his turf. George Rodger photographed the surrender of the German armies in the north to General Montgomery and took the good news to Denmark so fast that he found the Germans surrendering to *him*. Bill Vandivert met the Russians at the Elbe and went on to Berlin, entering Hitler's bunker. Ralph Morse shot the final German surrender at Reims. Dave Scherman, with Lee Miller, found Adolf Hitler's old flat in Munich; Scherman slept in Hitler's bed, and Lee bathed in the führer's tub.

When V-E Day finally came, on May 8, I did not feel much like celebrating. Thousands of Americans were still fighting and dying in the Pacific theater. Gene Smith was severely wounded on Okinawa on May 21. I was inducted into the U.S. Air Force on June 15 and ordered to the Texas panhandle for, of all absurd things, basic training. FDR had recently died, and now we had a new president—Harry S Truman. I had once found myself with him in an elevator, where we were introduced by *Life* photographer Tom McAvoy. A nice fellow, I remember thinking of Truman at the time. On August 6, Truman gave the order to drop the atomic bomb on Hiroshima, and the Pacific war was soon over.

From Texas I was sent to the Pentagon, to join the staff of *Impact*, the air intelligence magazine that had been founded by my former *Life* boss Ed Thompson. Its purpose was to enhance the morale and effectiveness of aircrews. The public never got to see it. *Impact* was the secret trade journal of the multibillion-dollar destruction business, if one could call it that. (Twenty-seven billion dollars was the cost of strategic bombing in Europe alone.)

Since World War II was now over, all we had to do was produce a seventy-two-page "Third [and final] Report of the Commanding General of the Army Air Forces to the Secretary of War." My job was to edit the pictures. Its language resembled that of a report to stockholders: "The Japanese have stated that air attacks killed 260,000, injured 412,000, left 9,200,000 homeless, and demolished or burned down 2,210,000 houses. Never in the history of aerial warfare has such destruction been achieved at such moderate cost. The combat efficiency of the B-29s was such that we were able to reduce Japan more economically than Germany." The report did not show the faces of the enemy—alive, maimed or dead, soldiers or civilians. We published aerial photos that systematically mapped the progressive devastation of air war—from a safe distance. Before, a city; after, a ruin. I found myself editing pictures with my eyes closed to any human feeling. The final issue of *Impact*, referring to a raid by B-29s on Nagoya, said succinctly, "Nobody doubted, least of all the Japs, that the blitz was a holocaust." A section on the atom bomb was headlined "Two Jolts Open New Military Vistas."

My Pentagon colleagues and I spent little time brooding over all this. We

This picture, taken twenty-seven hours after the atomic bomb dropped on Nagasaki, shows a mother and child awaiting medical treatment only two miles from the bomb's hypocenter. Such pictures were not published—*anywhere*, to my knowledge—at the time. Only *The New Yorker*, which devoted a full issue the following year to John Hersey's account of the bomb's aftermath in Hiroshima—without pictures—presented a detailed account to the public. What impact might this photograph have had as a *Life* cover? YOSUKE YAMAHATA, *August 10, 1945, Nagasaki/* © *Shogo Yamahata/Independent Documentary Group*

were all concentrating on one thing: how to escape back to civilian life as fast as possible. Ed Thompson came to my rescue by writing to someone in the War Department hierarchy—probably saying that I was not particularly useful as a soldier, anyway—and it worked. On November 7, 1945, I was "separated." Then I faced the real problem: my next assignment for *Life*. I didn't even know in what city we would live. Or in what country. My Chicago job was long gone. Time Inc. was facing a massive return of the employees who had gone into the armed forces, plus a return of war correspondents from overseas. Thompson offered me the number two slot in Washington. Fearing another Sherry Mangan scenario, I turned the job down and preoccupied myself with working on Andreas Feininger's *Feininger on Photography*, which Andreas had been authorized to put together on company time. I was getting a taste of *Life* limbo—a condition in which one could grow old (and many had). Clearly, it was time to go. This was the turning point of my career, a decision that would leave me poorer monetarily but richer—far richer—in experience.

   Life's national affairs editor, Roger Butterfield, told me that Bruce and Beatrice Gould, the husband-and-wife editors of *Ladies' Home Journal*, were looking for "a good picture man." I laughed and replied, "Roger, I'm not *that* desperate." But a day or so later, I mentioned the idea to Ed Thompson, who said, "Don't be a fool. The *Journal* is the best Curtis magazine." I lunched with both Goulds in their Rockefeller Center "workshop." We hit it off, and they gave me a trial assignment. I was to take a photographer of my own choice to their alma mater, the University of Iowa, to do a story on the lifestyles of returning veterans, who were then crowding American campuses on the GI Bill. I took Myron Davis, who was also quitting *Life*. The story was easy and obvious. I was surprised when the Goulds asked me to make the layout myself, ignoring their art director in Philadelphia. They ran it just as I had crudely pasted it up, with my text virtually unchanged. I had passed the test, and they offered me a job as an associate editor, with primary responsibility for pictures. Starting salary: $10,000 a year. Shortly after I accepted the *Journal* offer, a check for $3,500 came in the mail from Time Inc. I thought it was a mistake and confronted Wilson Hicks: "Wilson, what's this all about? I don't get severance pay. I wasn't fired!" He laughed but persuaded me to accept the check.

Ladies' Home Journal covers had traditionally favored fashions, brides (in June), and babies (most anytime). I introduced a new look by offering photographers $2,000 each for pictures of "Undiscovered American Beauties"—young women who had never modeled professionally. The first one accepted was Ruth Orkin's candid 35mm color cover of a New York housewife, who then began modeling. RUTH ORKIN © *1950*, *Meredith Corporation. Used with the permission of* Ladies' Home Journal.

11

Beatrice and Bruce
and Mary

oving from *Life* to *Ladies' Home Journal* meant far more than walking across Rockefeller Center. While *Life* could well claim to be "America's most powerful editorial force," the *Journal*'s influence was more pervasive. *Life* lectured America's leaders; the *Journal* addressed their female followers—in the millions. Calling itself "the magazine women believe in," the *Journal* dealt with women's daily lives and with their dreams.

For twenty-seven years, Bruce and Beatrice Gould edited and *lived* the *Ladies' Home Journal*, suiting the management of the magazine to their marital lifestyle. They had met at the University of Iowa. Starry-eyed and stagestruck, they had found newspaper jobs in New York in 1922—Bruce on the *Post*, Beatrice on the more distinguished *World*. They had written short stories and a play that had run seven weeks on Broadway, enabling them to buy a farm near Princeton, New Jersey. Its equidistance from New York and Philadelphia was to prove the geographical key to their future fortunes.

One day in 1935, George Horace Lorimer, chairman of the Curtis Publishing Company and the editor who had made *The Saturday Evening Post* into a national institution, asked Bruce Gould to take over Curtis's ailing *Ladies' Home Journal*. Gould was disinclined but accepted when Lorimer offered to hire *both* Goulds, as coeditors. Lorimer's idea of their relative worth was reflected in their starting salaries: $20,000 a year for Bruce; $5,000 for Beatrice. She had her revenge by agreeing to come to work only three days a week. Two of those three days, Tuesday and Wednesday, were in the *Journal*'s New York "workshop," atop the RKO building in Rockefeller Center, where the Goulds often spent the night, defying Rockefeller Center rules. Here were housed the "service" departments of the magazine, supervised by executive editor Mary Bass. The art department was in Philadelphia, along with the general editors who handled articles, fiction, and poetry under managing editor Laura Lou Brookman.

I was to work in New York, except Thursdays, when, with the Goulds and Mary Bass, I would take the eight o'clock train to Philadelphia, breakfasting with them in the club car. At least two Philadelphia editors came to New York each week to make the rounds of agents and authors. The Pennsylvania Railroad, with trains running every hour in both directions, offered a third base of operations. From Philadelphia's old Broad Street Station we proceeded to Sixth and Walnut. There, looking down on Independence Square and the Hall whose Liberty Bell had announced the American Revolution, was the Corinthian-columned marble headquarters of the Curtis Publishing Company, the most historic site in American magazine publishing. Upstairs, one could smell the paper and ink and hear the presses hum as millions of *Country Journals, Holidays, Jack and Jills, Ladies' Home Journals,* and *Saturday Evening Posts* came off the rotary presses and moved through the bindery to the old battery-powered, solid-tired Curtis delivery trucks, once one of Philadelphia's most familiar sights.

Bruce Gould had taken over the squash-court-size, walnut-paneled office of Edward Bok, the Dutch immigrant who had become editor of the Curtis "magazine for ladies" in 1889, at the age of twenty-six. He confessed in his third-person autobiography, *The Americanization of Edward Bok,* that women "had never interested him," but one eventually did: he married Mary Louise Curtis, the boss's daughter. In the next thirty years, Bok revolutionized women's magazines, developing "services" of all kinds, publishing the most popular authors and illustrators of the day, reproducing fine paintings and musical scores, and hobnobbing with presidents—whom he made contributors. Republican Benjamin Harrison was president when Bok assumed the editorship of the *Journal* in 1889; Grover Cleveland, a Democrat, succeeded him. Both wrote for the *Journal* when they left office. Theodore Roosevelt went one better: he agreed to a monthly interview, conducted in the White House barbershop ("I have only half an hour, when I am awake, when I am really idle, and that is when I am being shaved"). Woodrow Wilson submitted an article on Mexico and also sent Bok a piece by a woman friend "of great refinement," asking, "Will you do me the favor of reading the enclosed to see if it is worthy of your acceptance for the *Journal?*"

Bok refused patent medicine advertising. He crusaded against roadside billboards, unsanitary drinking fountains, the sale of fireworks, and venereal disease—the last a campaign that cost him 75,000 subscribers; one simply did not mention the subject in those days. Nor were some of Bok's other crusades popular: he railed against the domination of fashion by Paris couturiers, demanding "American fashions for American women." His readers could not have cared less. He did, however, successfully crusade against "dirty cities," and he saved Niagara Falls. When the falls was seriously threatened by greedy power companies, *Journal* readers, responding to Bok's editorials, flooded Washington with angry letters. On June 29, 1906, President Theodore Roosevelt signed a bill restricting the use of the falling water.

Edward Bok retired in 1919. By the time the Goulds took over in 1935, the *Journal* had slipped to fourth among women's magazines, behind *Good Housekeeping, Woman's Home Companion,* and *McCall's.* When I joined the staff in 1946, the *Journal* was again number one. The Goulds had taken vigorous action, immediately killing half a million dollars' worth of manuscripts and illustrations purchased by their predecessors. They upgraded "women's" fiction by going after and paying top dollar to such novelists as John Marquand, Rumer Godden, Daphne du Maurier, Edna Ferber, and James Michener. When novels had to be trimmed to create a serial or a "one-shot" (a condensation in one issue), they turned to Laura Lou Brookman. She was so adept at cutting that more than one author found his book improved. The Goulds built a stable of top illustrators, led by Al Parker, whose "Mother and Daughter" covers became a *Journal* trademark. They crusaded for prenatal care and against venereal disease, which remained a taboo subject, despite Bok's strenuous efforts. Beatrice testified before a Senate committee on the subject, and a *Journal* ad proclaimed, "Yes, I'll take a Wasserman"—the standard premarital test for VD was just becoming accepted. The Goulds appealed to readers to stop smoking but continued to accept cigarette advertising. Eleanor Roosevelt, the most respected woman in America, was a monthly columnist, to the dismay of the conservative Curtis board of directors.

On Mondays, when Bruce traveled alone to the Philadelphia office, a huge stack of manuscripts would await judgment. He could clear his desk faster than any editorial executive I have ever known. Checks would go out upon acceptance, every Wednesday, sparing contributors the agony of waiting for eventual publication. *Journal* covers normally featured models—young women or babies—in studio poses. I proposed a series of covers featuring women who had never modeled. We offered photographers $2,000 for each cover accepted plus a $500 fee to the model, and we were soon flooded with submissions. Most were imitations of precisely the kinds of covers we wanted to get away from, but photographer Ruth Orkin, whom I had known when she was a messenger at MGM in Culver City, came through with a set of 35-millimeter transparencies of a New York City housewife named Geraldine Dent, taken at a fruit and vegetable stand. The picture that caught my eye was one where Dent's bag of fruit had broken open and she had momentarily forgotten that she was being

For twenty-seven years it was the Thursday custom of Bruce and Beatrice Gould to tour the Philadelphia art department of the *Ladies' Home Journal*. Photostats and color proofs of display pages showed the progress of the next issue. Never in my time was the Goulds' authority challenged, even on the smallest detail. Pink, for example, was always sure to please when it came to decorating the home. JOSEPH DI PIETRO © *1949, Meredith Corporation. Used with the permission of* Ladies' Home Journal.

photographed. We used it for the March 1950 issue, which sold out—in fact, the *Journal*'s circulation hit an all-time high. It may have been the first time a 35-millimeter color slide was used on the cover of one of the "slicks." Engravers had preferred to work with large transparencies. This began to change.

Of greatest concern to the Goulds was the presentation of the special features they counted on to really sell the magazine. None was as important to them as "The Little Princesses," the inside story of life in Buckingham Palace as told by Marion "Crawfie" Crawford, the royal governess who raised Princesses Elizabeth and Margaret. In the days before the Royals became victims and accomplices of the media, the story was a publishing coup. It had been arranged with the help of Lady Astor and Dermot Morrah of *The Times* and had the tacit approval of the Palace. As designer, I hired freelancer David Stech, who had done the layouts for the Pentagon's *Impact*. Dave was one of those rare art directors who let the design flow from the pictures rather than force them into a preconceived pattern. We always worked together in virtual silence, our hands doing the talking as we shuffled pictures. Stech later became deputy art director at *Life*. I was sorry to lose him.

The Goulds encouraged experimentation—to a point. Early in 1947, I proposed that we photograph the faces of two women during childbirth: one having a spinal anesthetic, the other practicing "natural" childbirth, then coming into vogue. (Babies were much on my mind these days—Christopher Crosby Morris had recently been born to Dèle and me.) With photographer Gordon Coster, whose sensitive reportage I knew from *Life*, I traveled to the Chicago Maternity Center and to the University of Chicago's Lying-in Hospital. Both had remarkable records for safe natural-birth deliveries, practicing methods pioneered by obstetricians Joseph De Lee and Beatrice Tucker. Gordon and I accompanied a Maternity Center team to record a birth on the kitchen table of a West Side tenement. Picture editors on assignment are often accused of just standing around, but I found myself appointed a member of the team, assigned to gently hold the mother's left leg during several especially agonizing contractions. I returned to New York and made a dramatic layout. It was quickly killed. Beatrice was apologetic in her rejection, expressing her concern for a larger issue. "Sorry, John," she said, "but women who see these pictures will never want to try natural birth."

I had better luck with a series called "Baby's First Year" by photographer Wayne Miller. The series, which commenced with the birth of Miller's third child, Dana, was inspired by Wayne's photographs of his wife, Joan, during her first labor, four years earlier. Edward Steichen had exhibited the pictures at the Museum of Modern Art. Miller had been a star member of the Navy's "Steichen group" of photographers during World War II, and the "Captain," as Steichen loved to be called, came to regard Wayne as the son he had never had. For the *LHJ* series, I asked Wayne to record every major event, whether crisis or accomplishment, of the new baby's first twelve months. He agreed but later admitted that he at times had hated me, so intense was the invasion of his family's privacy. There were other dividends, however, besides the successful run in the magazine—the series became a book, with Dr. Benjamin Spock providing text.

To illustrate "The Unwed Mother," a plea by Joan Younger for greater compassion in dealing with their problems, I seized on the statistic that at that time one out of every twelve babies in the United States was born out of wedlock. I rented twelve high chairs and booked eleven one-year-old models, with their mothers, along with one illegitimate baby and its nurse from a New York foundling home. All were assembled for a group portrait in Gjon Mili's Twenty-third Street studio, the former Chinese nightclub to which I had taken Alice

Marble. Nobody was told which baby *it* was. The caption: "One of these babies was born out of wedlock." It was the simplest of all picture editorials: How could one stigmatize any *one* of those twelve beautiful babies?

Another challenge was the illustration of a piece by Margaret Mead, "Male and Female," in which the noted anthropologist told how primitive societies educate their children about sex. I asked Ralph Steiner and Mary Morris, then a married couple, to photograph two pubescent children, a boy and a girl of eleven or twelve, in the nude. They were photographed at separate times in the Steiner/Morris studio, but in the published spread the nude adolescents faced each other with only text between them. The layout was executed with such delicacy that no reader protested.

Mary Bass was almost nine months pregnant when we first met, the morning after Labor Day, 1946. Within the month, the *Ladies' Home Journal*'s executive editor celebrated her own labor day with a nine-pound son. The Goulds required me to report directly to them, but operationally I was placed under the delightfully loose supervision of this indefatigable woman, to whom journalism was life's blood. Mary's father was the Associated Press's Mexico City bureau chief, and her first husband had been the night city editor of the *New York Post*. He had died young, of tuberculosis; she had then married Basil Bass, a courageous New York attorney who represented talented writers and unpopular causes. Basil also died, and Mary went on to become a bride, and a widow, twice more.

Mary personified the *Journal*'s catchy promotion slogan, "Never underestimate the power of a woman." She never turned down a challenge. One day in 1939, the Goulds came back in high excitement from a vacation in Hawaii. They used vacations for brainstorming. "We want you to present to our readers a picture of life as it is lived in America today," they directed Mary, "what America eats, wears, and worries about." Thus was born the series called "How America Lives." Reporting on one family each month, it was planned to run for one year. It ran for twenty. Mary Bass produced the series, traveling 31,500 miles in the first year alone. As she wrote in a 1941 anthology collecting sixteen of the stories, families were chosen so as to represent a true cross section of American family life, "according to income groups and geographical distribution, population density and relative costs of living in different parts of the country." The challenge was to get them "to take us into their confidence—and into their homes."

The series required carefully coordinated teamwork. First a researcher, following statistical guidelines, would interview several possible families in a given locale and category. One family would be chosen, and a writer and photographer would be assigned to the principal story. Department editors would then help the housewife solve her problems, producing sidebars that would show, for instance, how to feed a family of five on ten dollars a week; how to furnish a nursery; how to sew a summer wardrobe. Many housewives were brought to the *Journal* workshop for advice, for fittings, or to try new ways of cooking or housekeeping. Department editors just as frequently went into the field to confront housewives with new ideas in their own kitchens.

In its first years, the pictures for "How America Lives" were taken by Martin Munkacsi, the talented and temperamental Hungarian who is credited with introducing action to fashion photography. Richard Avedon idolized Munkacsi. When the Hungarian died in 1963, Avedon wrote an elegy for *Harper's Bazaar* in which he told how, as a boy of eleven, he had covered the walls of his windowless Ninety-eighth Street bedroom "with my chosen view: a gleaning of five years' Christmas tuberculosis seals, three hundred Dixie Cup tops, and the photographs of Martin Munkacsi"—cut from the pages of *Harper's Bazaar.*

Munkacsi was born in 1896, in an area of Transylvania that is now Romania. He left home for Budapest at sixteen and, self-taught in photography, began covering sports for Hungarian newspapers. In 1927, he moved on to Berlin and freelanced for magazines, especially *Berliner Illustrirte Zeitung.* Ullstein, the Time Inc. of Germany, sent him on assignments throughout Europe, Africa, South America, and the United States. After Hitler's rise to power in 1933, Munkacsi joined the exodus of Jewish photographers. Had he not abandoned journalism for fashion, thus becoming dependent on making big money, and had he not suffered a succession of personal tragedies—three divorces, a daughter suddenly dying of leukemia, a heart attack—his work would undoubtedly have earned a higher place in the history of photography. Instead, his eminence is largely a result of his influence, not only on Avedon and fashion photography, but also on Henri Cartier-Bresson, who wrote of a 1930 photo of Munkacsi's, taken in Liberia, of three boys running into the sea, "It is that very photograph which was for me the spark that set fire to the fireworks . . . and made me suddenly realize that photography could reach eternity through the moment."

In 1940, Munkacsi was hired by *Ladies' Home Journal* for the unheard-of fee of $4,000 per story to shoot "How America Lives." In the next six years he photographed no fewer than sixty-five families. Unfortunately, they had begun to look the same to him. It was time to move on. In the spring of 1946, the Goulds asked their friend Edward Steichen what to do about photography in the *Journal.* He recommended two men from his gang in the wartime U.S. Navy. The *Journal* hired Joseph Di Pietro, a Navy lab technician, as a staff photographer, and began making assignments to Alfonso "Fons" Iannelli, who had covered combat as a Navy specialist First class. The "Steichen group" is known mostly for those who were commissioned officers: Horace Bristol, Barrett Gallagher, Fenno Jacobs, Victor Jorgensen, Charles Kerlee, Wayne Miller. Iannelli was only an enlisted man. Steichen deliberately chose the photographers for their diverse backgrounds, which included journalism, illustration, advertising, and marine photography. He revealed in his autobiography, "Off duty, almost every one of them sooner or later came to me separately and said he understood why he had been chosen for the job, but he couldn't understand why some of the others had been."

Shortly after Mary Bass returned from her brief maternity leave, she showed me a big batch of prints by Iannelli, on the family of a coal miner in Kentucky's Harlan County—known as "bloody Harlan" when the United Mine Workers organized there. Iannelli had spent weeks with the family, instead of the few days that Munkacsi normally devoted. I had never heard of Fons, who turned out to be a son of Chicago sculptor Alfonso Iannelli. Fons had learned photography by assisting Gordon Coster in Chicago. He was going through what he called "working psychoanalysis" to better project himself into the emotional situations he sought to record on film.

I was thrilled with the pictures. Fons and I made the layout on the floor. The eight-page story—perhaps the best layout I ever made unassisted by an art director—proved to be a turning point for the *Journal.* Miner Jim Perkins and his wife, Alice, lived with seven children in a four-room shack. Pigs foraged in the front yard. One picture spread documented, with red numerals, how eleven people (a daughter-in-law and grandchild completed the household) slept in three rooms, four in one bed, flies clearly visible on the face of one child. The text pointed out that "37% of the nation's families live on incomes of $1500 to $3000 a year."

This was a kind of journalism totally different from my experience at *Life,* where I was accustomed to covering the extraordinary, not the familiar. The Goulds believed that "journalism is at its greatest—and most absorbing—when it presents life as it is." We established a flat rate of $1,500 per story, plus expenses, and I told photographers to take their time. (At that time the average *Life* day rate was around $75.) I had no trouble attracting photographers. Choosing a photographer for "HAL" was like awarding a monthly Pulitzer Prize. I chose photographers more for their sensitivity and ability to develop a rapport with their subjects than for their technical talent.

Occasionally I chose a photographer on the basis of previously shared experience. I sent Robert Capa to Green Bay, Wisconsin, to do a story on a veteran of the Battle of the Bulge. Both remembered it all too well. I dispatched Ernst Haas to Rochester to photograph a couple from Czechoslovakia who had just escaped across the Iron Curtain. Ernst had married a Hungarian countess, whose family had just endured a similar adventure. In Los Angeles I asked Don Ornitz, son of one of the "Hollywood Ten," to shoot the story of an aspiring actor. In New York I commissioned Carl Perutz, who had virtually been born in the theater, to shoot a young couple who were trying to make it on Broadway. Joe Munroe, who had shot dozens of stories for *Farm Quarterly*, easily won the confidence of a twenty-two-year-old Tennessee farmer and his wife, even photographing them in bed—reading the Bible. Kosti Ruohomaa, a Disney animator before he turned to photography, was a natural for the story of a Maine farm, since he had grown up on one. He summarized the farmer's winter landscape in two pictures of footprints in the snow: one trail led to the house, one to the outhouse.

Roy Stryker, whose Farm Security Administration photographers had documented America in the thirties, was now director of photography for Standard Oil (New Jersey), also known as Esso. Esso's public relations experts had convinced the company to create a documentary photo archive, whose pictures would be offered to publishers for free, with credit to the company. Although a file of eighty-six thousand pictures was created (today it resides at the University of Louisville), Esso was never comfortable with the idea, and budgets were tight. Stryker could pay his photographers only $150 a week, so he was delighted when they enjoyed success at the *Journal*. Two of his people, Esther Bubley and Sol Libsohn, became "HAL" regulars. Bubley had the ability to make people forget she was even around; her pictures achieved incredible intimacy— she photographed a young Los Angeles couple, sitting at opposite ends of a couch, calmly discussing a divorce, and a Nebraska farm couple, lunching together in the middle of a cornfield in a daily rite reflecting their devotion. Working-class people felt especially at ease with Sol, who was the son of immigrants and a neighbor of painter/photographer Ben Shahn in Roosevelt, New Jersey, a town established by garment workers. Morris Engel was a photographer I could count on in almost any situation. Formerly on the newspaper *PM*, he had been a mainstay of the socially conscious Photo League, as was Sol Libsohn. Engel shot five of the finest stories of "How America Lives." One was the story of two young "homesteaders" in Idaho. They had successfully bid for their 160-acre farm in a lottery conducted by the Department of Interior's Bureau of Reclamation. Morris had been experimenting with a lightweight 35-millimeter handheld movie camera. He asked for $500 worth of film so that he could shoot a movie along with the stills. The resulting short, *The Farm They Won*, launched Engel's career in cinema verité.

It would have been easy to stay with such proven "HAL" photographers as Bubley, Engel, Iannelli, and Libsohn. Instead, I chose to experiment, using thirty different photographers on "HAL" in my six years of making those assignments. Geography was one factor. It made sense to employ such talented photographers as Myron Davis and Gordon Coster in the Midwest, Victor Jorgensen in the Northwest, the Hagels in California. One of my favorite selections

A young Manhattan housewife reacts to her baby's cry. ESTHER BUBLEY © *1950, Meredith Corporation. Used with the permission of* Ladies' Home Journal.

was of Lisette Model to shoot the story of a family who ran a Reno guest ranch where divorcees could board while meeting Nevada's residence requirements. Lisette, who had studied piano with Arnold Schönberg in Vienna, had no journalistic experience but had become a cult figure in photography, thanks to her portraits of outrageous people on the Promenade des Anglais in Nice. *PM* had published them in 1941 under the headline WHY FRANCE FELL.

When editing, I prefer to have the photographer at hand, to "soundtrack" me through any questions. Usually the choice is evident from the images themselves, but sometimes not. A good example came in editing, with Esther Bubley, the superficially prosaic story of a young Manhattan housewife confined in a small apartment. In Esther's contact sheets, I noticed a series of almost identical pictures of the housewife as she ironed clothes. In most, she was looking down at her work. However, there was one frame where her hands were ironing but her eyes had flashed up in alarm. "What happened?" I asked Esther. "That's when the baby cried." It was the housewife's decisive moment. We chose it as the lead picture of the story.

»MENSCHEN WIE DU UND ICH« von JOHN GODFREY MORRIS
— ein großer Bildbericht, dessen Veröffentlichung in dieser Nummer
beginnt. Er zeigt das Leben von zwölf Familien, die verschiedenen
Völkern angehören, verschiedene Sprachen sprechen, denen aber allen
eines gemeinsam ist: daß sie Menschen sind — wie du und ich.

HEUTE

NUMMER 63 • 1. JULI 1948 • 50 PFENNIG

In 1947 I assigned seven photographers to document the lives of twelve farm families in as many countries. "People Are People the World Over" ran in the *Ladies' Home Journal* for a year and was also published in the American-sponsored German picture magazine *Heute* in 1948. Little noticed at the time, "People Are People" would inspire Edward Steichen's "The Family of Man," a landmark photographic exhibition at New York's Museum of Modern Art in 1955. *John G. Morris Collection*

12

"People Are People"

Despite my happy immersion in a world of women, I hadn't lost touch with my old friends. Robert Capa was one. "I'm delighted to be an unemployed war photographer," he kept saying, but a new listlessness was also evident. If he was going to shoot picture stories, he at least wanted to be his own boss and hold on to his negatives. He kept turning over the idea he had talked about with friends for years—starting a picture agency owned by photographers. Chim and Henri, who had always been freelancers, had nothing to lose by joining. George Rodger and Bill Vandivert were both ready to leave *Life*, and their severance pay would get them started.

Before Capa got around to doing anything more about it, Ingrid Bergman happened to come to Paris. Capa and his buddy Irwin Shaw heard that she was at the Ritz, and they invited her to dinner, where the roguish photographer charmed her. Capa and Bergman ran into each other again a few weeks later in a rubble-strewn Berlin, and there their affair began. Capa photographed Bergman—fully clothed—inside a broken bathtub he found amid the ruins. She had been toying with the idea of leaving her husband, a severe Swedish doctor, but she was not sure whether she was ready to commit herself to Capa. Bergman had work in Hollywood—Hitchcock wanted her for *Notorious*—and since Capa had long flirted with the idea of making films, he was happy to follow her there in December, checking into the Garden of Allah Hotel. Capa, who seldom had a hard time assimilating wherever he found himself, actually had a rough time of it in Hollywood. Always a lousy driver, he racked up the first car he bought. By April 1946, he was back in New York. Bergman visited in May, and she was warmly received by Bob's mother, Julia, who made pleated skirts for Ingrid and her daughter, Pia. But a continuing romance was difficult. Bergman's and Capa's lives and fortunes were simply too far apart. He seemed relieved when work took him back to Europe. That spring, Bergman realized the affair was over, writing to a friend, "We are drinking our last bottles of champagne."

Now Bob was talking about going to Russia with John Steinbeck. Capa had moved into the Hôtel Bedford, where Steinbeck had taken a room during a marital rift. They met often at the bar and played poker with friends on Friday nights. Bob was morose and restless, reviewing the failed relationship with Bergman and perhaps also the one with Pinky. She had grown tired of waiting for Bob to commit and so had married his friend Charles "Chuck" Romine, a public relations officer for Troop Carrier Command. An unmarried and foot-loose Bob was okay by me, however. I figured that his trip to Russia, if it materialized, would fit beautifully into an ambitious scheme I was concocting for a worldwide picture series on family life—a "How the World Lives." I wrote a memo to the Goulds, proposing to "explain peoples to peoples in intimate, vivid terms, taking them not country by country but trait by trait, problem by problem." We would compare the families of farmers, a more universal occupation than locomotive driving. My working title: "People Are People the World Over." Dave Stech made a two-page layout that could be used month after month. Instead of running country by country, the series would show families in all the countries every month, as they went about their quotidian business and engaged in the common preoccupations of humankind. I then talked to Capa, who saw "People Are People" as an ideal assignment for his new group of photographers, about to be named Magnum Photos. The idea intrigued the Goulds, and it wasn't hard to persuade them that Capa and I would find a prototypical American family in their native Iowa. Bob and I took off for Des Moines on a Saturday afternoon. He soon donned an oxygen mask to alleviate a hangover.

The following morning we headed west on U.S. 30. We had not gone a hundred miles when we found just what we wanted, near the small town of Glidden: the family farm of Donald Pratt. Red barn, white farmhouse, tractor, cows and horses, two boys and two girls. Perfect. They were easily persuaded to cooperate. We agreed to start the following day.

It was now five o'clock on Sunday afternoon. As we drove back to our hotel in Carroll, Bob and I had a simultaneous thought: it would be nice to have a drink. We had not reckoned with the fact that Iowa was one of the few remaining dry states—totally so on Sunday. We had come unprepared.

On the outskirts of town, I spotted what we midwesterners call a roadhouse. The parking lot was almost empty, but I noticed that the door was open for business. Inside, we found a long row of booths, a few tables, and a dance floor.

It was one of those places where, if you were smart, you brought your own liquor and bought setups.

A waitress came up, with the usual "What'll it be?" With my most imploring smile I said, "Could we have two beers?"

"Of course not. It's Sunday."

Resigned to Coke, in mock desperation I demanded, "Then just bring us two Scotch and sodas."

To which she replied, "Ballantine's? Haig and Haig? Johnny Walker?"

We roared. If Iowans bend the law, they do it for good reason. We drank to Magnum, but not with champagne.

That night at the hotel I found a message from my sister, Mary. She had flown that afternoon to Chicago. My father had just had a heart attack. Leaving Capa behind in Iowa to do the story alone, I flew to Chicago the next morning and joined my sister at my father's bedside. I could not remember ever seeing him sick in bed. In all but religion and politics, he had long inspired me, his only son. He wanted no doctor, only a Christian Science practitioner to read to him. On Saturday afternoon, he asked for the Twenty-third Psalm. Mary held his hand and I read, "The Lord is my shepherd . . ." And he was gone.

John Dale Morris, born on a Missouri farm in 1869, was a gentle man who came up the hard way. A born salesman, he started out selling dictionaries, then encyclopedias. He founded John D. Morris & Company of Philadelphia, to publish sets of the classics. By 1902, he was worth a quarter of a million dollars, but five years later he went broke in the Panic of 1907. Almost simultaneously, his first wife died in childbirth, the baby as well.

My mother, Ina Arabella Godfrey, the daughter of a doctor in the village of Colon, Michigan, studied the classics in Latin and Greek and made the "grand tour" of Europe before going to work for John D. Morris & Company. She and the handsome widower fell in love. They married in 1908 and had my sister, Mary, in 1909. Mary did not welcome my arrival in 1916, in the Philadelphia suburb of Maple Shade, New Jersey. She pushed my pram down the street, trying to sell me, but got no takers.

In 1918, my father was offered a job at Chicago's La Salle Extension University. We settled in the quiet and comfortable neighborhood of Hyde Park, which embraced the campus of the University of Chicago. I think of Hyde Park as my home to this day. The residence of my childhood was a three-story apartment building, now a century old, at 5515 Woodlawn Avenue. In those years my father was seldom home. Business took him away on long trips. For two or three years he even lived in New York, coming home occasionally on the overnight *Twentieth Century Limited*, which among its many luxuries boasted a barbershop. His arrivals were like Christmas, his valises full of toys from F. A. O.

Schwartz, tools from Hammacher Schlemmer, saltwater taffy from Atlantic City.

The Goulds were delighted with Bob's pictures of the Pratts of Iowa. We agreed on a budget of approximately $15,000, including expenses, to cover the rest of the world. I knew it would be tight, so I rigidly prescribed the rudimentary picture situations that must be covered, in addition to making a family portrait: farming, cooking, eating, washing, bathing, playing, studying, shopping, worshiping, relaxing at home, traveling, sleeping.

Capa very naturally wanted to make the whole thing a Magnum project. Magnum's photographers were going to loosely divide the world among themselves: George Rodger would cover Africa and the Middle East, Henri Cartier-Bresson would go to Asia, Capa and Chim would cover Europe. If one photographer failed to shoot even one of the prescribed subjects, however, it would throw off the whole series. Therefore, I refused to assign China and Japan to Cartier-Bresson. I simply could not see Henri following such a simplistic script. I commissioned Horace Bristol for those two countries; he had left *Life* to join Edward Steichen's Navy unit during World War II and was living in Tokyo. George Rodger shot families in Egypt, Pakistan, and Equatorial Africa; Chim handled France and Germany. Capa found Magnum "stringers" for England (Larry Burrows), Italy (Marie Hansen), and Mexico (Phil Schultz); Capa himself had taken care of the United States (Iowa) and agreed to do the USSR. Worldwide shooting would begin in the summer of 1947 and would be completed by fall.

Just after I returned to New York from my father's funeral, Capa told me that Steinbeck had gotten his visa for the USSR; Bob's had not come through, but Steinbeck had told the Russians that he would not go without Capa, so they were hopeful. I confirmed the Russian family assignment to Capa and made an additional one: "Women and Children of the Soviet Union." It was so vague that we didn't discuss money.

Capa returned from Russia in October and asked me to meet him for lunch at the Algonquin. I took it as a bad sign, and I was right. First, he told me the really bad news: he had not shot the Russian family—he and Steinbeck had been toured around too fast. However, as a consolation prize he had photographed a family in Slovakia on the way home; at least it was behind the Iron Curtain. Second, the Russians had constantly frustrated him, forbidding him, for example, to shoot in a Stalingrad tractor factory because it had made tanks during the war and was still considered militarily sensitive. As a final blow, the censors had taken away Capa's rolls of film for inspection and had developed them—badly. Capa was sure he had blown the trip, but, having already salvaged as best I could one major Capa story—the surviving D-Day negatives—I knew to insist that I see everything. Several days later we met in his room at the

This *Ladies' Home Journal* cover by Robert Capa introduced an unprecedented sixteen-page picture story by Capa, with captions by John Steinbeck, on "Women and Children in Soviet Russia." I arranged to pay Capa $20,000 for his pictures; Steinbeck got only $3,000 for his words. The issue sold out. *Copyright © 1998 Estate of Robert Capa. Cover © 1948, 1950, Meredith Corporation. Used with the permission of* Ladies' Home Journal.

Capa had photographed a Soviet Union I had not seen and could not have imagined at the time. The very commonality of the scenes lent them interest. *Copyright © 1998 Estate of Robert Capa*

Bedford. He had a huge stack of 8-by-10-inch proof prints, and they were technically not as bad as he had made them out to be. I began shuffling through them. It was a Soviet Union I had not seen and could not have imagined—not the heroic prewar images of the propaganda magazine *USSR in Construction*. Not the grainy Sovfoto releases from the battlefronts of World War II. Here were children lined up to see Lenin's tomb, but also playing chess in the park, studying piano and ballet, herding geese. Here were farm women dancing barefoot after the harvest. Here were priests, traffic cops, Volga boatmen.

I had gone through perhaps two hundred black-and-white prints, with mounting excitement, when I remembered that I no longer worked for *Life*. To make a big splash in the *Journal* would require a minimum of color—to compete with our gaudy fiction illustration and fashion. On demand, Capa handed over a dozen or so rolls of 120 Ektachrome in strips, unmounted. I don't think he had really looked at them. Again—not so bad; certainly a fair number were reproducible. I *had* to have a color cover, and eventually I found one frame, *just* one frame, that was strong and tight enough. It showed a peasant woman in her babushka, kneeling at work in a field, looking straight at the viewer. Bob told me the story behind the picture, which would never be told in the *Journal*. She had waved a cucumber at him, saying, with a wide, toothless grin, "Men should be as impressive as cucumbers!"

I pulled that one transparency, told Capa I wouldn't need the rest of the pictures until the following week, and warned him, for his own good, not to show them to any other magazine. I took the transparency straight to Dave Stech's studio and asked him to make up a full-scale *Journal* cover. The following Tuesday, I took the cover mock-up, hidden by an overlay, into Bruce Gould's small New York office and set it down in an armchair facing him and Beatrice. I said nothing as the Goulds began turning over the prints, at first mechanically but soon more slowly as they saw more and more of interest. After a while, I saw Bruce glance curiously at the hidden mock-up. Finally, having looked at every print, he asked, "Well, what do you propose?" Taking off the cover flap, I replied, "A cover and sixteen pages." The Goulds laughed, as I knew they would, but Beatrice's next question was more serious: "Is this exclusive? Will *Life* get anything?" I explained that the *New York Herald Tribune* would syndicate a Steinbeck series to newspapers, with some Capa photos, but that we would have first magazine rights and Steinbeck would write short text blocks to our layouts.

Bruce looked at Beatrice. He must have seen affirmation in her eyes, so he asked me the price. I made a fast calculation, knowing that the Goulds were accustomed to paying $25,000, or even more, for prime magazine properties. My instinct told me that unless the price was on that level they wouldn't think the Russian story worth the space. "Twenty-five thousand for Capa's pictures," I replied without blinking. "As for Steinbeck . . ." I shrugged, secretly astonished by my own audacity. Bruce mused over this. "See if you can get it for twenty," he said. "I'll handle Steinbeck."

I went to my office, feeling a little dizzy, and made arrangements to meet Capa at the bar of Toots Shor's at noon. I knew that Bob would have been thrilled by a sale of $5,000. But $20,000! He was overwhelmed. Meanwhile, Bruce Gould called Elizabeth Otis, Steinbeck's agent, and bargained her into accepting $3,000 "for a few captions." The resulting story, a cover plus sixteen pages of alternating color and black and white, ran in the February 1948 *Ladies' Home Journal,* and I must say it looks just as good to me now as it did when Stech and I laid it out. John Steinbeck was not particularly happy about writing copy to fit the layout, and I had to make the final adjustments without consulting him. I've always thought this paragraph sounds just like Steinbeck: "The old mother . . . laid our beds in the straw of the barn. She had a face like all the kind old grandmothers in the world, and she had killed two Germans with a pitchfork." We saw the story as a plea for peace and sanity in a world that was becoming mad with fear. It was a time when statesmen of goodwill were in short supply. Steinbeck's last lines were "In a field of cucumbers, we found this boy named Grischa, wearing a hat of marsh grass. He cried: 'But these Americans are just like us!' "

The February 1948 issue quickly sold out, but the *Journal*'s promotion people were loath to boast about it. For them, Capa was too great an aberration from the *Journal*'s normal cover formula: mothers and daughters, brides and babies. Neither did they take great notice when we began, in May, the "People Are People" series. I introduced the families in the first installment:

Here are eighty-eight of the two billion people who inhabit the planet Earth. They are twelve families who represent twelve countries, three races and five religious faiths. They speak eleven languages. They are posing for a photographer sent by an American magazine, the *Ladies' Home Journal.* In the past few months the *Journal,* like a magazine on Mars, has sent photographers to inquire into the lives of families the world over. These, then, are the families you will meet each month in this series, in the order in which the sun awakens them. The Okamotos, of Oshika, Japan—whose twelve annual taxes include a cow tax and a supplementary cow tax. The Ho Fu-yuans, of Kia-ting, China, who would not permit their little girl to be photographed lest evil spirits cause her death. The Mohamed Usmans, of Patni, Pakistan—a couple who had not met before their wedding, but whose marriage has lasted thirteen years. The el Gamels, of Manayel Shebein el Kanater, Egypt— whose donkeys are descended from those in the Bible. The Zamba Alumas, of Lujulu, Equatorial Africa—where every girl's first task of the day is to gather fresh leaves for her skirt. The Baloghs, of Furolac, Czechoslovakia—where weddings last three days and wolf meat is considered a delicacy. The Guercinis, of Greve, near Florence, in Italy—whose spotlessly clean house is painted yellow because the neighbors' are red. The Stieglitzes, of Wollau, Germany—who fell in love at a village dance and were married in the year Hitler came to power. The Redouins, of Fossés, France— who sent messages by carrier pigeons to England during the late German occupation. The Hiatts, of Hook Norton, England—who like to read Western stories and whose favorite pub is The Gate Hangs High. The Pratts, of Glidden, Iowa, U.S.A.—whose nine-year-old girl would rather ride a pony bareback than do anything else in the world. The Gonzalezes, of Moravatio, Mexico—where cockfights are legal and it is the custom to "steal" a bride from her parents. The conclusion of our survey will surprise only those who write newspaper headlines. It is simply that people are pretty much people, no matter where you find them.

The series made little stir at the time, but it made me a lasting friend. Edward Steichen took notice. He was then director of photography at the Museum of Modern Art, and he borrowed the pictures to create Fifth Avenue window displays honoring the United Nations on its 1949 birthday. Steichen began to dream, sharing his hopes with me, of an exhibition he would eventually call "The Family of Man."

Roy Stryker (*wearing glasses, top right*), who had directed the Farm Security Administration's photographic project, appears to be just one of the students at the final session of the University of Missouri's first Photo Workshop in 1949. I made an exhibition layout from the weeklong collective coverage of the twenty-three paid students. © RUS ARNOLD

13

The Missouri Workshop

In the *Journal* years, I used to lunch regularly with Roy Stryker. One day in the spring of 1949, he announced over lunch that he needed my help "in Missouri." In retrospect, it was one of the most flattering invitations of my professional life—to teach at the first Missouri Workshop, a program of photography and photojournalism that is now legendary in photographic circles. The Missouri Workshop was founded by Clifton "Cliff" Cedric Edom, who taught photography at the University of Missouri's School of Journalism. Edom, unlike most journalism professors, had begun his career as a photoengraver. He was also an amateur photographer. In 1943, seeking to combine journalism with his hobby, Cliff enrolled as a thirty-five-year-old freshman in the University of Missouri's School of Journalism. His wife, Vilia "Vi" Edom, stayed on her job to help put him through school and became his principal assistant at every workshop. When the school's photography instructor went off to war, Dean Frank Luther Mott gave Edom the job. Dean Mott soon found that he had a man who shared his ambition to make Missouri the world's preeminent journalism school. Edom took up the cause of "photojournalism," a term he seems to have invented. His first move was to begin a national competition for Pictures of the Year, which continues at Missouri to this day, conducted jointly with the National Press Photographers Association.

The press photos submitted for Edom's annual contest often represented the kind of photography that he personally deplored: carefully contrived clichés featuring New Year's babies, Easter chicks, and Halloween witches; well-worn oddities such as the horse laugh, the airborne shortstop, the crying beauty queen. Edom rebelled: "I felt that there was a demand for 'depth reporting' as opposed to the shallow flash-on-camera, stand-'em-up and mow-'em-down technique then in vogue." Edom found his major inspiration neither in the daily press nor in the picture magazines. He found it instead in Roy Stryker and his Farm Security Administration photographers. The two met at a 1945 convention in Oklahoma City. They walked around the town for hours, spending a full hour in an Army and Navy store. Stryker told Edom, "It's in places like this where you learn about people, about their economy and what makes a community tick." From this Oklahoma City promenade came the idea for the now-celebrated University of Missouri Photo Workshop, held for one week each year in one of Missouri's many small towns. In forty-eight years, the workshops have drawn more than two thousand student photographers and revolutionized the teaching of photojournalism.

I had never worked with Stryker, but I had enjoyed hanging out with him in New York. He loved to talk of his boyhood on a ranch in Colorado and of his father, a radical populist, who would lead the family in prayer: "Damn Wall Street, damn the railroads, and double-damn Standard Oil." Roy viewed the double-damn with particular irony. "I often wonder what the old man would say if he knew I spent ten years of my life not only working for Standard Oil but having a wonderful time of it," he said with a laugh. He had spent nine months in France with the American Expeditionary Force in World War I but had never seen action—and had never, as far as I know, left the United States again.

As a student at Columbia University, Stryker came under the influence of two great professors. One was geographer J. Russell Smith, whose thousand-page *North America* first appeared in 1925. It became Stryker's Bible. He made his photographers read it—or at least say they had—before going into the field. The second professor was Rexford Guy Tugwell, who gave Stryker his first assignment in picture editing, to illustrate his book *American Economic Life*. One third of the pictures came from Lewis Hine, who had been courageously photographing America's poor and oppressed for three decades—his photographic testimony for the National Child Labor Committee resulted in legislation banning children from working in factories (although they were soon enough dispatched to the fields).

In 1933, Franklin Roosevelt called Tugwell to Washington to be part of the "Brain Trust" of the New Deal. His assignment: to create an agency to address the plight of the American farmer, who was being forced off the land by depression, drought, and mechanization. Tugwell named Stryker "Chief of the Historical Section" of the Farm Security Administration. Stryker assembled a diverse and talented photographic team, including some whose images would become central to the history of photography: Arthur Rothstein, Carl Mydans, Walker Evans, Ben Shahn, and Dorothea Lange. Also on the team: Russell Lee, Marion Post Wolcott, Jack Delano, John Vachon, and John Collier. When FSA was absorbed into the Office of War Information, Stryker helped launch the careers of Esther Bubley and Gordon Parks. And with Standard Oil, Roy's roster grew again.

Stryker and Edom were neither photographers nor journalists, so for the first workshop they invited Harold Corsini, a Standard Oil freelancer, and Rus Arnold, a Chicago portrait photographer and lighting expert, to teach photography; the picture editors were Stan Kalish of the *Milwaukee Journal* and me.

Our twenty-three paying students (who each paid thirty dollars plus expenses) came from seven states, drawn by some invisible grapevine since there had been no advance publicity. Four were photographers from dailies; six people worked for weeklies and house organs (mostly as editors); seven were students and teachers; two were in oil company public relations. There were two "freelance" photographers (one studio photographer and a Kansas City housewife who called herself a "pictorialist"). Only one photographer worked with 35-millimeter; the others used 4-by-5-inch and 120 film. We told them that there would be little formal instruction. The subject of study was the city of Columbia, seat of the university; each student was to shoot a story or theme in pictures. Students could work in teams if they chose. Edom laid down one law: *Show truth with the camera.* No setups. Tell it as it is. Let the story unfold. Observe, but don't direct. And be respectful of people's privacy.

First, we all took "a course in curiosity." We boarded a school bus to tour the town, from snooty Stephens College to Sharp's End, the "Negro district." The university was still segregated. Blacks were sent to a separate state institution. We were briefed on the city by a historian, by the prosecuting attorney, and by one of Columbia's old-timers.

Each night, the faculty selected frames from the day's take for projection and discussion. Students could speak up to define their objectives or not, as they wished. On Friday, each student was required to take his pictures and make a "magazine" layout of one to four or more "spreads," trying to bring coherence to the story in form and content. The resulting layouts were then critiqued. The results amazed everyone. Almost all found themselves shooting the best pictures of their lives.

On Saturday morning, we met with the class for one final session. Looking at the assembled layouts, I observed that there was sufficient quality and quantity for an overall exhibition on Columbia. Challenged by Stryker and Edom, with Stan Kalish as assistant, I spent the next three hours grouping pictures that I chose from the work of all the photographers into rough layouts, making a seventy-five-picture, thirty-six-panel exhibition. The group show on the town became an annual tradition.

Stryker and I stayed in touch, and we kept each other abreast of the new talent in the field. One brilliant prospect I sent on to Roy was Elliott Erwitt, who had come to see me at *Ladies' Home Journal*. I have always made it a policy to see every serious photographer who seeks me out, whether I have work for him or not. Elliott was a slight, deceptively shy young man in a sweater who looked to be a teenager but who was actually twenty. He handed me a group of about forty prints and stood by. I realized that they had nothing, but *nothing*, to do with the *Ladies' Home Journal*. They were real but surreal—astonishing pictures of pigeons, masks, kites, statues, dogs acting like people, people acting like dogs. I was intrigued, but I couldn't get much out of the young photographer except that he was desperately broke. At that moment I had no assignments to make, and if I had, I wouldn't have had the slightest idea what pictures would have resulted. But here was a talent that had to be kept going. I went to a phone in the outer office and called Stryker at Standard Oil: "Roy, I have a genius on my hands, and he's hungry. Help!" Erwitt left Stryker's office the next day with a hundred dollars in cash and an assignment to shoot the Bayway refinery. In 1950, Stryker left New York to found the Pittsburgh Photographic Library. Erwitt tagged along. One day he came to New York and dropped in to see me, no longer so shy. I keep a card file with names and numbers of photographers. I pulled out Erwitt's card, to update it. I found I had written, from the first interview, "Simply a genius." We would meet again, at Magnum.

In 1962, Roy Stryker retired to his beloved Colorado. He was perhaps the most dedicated man ever to work in documentary photography. He thought that pictures should always ask questions. He had his critics on both left and right, which pleased him. He put his mission very simply: "We introduced Americans to America." Stryker arranged for the Farm Security Administration files to go to the Library of Congress, where they remain, a national treasure. My only problem with Roy concerned the FSA negatives. Not only did he deny photographers the ownership of them (which was perhaps impossible under U.S. government regulations), but he took it upon himself to destroy those he rejected for various reasons: a total of perhaps 100,000 of the 270,000 shot by FSA photographers. It was past history when we first met, but I regret that I never asked him about it.

Cliff Edom proudly poses with his 1976 textbook, *Photojournalism*, a word he seems to have coined as a young professor at the University of Missouri School of Journalism. Interestingly, Edom did not confine the term "photojournalist" to photographers; it also included picture editors.
© CHARLIE NYE

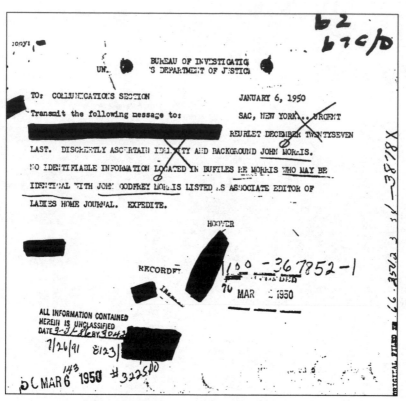

A 1991 check of my FBI file under the Freedom of Information Act turned up this 1950 telegram from J. Edgar Hoover to his New York agents, instructing them to "discreetly ascertain identity and background John Morris . . . expedite."

14

Red-baited

World War II had left me unscathed, but, like many other innocent Americans, I almost became a casualty of the Cold War. My crime: defending the Photo League, a New York organization of socially conscious photographers that had been founded in the early thirties. The Photo League held discussions and exhibitions, ran a school for aspiring photographers, and conducted group photographic projects, such as "Harlem Document." Some of America's most distinguished photographers supported the League: Paul Strand, Lewis Hine, Margaret Bourke-White, W. Eugene Smith, Ansel Adams, Aaron Siskind. I had spoken twice in their symposiums and had contributed to their bulletin, *Photo Notes.*

In 1942, a young woman named Angela Calomiris, then working for twenty-seven dollars a week as a playground director, joined the Photo League, determined to become a photojournalist. Not long after, two men came to her apartment and introduced themselves as agents of the Federal Bureau of Investigation. Appealing to her patriotism—she was the daughter of poor but proud Greek immigrants—they asked her to become a "plant" in the Communist Party. The FBI considered the Photo League a Communist front; her membership would give Calomiris good cover for infiltrating the Party. During the next seven years, she rose to financial secretary of its West Midtown Branch, taking the Party name "Angie Cole." Meanwhile, she used her camera to take mug shots of Party members for the FBI, to whom she was known as IS-342.

In 1947, members of the Photo League were astonished to find that the League had been placed on the U.S. attorney general's list of "subversive" organizations under the terms of the Smith Act, or Alien Registration Act of

1940, which made it a crime to advocate violent overthrow of the government or to be a member of any group devoted to such advocacy. Very likely there were Communist Party members in the Photo League, but most of the League's members were concerned primarily with photography, not politics. American Communists were always few in number.

On the morning of April 26, 1949, a federal marshal ushered Angela Calomiris into the courtroom of Judge Harold R. Medina to testify in the trial of eleven members of the National Board of the Communist Party under the Smith Act. In five days of testimony, she told how she had been "recruited" into the Party and worked her way up in it. On the first day she mentioned the Photo League, naming Sid Grossman, her devoted teacher, as a Communist. She knew Sid was a Party member because she had recruited him herself.

A few months later, Angela Calomiris appeared at my office to show me her portfolio. "So you really are a photographer?" I asked with unveiled cynicism. I went on, incautious and self-righteous: "I'm not even going to comment on your pictures. Even if I thought they were good, I wouldn't give you an assignment. After what you've done, I could never trust you." The interview was over.

Two years went by, and the Cold War intensified. I had almost forgotten my encounter with Calomiris when Westbrook Pegler called. A former sportswriter, he had turned into an archreactionary, an all-out foe of Franklin Roosevelt and the New Deal. As a columnist for the Hearst newspaper syndicate, he was a leading Red-baiter. Pegler wasted no time: "John Morris? You're the photo editor of *Ladies' Home Journal?*" I acknowledged I was, instantly alarmed by his gruff tone. "Angela Calomiris says that you denounced her in your office as an FBI spy. Is that true?" I had to think about this for a minute. "I told her she had done a disservice to her fellow photographers," I explained to Pegler. "She hurt a lot of innocent people."

I wondered what Pegler would do. I did not have to wait long. On September 19, his column was headlined GIRL SPY FOR FBI RECOUNTS INSULT BY PICTURE EDITOR. I was an easy target. Pegler was delighted to attack the *Journal* as well, since Eleanor Roosevelt, whose monthly column ran in the *Journal,* was anathema to him: "The *Ladies' Home Journal* cleverly turned political and supported the New Deal during the long reign of Eleanor Roosevelt as queen of the magazine." Pegler kept up the attack for three more days, winding up with an exhortation headlined U.S. SHOULD EXECUTE ALL COMMUNISTS AS ITS FOES and beginning, "The only sensible and courageous way to deal with Communists in our midst is to make membership in Communist organizations or covert subsidies [sic] a capital offense and shoot or otherwise put to death all persons convicted of such."

In those paranoid days, such nonsense was all very embarrassing to the Curtis Publishing Company, as well as to the Goulds, who had shocked their Republican peers when they began publishing Mrs. Roosevelt. While ignoring the attack in the pages of the *Journal*, Bruce Gould wrote a humiliating two-page letter of apology to readers who inquired, explaining that "Mr. Morris has never been a Communist, nor does he have Party leanings" and recounting my record of conscientious objection and war service. The Goulds invited Angela Calomiris to come in for a personal apology. It was a relief to me when she told them that she "wouldn't take a job with the *Ladies' Home Journal* if it were the last magazine on earth."

When I finally obtained my highly censored FBI file in 1991 under the Freedom of Information Act, I found that the New York office of the FBI had reported me to Washington in December 1949, probably on a tip from Calomiris. There's no way to know, since names of informants are crossed out—"freedom of information" does not include the names of one's accusers. J. Edgar Hoover himself sent a telegram back to New York in January, ordering his agents to "discreetly ascertain identity and background John Morris . . . expedite."

New York's "discreet" inquiry led nowhere. After checking its "paid confidential informants," FBI New York reported on March 5, 1952, "The subject of this case is not being recommended for a Security Index Card in view of the fact that information developed to date fails to reflect that he is or ever had been connected with the Communist Party. . . . This case is therefore being considered closed." My file was kept open, however, for another fifteen years. I can only speculate why. One likely reason was that in 1949 I had joined a group of writers and publishers who met regularly at the Greenwich Village home of Jack Goodman of Simon and Schuster to combat McCarthyism. Among my "fellow travelers": Arthur Miller, William L. Shirer, John Hersey, Edgar Snow, Joseph Barnes, Louis Untermeyer, and Ira Wolfert. Even to attend these meetings was to risk blacklisting and exposure, but we made no effort to hide our activity. On the contrary, the group sought, through newspaper and magazine pieces and radio broadcasts, to reestablish the American tradition of free speech and the right of dissent. Despite distinguished bylines, we got almost nothing published.

Bruce Gould would have fired me instantly if he had thought I was a member, or even an *ex*-member, of the Communist Party. The Goulds were surprised, but not shocked, when they polled their editorial staff in 1948 and found that seven out of fifty-nine of us intended to vote for the Progressive Party's Henry Wallace rather than for the Republicans' Thomas Dewey or the Democrats' Harry Truman. The atmosphere at the *Journal* was nonpolitical and permissive. Nevertheless, I felt terribly frustrated. It was *Life*, not *Ladies' Home Journal*, that was calling the shots in public affairs, and *Life*, under Luce's leadership, was mounting a crusade against communism. I still identified with *Life* and scrutinized every issue. In contrast with the wistful idealism of the *Journal*'s "People Are People" series, *Life*'s February 27, 1950, cover showed an atom bomb exploding. The issue led with this bold headline: "War Can Come; Will We Be Ready?" Harry Luce was up to his old tricks. Having mobilized the United States for World War II, he was now beating the drum for World War III. I proposed that the *Journal* try to revive the militancy of women. The Goulds were obviously thinking along similar lines, and during the next year, 1952, a presidential election year, they ran a series called "Political Pilgrim's Progress," focusing on women who were making a difference in their own communities.

My relationship with Bruce Gould was notable for its candor. When I told him that the Morrises were going to build a house in Armonk, north of Manhattan, rather than in New Jersey, I knew he would read this as a sign that I saw no real future with either the *Journal* or with the Curtis Publishing Company. At our first interview, Gould had asked me, "What magazine would you like to edit if you had the choice?" My answer was simple: *Life.* By 1948, however, my ambition had grown—I wanted to edit my own magazine. Whenever this subject arose of what I *really* wanted to do, Bruce's response had been to raise my salary another notch. But in 1951 "my own" magazine almost happened. Philadelphia publisher Walter Annenberg asked me if I would be interested in editing a new picture magazine of my own design. He was in a hurry. Dave Stech and I went furiously to work in our spare time, dummying a handsome monthly to be called *Watch: The World in Pictures.* Three weeks later, Annenberg's assistant phoned to call the whole thing off. "Walter's changed his mind. He's got another idea." It turned out to be *TV Guide.* A wise decision. In 1988, Annenberg sold it to Rupert Murdoch, tossing in his other magazine properties, for $2.8 billion.

APRIL, 1953

WATCH *the world in pictures*

THE LITTLE WORLD
OF
SAN NICOLA

PROFILE OF AN ITALIAN VILLAGE

This is the one and only cover of *Watch*, a magazine that Philadelphia publisher Walter Annenberg asked me to start for him, only to change his mind—in favor of publishing *TV Guide*. *Watch* was to have been an international cultural monthly. (I took this picture of a French peasant mother and child in a chateau near the First Army press camp in Normandy. They had lost their home in the bombardment of Normandy.) DESIGN: DAVID STECH; PHOTO: JOHN G. MORRIS

Little did we realize it at the time, but this happy gathering at the home of Paris *Vogue* editor Michel de Brunhoff, shortly after the Liberation of Paris, brought together three of the four principal photographer-founders of Magnum: Robert Capa (*far left*), David "Chim" Seymour (*center, without a tie*), and Henri Cartier-Bresson (*far right*)). Only George Rodger is missing. I am seen peering over Capa's shoulder. *Vogue*'s Lee Miller is in uniform at bottom right; *Life*'s Bob Landry is at bottom left. *John G. Morris Collection*

15

"Nothing but Champagne!"

O n May 22, 1947, two days before I flew to Iowa with him for "People Are People," Robert Capa invited me to have drinks at Bill and Rita Vandivert's Greenwich Village apartment to celebrate the launch of an international cooperative picture agency. It had been agreed upon several weeks earlier at the Members' Penthouse of the Museum of Modern Art. The attendees at that meeting were Capa, Chim, the Vandiverts, and Maria Eisner, the only member of the group who had any experience in this sort of venture—she had founded Alliance Photo in 1934. At the Vandivert party the champagne flowed, and the agency was christened Magnum Photos.

Its founders were determined that Magnum would be a great picture agency. I was the one "outsider" at the Greenwich Village gathering, and properly flattered by the invitation, but in truth I was there because I was Magnum's only certain American customer. The paperwork had been completed that day, and Capa's enduring dream of running his own picture agency was now a reality. Since most of the photographer-founders were far away—George Rodger in Cyprus, Henri Cartier-Bresson in California, Chim somewhere in Europe—Rita Vandivert wrote to them to explain it all: "There are seven of us in the . . . organization—five photographers—Henri Cartier-Bresson, Capa, Chim, George Rodger and Bill Vandivert. In addition there are two females, Maria Eisner to run the Paris office and cover all of Europe, and myself to run the New York office. I am the President, all the rest of you are also Vice-Presidents, and Maria is Secretary and Treasurer."

Rita assured George and Henri that each would have to invest only $400 and that expenses would be kept to a minimum. The New York office, for the time being, would be Bill Vandivert's studio at Union Square. The Paris office would be Maria's apartment at 125 rue du Faubourg Saint-Honoré. It was planned that the members would all meet at the end of the first year, and, as Rita wrote, "celebrate it with nothing but champagne!" At the end of the first year, however, there was not much to celebrate—no profits, anyway—and both Vandiverts resigned.

The Magnum staff, largely recruited from the ranks of relatives and girlfriends, worked more for love than for money in those early years. The most professional was the Milan-born Paris bureau chief, Maria Eisner. At Alliance before the war she had sold not only Capa's and Chim's pictures from Spain but also occasional photos by Cartier-Bresson. Maria had been trained in Berlin by the legendary Hungarian picture agent Simon Gutmann, a Capa crony. It helped that Maria spoke four languages.

In 1948, Magnum's second year, the worldwide network of "old boys" spread out. Cartier-Bresson went to India with his wife, Ratna, a Javanese former dancer known as "Elie." He would win his first Overseas Press Club award for his coverage of the death of Mahatma Gandhi. In March 1948, George Rodger sailed to Cape Town, South Africa, to start an epic journey overland to Cairo with his English wife, Cicely. Their plan was to make their home in Nicosia, Cyprus, and raise a family while George covered the Middle East. Chim succeeded in getting a United Nations Educational, Scientific, and Cultural Organization (UNESCO) assignment to cover the "Children of Europe." Capa went off to cover the birth pangs of Israel and that fall returned home to Budapest for a story in *Holiday* more memorable for his charming text than for his pictures. International projects were vital to Magnum's success. Capa and I tried hard to come up with a sequel to "People Are People." In February 1949, in a memo to Bruce Gould, I proposed a series on major cities. Capa offered to shoot Rome or Paris for a sample layout. Gould didn't buy it, nor did he buy a series called "Youth and the World," for which I wrote the prospectus. Although I wasn't yet officially a Magnum staffer, my allegiance was clear.

One day in October 1949, a cable came from George Rodger in Cyprus: "My darling Cicely and baby died in childbirth." In shock, I passed the message to my young *Journal* assistant, Lois "Jinx" Witherspoon, who had traveled with George and Cicely in Africa on her 1948 vacation. She almost fainted. A few months later, George came to New York, and Jinx took a brief vacation from the *Journal* to be with him. The next fall Jinx left the magazine to join George as his researcher in West Africa. A decade after Cicely's death, George finally achieved the home he sought, in the village of Smarden, Kent, England, married to Jinx. The couple had three children.

In 1951, Capa sold the project "Youth and the World"—in Europe called "Generation X"—to *McCall's*. He withdrew it six months later, however, in courageous disagreement with the superficial editorial treatment proposed by *McCall's* editor Dan Mich. Magnum was in turmoil, but Capa salvaged the situation when he sold the series to *Holiday's* editor, Ted Patrick, with whom he had established a drinking relationship at "21." (The first time Capa went to "21" a doorman took one look at him and refused him entrance until Capa explained, "But I have to meet the photographer Robert Capa!")

In 1949, Maria Eisner married and relocated to New York. It was my habit to stop by the Magnum office once a week to discuss story ideas with the New York–based photographers. In return, Magnum Paris sold my "People Are People" to *Heute* in Germany and a story on the 1950 congressional elections to *Epoca* in Italy.

By Christmas 1951, it looked as though Magnum would make its first profit—perhaps as much as $700. A celebration was in order, and Capa booked a private bar at the Algonquin Hotel, declaring it open to "friends of Magnum," of which there was suddenly a multitude. At the height of the festivities it began to snow, and the celebrants decided to hunker down for the night. The final bar bill more than matched Magnum's profit for the year.

By February 1952, Capa felt confident enough of Magnum's future to write his first, and uncharacteristically formal, "Report to the Stockholders of Magnum." Werner Bischof and Ernst Haas had joined the four original shareholders, and three photographers were being groomed for the privilege: Fenno Jacobs, Carl Perutz, and Homer Page. Capa's purpose was to show that Magnum was doing okay and he was not: "After five years Magnum is solvent and I am bankrupt." He did not mean this literally; he was simply proposing that he be adequately compensated with a generous expense account (which Magnum could not afford). This was the background of our discussion later that year. Bob was tired of being Magnum's indispensable man. He wanted to resume his own career, but he was determined to ensure Magnum's future. Rather than put it into the hands of businessmen (Black Star had shown interest in a merger the previous year), he decided to approach someone who shared his journalistic convictions. He asked me to be Magnum's chief executive— though he did so without overwhelming enthusiasm for his decision, I should add. I was a difficult choice. By appointing me, Capa would lose one of Magnum's best customers in order to incur Magnum's biggest expense. In its first fiscal year, the agency's New York billings had been $40,000, of which $28,000 had come from my *Ladies' Home Journal.* The first five years of Magnum had been rough, but now the fragile international cooperative seemed out of danger and could "afford" me, Capa said. I would be paid twice what any previous bureau chief had received (*only* $2,000 a year less than my current pay at the *Journal*). Capa felt he could justify such a salary because I would be responsible for selling around the world, not just to the U.S. press. With the sense that we were both putting our necks on the line (again), Capa and I made the deal between Christmas and New Year's. I resigned from the *Ladies' Home Journal* in early January 1953, parting from the Goulds with warm feelings all around. To celebrate, Capa and I agreed to meet for lunch at the Oak Room of the Plaza Hotel. We had one thing left to settle: my title. Standing at the bar next to us was T. S. Matthews, who had just resigned as executive editor of *Time,* and was perhaps celebrating too. Clapping me on the shoulder, Capa said, "How about executive editor? This is the kind of place for us executives to meet!" Just before returning to Paris, Capa called a meeting of the Magnum "family"—photographers, staff, wives, and lovers. He stood on a chair to make an announcement, pointing to me: "Well, children, from now on you take your problems to him!"

George Rodger, who had covered World War II on a dozen fronts for *Life*, staked out Africa as his territory when Magnum's founders divided up the world in 1947. Always an adventurer, he felt equally at home in jungle or desert—before settling down in a village in Kent. *Copyright* © GEORGE RODGER/*Magnum Photos*

Following Capa's tips I won handsomely on my first Sunday at Longchamp in May 1953. Inexplicably, he did not take his own advice and lost. Somehow our friendship survived. © HENRI CARTIER-BRESSON/*Magnum Photos*

16

"Personal and Confidential"

Magnum's basement office in the brownstone at 17 East Sixty-fourth Street was desirable for its address—adjacent to the Wildenstein Gallery—and low rent, $250 a month, but little else. I shared a front room with Inge Bondi, who had been acting as interim manager. Inge, a British-raised Berlin refugee, had been hired by Maria Eisner. She quickly showed an aptitude for the picture business. Our relationship was a bit strained at the start. I thought of her as a kind of child prodigy, confirmed by the middy blouse in which she occasionally came to work. I'm sure she thought of me as someone whom she would have to train. Eventually we worked it out.

My most pleasant task upon joining Magnum was to negotiate, with Ray Mackland, who had succeeded Wilson Hicks as *Life*'s picture editor, a price for a color essay called "New York: Images of a Magic City." It was by Ernst Haas, a rising star in Magnum's expanding firmament. The price was $20,000; thereafter we sold Haas color to *Life* at $1,000 a page. Haas was one of only two photographers Magnum admitted to membership in its first seven years; the other was Werner Bischof from Zurich. Both were so handsome that they could have made it on looks alone, but there was never a question of their photographic credentials. Ernst had made a photo sequence of Austrian prisoners of war returning to Vienna in 1947, a "news story" so powerful that it looked fresh when editor Warren Trabant published it months later in the American-backed Munich picture magazine *Heute*. With *Heute*'s Vienna correspondent, Inge Morath, Haas arrived in Paris on Bastille Day 1949. They walked all the way to Magnum from the Gare de l'Est (about two and a half miles) to save money. Ernst had accumulated a $1,200 credit through Magnum's resale of his story.

He was fond of recalling how "Capa took me out to lunch and congratulated me on becoming a 'shareholder.' " Haas asked what that meant. "It means," said Capa, "that your money is in Magnum, that Magnum is a nonprofit company, and that you will never see your money again."

Haas arrived in New York in 1951, dead broke. He had a way of making his penury sound so funny that friends vied with one another to help him out. My *Ladies' Home Journal* office was one of his first stops. Not only was I good for a free lunch, but I gave him a "How America Lives" assignment. A few months later Haas went to New Mexico on Magnum's "Generation X" project. When finished, he hitchhiked around the state, photographing "The Land of Enchantment," as New Mexico bills itself. Ernst came to show me his delightful, satirical images, but they were of no use to the *Journal.* I asked him to leave them anyway and invited Dick Pollard, the *Life* editor who had been my guide to Hollywood, to come by the next day. I knew they would be a hard sell at *Life.* Pollard agreed to ignore channels and take the pictures straight to Sid James, *Life*'s acting managing editor, who gave the story six pages. It was the breakthrough Haas needed. In New Mexico he had shot several rolls of Kodachrome, all he could afford. *Life* now agreed to give him as much color film as he wanted—but no story guarantee. For months Ernst roamed New York with his cameras, making photographic poetry out of the familiar urban scene. Then he spent days with light box and projector, editing his thousands of slides down to a tray or two. He rehearsed for the final projection session as if it were a Broadway opening. He had a hit. Thompson agreed to twenty-four color pages divided between two issues, a record. Haas would become known as the world's preeminent color photographer.

Ten days into my Magnum tenure a fat special delivery letter arrived from Paris marked "Personal and Confidential." I was dismayed to see that it had already been opened. Its contents were dynamite: a two-page single-spaced letter from Capa enclosing a copy of a three-pager from him to his friend Ted Patrick, editor of *Holiday.* Both had been dictated to Margot Shore, Magnum's fast-thinking new Paris bureau chief. Bob's letter to me began, "In your new existence you should be careful that if you see a letter marked 'Personal and Confidential,' you should dissolve three tablets of vitamins in a glass of whiskey before opening." I then read his letter to Patrick:

> This is a subject about which many books have already been written, but nobody knows how does it feel before it happens. . . . Well it happened simply. Four days after my arrival back to Paris in the form of a form letter inviting me to pass by the Consulate with my passport. Although this type of invitation is not very coveted in our

time, me feeling dreadfully innocent, I presented myself and when I left the Consulate I had only my comb in my inside pocket. The gray-haired lady said that she was sorry but she had instructions from Washington to pick up and hold my passport because I was alleged being a Communist. I also had the right, she said, to write an affidavit proving the contrary. Well, I was pretty well dazed, returned to my hotel, and began to chew my life in every direction. After about seventy-two disgraceful hours, I wrote a ten-page synopsis about my whole life, in which I carefully explained that not only have I never been one, but why I have never been one; all my contacts, moves and history. And although it was sad that one has to write that sort of thing, I felt somewhat better when I rushed back to the Consulate and swore that my story was true.

The remainder of the letter to Patrick, and the one to me, related how Capa was fighting back. He had consulted attorney Morris Ernst, who happened to be in Paris. Ernst had a good reputation for his handling of civil liberties cases but did not believe in civil liberties for Communists. Since Capa wasn't a Communist, Ernst told him he would see what he could do. It was a grave problem for Magnum. Capa, our biggest earner, was overdue to join John Huston and Humphrey Bogart on location in Italy to cover the filming of *Beat the Devil*. He was also supposed to do a story for *Holiday* on Cortina d'Ampezzo, the Italian ski resort. Without a passport, Capa could not function.

The following week Morris Ernst, who had already extracted a $500 retainer, was talking about "immediate payment" for services to date and presented us with a bill for $4,600. He had made a few phone calls that resulted in Capa's passport being returned to him, but with severe restrictions. It was good for travel only in France and Italy, and for only two months. At least Bob could join Huston's movie company for a few weeks. Capa was by now deeply suspicious of Ernst and theorized that the lawyer had vastly overestimated Capa's earnings. He wryly observed in a letter to me, "By now I am between two fires and I have to convince the State Department that I am a photographer and not an instrument of the Russian world revolution, and we have to convince Mr. Ernst that I am a photographer and not a representative of international world capitalism." We decided to pay Ernst another $600 and to press for further progress. Things looked worse than ever. Capa considered making appeals to the generals who knew him from World War II: Matthew Ridgway, Gavin, even Eisenhower. In some desperation, I spent Saturday, April 18, preparing a background dossier on Capa and Magnum, and fired it off to Ernst with the strong suggestion that he go to argue the case personally with the all-powerful Ruth Shipley, head of the State Department's Passport Division. Ernst agreed and saw her the following Wednesday. He never learned (or never told us) the nature of the accusation against Capa—"a case of mistaken identity" was the reigning supposition—but the direct plea to Shipley worked, and Capa's full passport was restored. I settled with Ernst. I don't recall how or where we found the money. Case closed. "Now you can buy your ticket to Paris!" Capa told me.

I could not, however, just drop everything in New York. There were too many other problems. I was all too conscious that Magnum's stars were Europeans. I had to raise the status of the Americans. Many photographers had tried to work with Magnum's New York office in its early days but discovered, as did founder Bill Vandivert, that they could do better on their own. In 1951, however, four came along who stuck it out: Eve Arnold, Burt Glinn, Erich Hartmann, and Dennis Stock. All four grew with Magnum, and Magnum grew with them. If there is a Magnum "school," they were its first adherents.

Eve Arnold, a student of Alexey Brodovitch, the *Harper's Bazaar* art director who taught at the New School for Social Research, was sensitive to people and to social issues. She also had a lot of guts. She decided to cover the McCarthy hearings on her own. Not knowing what to make of her, the senator tried to take her into his camp, throwing a friendly arm over her shoulder during a recess—an act which immediately alienated her from the rest of the press. But he was cozying up to the wrong photographer. Eve's pictures perfectly captured the viciousness of Joseph McCarthy and his cohorts, Roy Cohn and David Schine. Eve also captured "personalities," as movie stars were described in those days, such as Marlene Dietrich, James Cagney, and Joan Crawford. Eve's are probably the warmest and, in their way, the most sensual, pictures ever taken of Marilyn Monroe, who adored the diminutive photographer and confided in her. Eve pursued her own photographic projects, sometimes with little promise of economic reward. She chronicled the life of the township where she lived on the north shore of Long Island, focusing on a family whose ancestors had settled there in the seventeenth century. After she had worked on it for five years, *Life* bought it, with the added dividend of a *Life* assignment on Malcolm X and the Black Muslims. On and off for two years, Eve followed Malcolm X from Washington to New York to Chicago and back to New York. In Chicago she was called at eight each morning in her hotel room by someone with a southern accent saying, "Get the hell out of town before it's too late." Finally her story was completed and laid out by *Life* for ten pages, only to be killed at the last minute—it had been placed opposite an advertisement for Oreo cookies with the copy line, "The greatest chocolate cookie of them all." Both Nabisco and the Black Muslims would have been outraged.

Erich Hartmann came to Magnum in 1951 with little experience. Quiet and reflective, he loved the challenge of making still life exciting. His breakthrough came with his first *Fortune* cover and portfolio, on the Great Lakes in wintertime. Thereafter he became a successful industrial journalist, adept at interpreting high-tech subjects.

Dennis Stock won first prize in *Life*'s highly touted Young Photographers Contest in 1951, with his story of the arrival of a shipload of displaced persons at one of New York's Hudson River piers. He had been working for Gjon Mili, making twenty-five dollars a week. Mili decided that Dennis was ready to make it on his own, and Capa agreed to try him at Magnum. Dennis is probably best known today for his 1955 essay on James Dean—and specifically for a single image of Dean, in Times Square, walking the "Street of Broken Dreams," his shoulders hunched, his head pulled low inside an overcoat. The essay appeared in *Life* and did much to help make the short-lived actor a cult figure.

Harvard-educated Burt Glinn was stringing for Magnum in Seattle while also working for *Life*. Eventually he got up his nerve to make the jump to Magnum as a full-timer, and he became our biggest money earner (he would one day assume Magnum's presidency for a record three terms). While Burt occasionally covered hard news, he was principally employed as a regular shooter for *Holiday*, and here he adopted the lifestyle that gave him the polish and contacts necessary to attract lucrative corporate accounts for annual reports.

During the Capa passport crisis, my young friend Elliott Erwitt showed up at the office. He had just been discharged from the U.S. Army. Capa had told him, in Paris, to see me about joining Magnum. I asked how long he had been out of the Army. "About three hours." I was delighted. But there was a hitch. He needed $200 in cash to fly to Bermuda and marry his Dutch girlfriend, who was six months pregnant. She could not immediately enter the United States except as the wife of an American citizen. Despite his record with Stryker and despite the fact that he had placed second to Dennis Stock in the *Life* contest, Erwitt represented a risk. Magnum had no business advancing the money. Taking a leaf from Capa, I decided to bluff. I called William Lowe, the ambitious young executive editor of *Look*, telling him that I needed a $200 guarantee for a story in Bermuda right away. The subject: college spring break. When I leveled with him, Lowe bought it, and Erwitt accomplished his mission in Bermuda, returning to New York with his bride. The couple settled in an Upper East Side tenement, and Erwitt made some delicately poignant photographs of Lucienne—"Looie"—Erwitt, both pregnant and with their newborn. Two became classics in "The Family of Man" exhibition, and Erwitt went on to become one of Magnum's most successful photographers, brilliant in his versatility. As Magnum's president in 1961, he would have the dubious privilege of firing the executive editor—me.

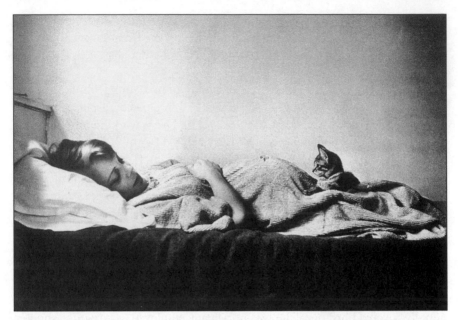

When Elliott Erwitt came to see me about joining Magnum in the spring of 1953, he presented a delicious challenge: to get him a $200 cash assignment that would permit him to go to Bermuda to marry his very pregnant Dutch girlfriend, thus enabling him to bring her to the United States legally. *Look* magazine provided the money. Lucienne "Looie" Erwitt soon provided the baby. Elliott produced this picture, later shown in "The Family of Man" exhibition at the Museum of Modern Art in New York. © ELLIOTT ERWITT/*Magnum Photos*

A day or so after I'd dispatched Erwitt on his honeymoon, another photographer walked into our offices to announce that he wanted to join Magnum. It was the twenty-nine-year-old Swiss-born Robert Frank, just disembarked from the *Mauritania.* He had been making a living doing fashion photography, but it was his sensitive, provocative images of the street, in Europe as well as America, that had begun to attract the attention of the photographic community. I admired Frank's talent as much as I did Erwitt's. They even happened to be friends. But I simply did not know how to cope with two hungry newcomers in one week, and I put him off. I doubt that he ever forgave me, because when, four years later, I joined a small Magnum delegation to talk with Robert Frank about membership, it just didn't work out. By then he had successfully traveled a long and lonely road, thanks to two Guggenheim Fellowships. His resulting book, *The Americans,* is perhaps the most passionately admired and hated book in twentieth-century photography, its portrait of our country so bleak and depressing that no U.S. publisher would touch it until it had been published in France by Robert Delpire. I have often wondered what would have happened if Robert Frank had walked into Magnum ahead of Elliott Erwitt.

. . .

Faced almost daily with such issues—constantly hustling and being hustled, bandaging individual egos while trying to balance the needs of an unruly collective, chasing after thousands of dollars while worrying over nickels and dimes—I soon began to realize that my job was basically impossible. For one thing, the economics were against me—and "us." Magnum's own revenues were simply a percentage, normally 30 to 40 percent, of billings for assignments and for stories shot on "speculation." For stock pictures the split was usually fifty-fifty. The lower the percentage taken by Magnum, the better—as the photographers saw it. Thus it seemed in their own interest to keep office overhead—including staff—down, and to get their own expenses "off the top"—deducted from the gross billing before Magnum took its commission. Such expenses might include those of a girlfriend, doing double duty as researcher. We were always desperately short of capital, and accumulating any seemed an impossibility. Often it took a miracle to meet the payroll; it was disastrous if two photographers demanded large withdrawals against their credit balances at the same time. The core idea was not for Magnum itself to make money. The idea was to make money for the individual photographers, all of whom freelanced, with neither salaries nor guarantees from Magnum. If one was up, another was down. It amounted to collective insecurity. The publishing industry had little interest in our problems. Postwar profits were based on prewar practices. The American Society of Magazine Photographers was just beginning to fight for a day rate of $100. Life had raised its basic page rate to $150 for black and white, $300 for color—and its circulation was more than 5 million. Look, like Life, concentrated its resources on staff production and demanded the right to resell pictures made by freelance photographers on assignment. The Saturday Evening Post went even further and demanded the surrender of negatives. Retention of negatives was the basic principle underlying Magnum's existence. Even magazines that gave us second rights were apt to hold material so long that it became unsalable. Freelance photographers were often obliged to absorb all their direct expenses—and of course had to pay for their own equipment and insurance. Newspapers were still paying five dollars and less for a picture. Something drastic would have to be done. Worldwide distribution—selling the same story everywhere—seemed to be the answer.

On May 17, 1953, after the usual sixteen-hour flight, my TWA Constellation landed at Orly. Capa was there to meet me. Flashing a press card, he had driven right onto the field in the hand-me-down Ford convertible of *Life* photographer Yale Joel. I would have preferred the safety of a taxi: Capa's driving was as dreadful as ever. Fortunately, there was little traffic that Sunday morning, but I held my breath as he circumnavigated the place de la Concorde, cursing to obtain the right of way, cruised along the Champs-Élysées, and finally pulled up in front of his hotel on avenue Montaigne. Several of Capa's clique were sitting outside, drinking coffee and munching croissants. I was reintroduced to Irwin Shaw, whom I had last seen in uniform, and met Lionel "Bobby" Birch of *Picture Post*, visiting from London; model Suzy Parker, who had been taking lessons in photography from Capa; and Noel Howard, a former Free French fighter pilot, now an amiable fixture in the film colony and a kind of mascot for Capa.

It was not the kind of day to talk business, yet it was too early for serious eating or drinking. Looking at his watch, Capa declared that we could easily make the first race at Longchamp. We checked me into the hotel and took off. Despite my working visits to Saratoga with Alfred Eisenstaedt and W. Eugene Smith for *Life*, I had never placed a bet on a horse. Capa agreed to be my instructor. For the first race, the Prix Blangy with a purse of 300,000 francs, we placed my bet on a filly called Hasty Heart. The odds were three to one, and I won. For the second race, I bet on a horse owned by Baron Guy de Rothschild. Again I won. Meanwhile, Capa was losing. In the third race my horse came in fourth. Capa then introduced me to the intricacies of the *jumelé*, meaning twin bet, where you win if you pick the first two horses in order. I won. By now I had an armful of francs and Capa had lost just as heavily. It was a bit too much for him, so I tactfully lost for the rest of the afternoon.

I had agreed to make my entrance at Magnum when I woke up on Monday, but it was past noon when Capa called, asking, "Aren't you even coming for lunch?" Embarrassed, I hustled across the Champs-Élysées to the apartment building at 125 rue du Faubourg Saint-Honoré that housed Magnum. To my American eyes the place looked utterly impractical. There was a sign indicating that one could take the elevator up but not down. It was time for the daily two-hour lunch break, and the office was practically empty. Capa announced, "Today you will have a surprise!" We walked briskly to one of his favorite restaurants, and there, apéritif already in hand, was Pinky. She had literally sailed into town that morning, aboard the yacht of some English friends. It was now moored on the Left Bank just below the pont de l'Alma. She and Bob were now just friends. Our reunion continued through the afternoon, winding up with martinis on the deck. Was this to be my new lifestyle? I couldn't, and fortunately didn't, believe it.

On Tuesday, I finally got to look around the Magnum office, an apartment of *trois pièces*: living room, bedroom, kitchen and bath, or rather *toilette*, as the tub had been shelved over. The living room, with windows overlooking the street and the church of Saint-Philippe-du-Roule, was lined from floor to ceiling with cardboard boxes of prints and albums of contact sheets. An editing table ran down the center, and there was a reception couch adjacent to the door. A vague mood of quiet conspiracy prevailed, except when one of the raucous French phones suddenly rent the air with its ungodly jangle.

Of the paid inhabitants, only four, as far as I could make out, were privileged to have real desks. In addition to Margot, they were those who did the business: Susie Marquis, a Hungarian cousin of Capa, who dealt with the magazines; Monsieur Ringard, a brother-in-law of the Russian violinist David Oistrakh, who peddled pictures to Paris publishers; and a bookkeeper, the matronly Madame Presle, who collected and counted the money and made out the photographers' statements. She was also the incorruptible custodian of the "black cash." Michele Vignes, a bright young lady of good family who eventually became a successful San Francisco photographer, had just been hired to keep things in order. Finally, there was a messenger, who hung out in the kitchen, and Georges Ninaud, the lovable but often tipsy *gérant*. He was legally responsible for the office and consequently was encouraged to stay away as much as possible.

The basic problem of the office was that there was no place to sit down—certainly not for me, a visitor. This made things difficult for the floating population of photographers and even for customers. The photographers often took refuge, sometimes for the night and with a friend, in the back room, which was further occupied by laundry, luggage, and camera cases.

It would have all been quite impossible except for the bistro downstairs. This was the true conference room, its seating democratic and flexible. There was no rent except the price of drinks, and one could linger over a *café crème*, a *pression* (draft beer), or a *citron pressé* for hours. Food was available, but the custom was to "go out" to lunch; one never ate dinner in the bistro unless truly desperate. The pinball machine was active at all hours.

I learned that Cartier-Bresson had left Paris on a *Holiday* assignment the day before I arrived, taking with him his wife, Elie, plus Inge Morath as researcher. I didn't know whether to read this as an insult or as a boast—showing that *he*, at least, was devoted to the job. I was sorry to miss him but delighted to hear that Werner Bischof, the one Magnum member I had not met, would arrive from Zurich the next day, with his wife, the lovely dark-haired Rosellina. True Europeans, they minimized their expenses in Paris by staying in a hotel where many clients left after an hour. Werner was one of the two star photographers of the distinguished Swiss monthly *Du*. The other was Emil Schulthess. Occasionally *Du* turned an entire issue over to one of them. Joining Magnum had been a difficult decision for Werner, who took his obligations to Rosellina and the family they hoped for with utmost seriousness. He had been profitably represented by Black Star, but after meeting Capa he wrote to Rosellina, "What is important to me is that they [Magnum] are all sound people and socialist-inspired."

With Paris as my base I began to make the rounds of our agents, clients, and photographers in Germany, Italy, Switzerland, and England. First I flew to Munich, where I saw for myself what the war had done to Germany. Rubble and ruins everywhere, eight years after V-E Day; men and women on crutches, in wheelchairs; shortages, it seemed, of everything but beer, but at least nobody looked hungry. And a friendliness toward me, the erstwhile enemy, that was difficult to comprehend. I was met at the pockmarked airport by Erich Lessing, then Magnum's Vienna "correspondent photographer" (a term with more cachet than "stringer"), later a member. He had come to show me around. He introduced me to Paula Wehr, the old-time agent who then represented Magnum, operating from her home. Then we visited Herbert List, whom the label "correspondent" scarcely fit. The patrician List had left his family's coffee business in Hamburg for a career in photography, inspired at first by Andreas Feininger, later by Man Ray and George Hoyningen-Huene. List was a father figure to Max Scheler, whose own father, a distinguished German philosopher, had died seven months before Max's birth in 1928. From Herbert, Max had acquired impeccable taste, but in addition Max was an aggressive, restless journalist whose five languages enabled him to operate successfully in many countries. He needed more security than Magnum provided, so he left to become a staff photographer at the German picture weekly *Stern* and still later became the pioneering picture editor of the German picture monthlies *Geo* and *Merian*.

Milan, rather than Rome, was the mecca of Italian publishing. In Paris, Chim commanded, "Meet me in Milan. I will take you around." Italy was Chim's adopted country. Chim had always been a man of mystery to me. He bore a real resemblance to Peter Lorre, and he would have made a perfect movie spy, with his soft voice, heavy accent, thick glasses, and delicate hands. Conservatively tailored and shod, he once admonished me, "John, you *must* get better shoes." Chim proudly showed me around Milan, first calling on Arnoldo Mondadori, head of the house that published the picture weekly *Epoca*. Mondadori thought of himself as the Henry Luce of Italy and revered *Life*, which produced many a "copycat" sale for Magnum. Chim and I lunched with Vincenzo Carrese, our new Italian agent—a previous one had absconded with Magnum's money. That evening, sitting with Chim in the choicest seats of La Scala, I reflected that working for Magnum had its rewards, even if not financial.

On my way back to Paris I stopped overnight in Zurich, my first time in Switzerland. Rosellina Bischof, who spoke five languages fluently, introduced me around. Werner had gone off to Finland on a *Holiday* assignment but would return to London to cover the coronation of Queen Elizabeth as one of the *Life* team. Capa also went to London with the vague intention of covering the coronation, but he seemed to have spent the day celebrating with Lauren Bacall and Humphrey Bogart. Ernst Haas and I joined Capa the next day. Magnum had no London office, but it did have a headquarters. Capa had found a congenial hotel, the Pastoria, just off Leicester Square. Ernst and Werner had come to know, respect, and love each other, as both did Capa. I had known Bischof only through his pictures. On that day in June, I was admitted to their brotherhood, little knowing that it would be the last time we four would be together.

Back home, I fast returned to reality. I had made some important contacts on my European tour, but it was now clearer than ever to me that there was no way our tiny transatlantic staff could service the diverse needs of so many photographers—more than twenty if one counted the "associates," although that term was not yet in use. I pointed out this bit of obvious news to Capa and received in reply a terse memo from him: "We are absolutely against any present enlargement of our offices and office budgets." Here was a real crisis in my relationship with Bob. I thought of resigning but instead waited ten days to reply, calmly, that income was up 20 percent from the previous year—good, but we could do much better. "For a group of the world's great photographers," I wrote, "you are grossing far too little money. This isn't your fault—you simply haven't a strong enough team working for you." I then made my case for enlarging the staff, pointing out that for every additional dollar spent on the offices, two would accrue to the photographers as revenue increased proportionately. Thanks to a sharp upturn in business, Capa gave in. I began slowly—and slyly—adding staff.

In December 1953, Werner and Rosellina Bischof came to New York for the first time and spent Christmas with us in Armonk. Rosellina confided to Dèle that she was four months pregnant. Werner's intention was to add photographs of North and South America to his archive, already so rich in Europe and Asia. A young executive named Jean Riboud, from the international oil engineering firm called Schlumberger, had offered a string of assignments that would permit Werner to drive the length of Latin America. At the time, it seemed a godsend.

ABOVE: **Werner and Rosellina Bischof, New York, 1953.**
© PETER BALLY
LEFT: **Robert Capa, Paris, 1952.**
© RUTH ORKIN

17

Disaster

Magnum's greatest concern was Capa himself. In late May 1953, his back had begun tormenting him. One day it was so bad that he simply lay down on the floor of the Magnum office and wept. He tried codeine, traction, and even treatments at a London nursing home—nothing seemed to work. His girlfriend, Jemison "Jemy" Hammond, arrived from New York, and together they went to Saint-Jean-de-Luz, near Biarritz, where John Huston's wife, Enrica (known as "Ricki"), had invited them to come and play with old friends. When Capa had a spasm, he would lie facedown while Ricki walked on his back to massage it.

Luckily, by fall Bob had recovered sufficiently so that we could begin corresponding about a worldwide project tailored just for him. The theme: "A famous war photographer looks for Peace on Earth." The truth was that photography had begun to bore him, however, and he didn't know where else to turn. Covering movies, even though he didn't have to make the conventional "stills," was more satisfying socially than professionally. It paid as much as $750 a week plus expenses. Capa tended to gamble his share away—Huston and Bogart regarded him as an easy touch. Magnum's affairs were looking up, but Capa was broke as usual. He decided to forgo his usual holiday trip to New York. He went instead to Klosters, hoping to strengthen his back on the ski slopes—and just managed to avoid skiing over a cliff. While there, he received an offer that he could not refuse. *Mainichi,* the huge Japanese newspaper chain, proposed to start a magazine, *Camera Mainichi,* and invited Capa to Japan for six weeks, with freedom to shoot whatever stories he wished, at their expense. In addition, they would supply him with the latest Japanese cameras, lenses, and film. En route to Tokyo, Capa stopped briefly in Rome to see friends, including Lauren Bacall. One showed him a copy of *The New York Times* for April 7, 1954, with a letter I had written to the editor, attacking the doctrine of massive retaliation. I'm sure he was not surprised by my sentiments. I had just sent him a Fellowship of Reconciliation pamphlet on "The Children of Nagasaki" to suggest that he do a story, perhaps for *Holiday*, on "A Child of the Bomb." When he got to Japan, Capa broadened the idea, photographing children wherever he went. He seemed happy, writing from Tokyo to the Paris office, "I am here now five days and these are the first five minutes free. *Mainichi* is driving hard, but the country is lovely, exciting, and taking pictures is fine. By now I have received five cameras, fifteen lenses, thirty bunches of flowers, and made many speeches, and there are days when I can get away by eating only one Japanese, one French, and one Chinese lunch."

Two weeks later, I happened to have one of my periodic lunches with Ray Mackland of *Life*. Ray told me that he had to find a temporary replacement for staff photographer Howard Sochurek, who was covering the war between the French and the Vietminh. Knowing that Capa was in Japan, Mackland asked if Bob would cover for the four weeks that Sochurek would be back in the States. I said I didn't think so, but I would have to ask him. Mackland offered a basic guarantee of $2,000 plus expenses for the four weeks, and I queried Capa by cable, assuming—and hoping—that he would turn it down. That night in Tokyo, Capa had a late dinner with Sochurek at the Press Club. Howard, who was just back from photographing the French positions at Dien Bien Phu, reported that Capa seemed "bored, undecided, saddened by the loss of life among people with no influence on their own destiny." He had not decided to accept the assignment when the two parted after midnight. But the next morning, April 30, Capa cabled back to me that he would accept the assignment. I was horrified, that night in Armonk, thinking over the dangers we had shared, and survived, in France. I decided to call him in Tokyo. The connection was poor: "Bob!" I yelled. "You don't have to go! It's not *our* war!" "Don't worry!" he screamed back. "It's only four weeks!" But I knew Capa well enough to know that he was breaking his own commandment, once expressed very simply to Martha Gellhorn: "In a war you must hate somebody or love somebody, you must have a position or you cannot stand what goes on." Capa had always stuck to that rule, most recently photographing war on the Israeli side, with which he could easily identify, in the 1948 conflict that had established the Jewish state.

Clearly Capa didn't hate the Vietnamese, nor did he love the French military regime, although he enjoyed the camaraderie of the soldiers themselves, some of whom he knew from the liberation of France. Harry Luce saw things differently. He saw France as our ally and Vietnam as an active front in the Cold War, which we had fought so hard in Korea. Unlike other American publishers, Luce insisted on constant coverage of Vietnam. Howard Sochurek had first been sent there in 1952. He reported quite graphically on how our friends the French were getting killed in that "dirty war," as *Life* described it. In 1953, Sochurek was relieved by David Douglas Duncan, whose 1950 "Christmas in Korea" story had brought new realism to *Life*'s coverage of war's horrors. Duncan, an ex-Marine, had found the French lying down on the job. He cabled Ed Thompson that the war was A HOPELESS QUAGMIRE, SUCKING MEN AND MONEY OUT OF SIGHT, AND MAY PROVE FATAL UNLESS WE FACE THE ISSUE SQUARELY. . . . ALL HANOI BETS ARE AGAINST US [*LIFE*] SOUNDING OFF SINCE APPARENTLY THEY CANNOT GET [the truth] PRINTED . . . BECAUSE IT SEEMS ANYONE WHO SOUNDS OFF GETS TAGGED AS A "COMMIE." Thompson replied: "I THINK YOU HAVE A HELL OF A NERVE SOUNDING OFF AT THIS POINT ABOUT BETTING WHAT WE WOULDN'T PRINT."

Duncan stayed in Vietnam ten weeks and, as was becoming his habit, brought his story directly to New York himself, arriving unexpectedly on a Saturday. Sid James, sitting in for a vacationing Thompson, was closing an issue and needed a strong lead story. Both he and Duncan were in luck.

That same Saturday night, Henry Luce was having dinner with French government leaders in Paris. He assured them that we were on their side. When the "defeatist" story appeared, Luce was seriously embarrassed. Diplomatic protests were lodged in Washington. When Luce returned to Rome, where Duncan was based and where Mrs. Luce was the American ambassador, there followed the only direct confrontation between the editor in chief and a *Life* staff photographer in the history of the magazine. In a two-hour session on the evening of September 2 in the embassy garden and another the following noon, Luce raged at Duncan. Duncan defended his story as "true, but (perhaps) untimely?" Luce did not disagree. Duncan wrote to Ed Thompson, "So I said that if my presence on the magazine was distasteful to him, and in any way made your job awkward, then the logical thing for him to do was to fire me. He said 'No,' that was not what he meant."

Sochurek was returned by *Life* to Indochina to replace Duncan and courageously covered the resupply of the French fortress at Dien Bien Phu. Now it was about to fall. Rather than dissuading Capa, I now believe that the knowledge of these conflicting journalistic views may have actually spurred him to go and take a look for himself. He and Duncan had long been friendly rivals. Sochurek represented a new generation, but Capa's competitive instinct was strong and he had answered many a challenge to his courage. Even worse, Capa had been hailed as the world's greatest war photographer. It was a curse that had originated with the publication of the "Dying Spanish Soldier," which had made him world famous. Ever after, André Friedmann was forced to live the Capa legend. (Fortunately, he never knew that the very authenticity of his picture would be questioned, by an English journalist named Philip Knightley, in 1975. Such doubts were laid to rest in 1996, when the dying militiaman was finally identified as a twenty-four-year-old mill worker from Alcoy, near Alicante. He was killed on September 5, 1936, on the Cerro Muriano front near Cordoba, only seven weeks into the Spanish Civil War. The discovery was made by Mario Brotons, also from Alcoy, who had fought on that front himself as a teenager. By searching military archives in Madrid and Salamanca, he found that while many men were wounded that day on the Cerro Muriano front, only one man died: Federico Borrell, maternal surname Garcia. Federico had a younger brother named Everisto, who also fought in Cerro Muriano. In 1996 the English journalist Rita Grosvenor, who lives in Spain, interviewed Everisto's widow, Maria, for *The Observer.* Maria said, "Everisto told us Federico had been killed. He hadn't seen what happened because he had been in a different position. But his friends had told him they saw Federico fling up his arms and immediately crumble to the ground after being shot in the head. He died instantly, they said.")

By the evidence of the letter he wrote to me from the Tokyo *Time/Life* office on May 1 (the day after my phone call) the "Capa legend" was not on Capa's mind. Rather, Capa's inherent curiosity, and his answer to the challenge of a given subject, are apparent:

> I am sorry I was kind of short on the phone but long distance calls always scare me. I much appreciate your calling but be assured I didn't take the job from a sense of duty but with real great pleasure. Shooting for me at this moment is much fun and possibly shooting on a very complicated subject but down my own alley is even more so. I know that Indochina might be only sheer frustration but somehow it should be one story anyway. So I am off and will be back here in four weeks and mid June in Paris if lots of unresistable offers are not stopping me. I was very glad to hear your happy voice about things in general.

We had spoken for the last time. I would receive one more communication from Capa, an undated letter from Hanoi that began "My John, just returned from Laos. . . . I intend to make one more story."

I had agreed to spend a vacation week teaching at the sixth annual University of Missouri Photo Workshop. The town, oddly enough called "Mexico," was not far from the birthplace of Mark Twain. For some reason we attracted only fifteen students, but among them were two who would become famous in our profession: W. E. "Bill" Garrett, a Missouri graduate student, who would become the editor of *National Geographic*; and Thomas J. Abercrombie, then a *Milwaukee Journal* staff photographer, who would become an intrepid photographer/writer for the *Geographic*, its first to land at the South Pole and its first to photograph inside Mecca.

The morning after the workshop ended, I was awakened by a call from Inge Bondi at Magnum, New York. She was sobbing. "John, I have terrible news. Werner is dead. Dead! His car went over a cliff in Peru and they've just found him. The Swiss consulate just called." Immediately I thought of Rosellina Bischof in Zurich, ready to give birth to a second child any day. Did Rosellina know? Inge thought not. I asked Inge to get in touch with her doctor and to keep the news off the wires if possible. I hurried back to New York. Tom Abercrombie was driving to Milwaukee and offered to drop me at the Chicago airport. The trip seemed to take forever. I was overwhelmed by happy and sad memories of Werner and Rosellina. I recalled our Christmas together in Armonk. In February, the Bischofs had left New York by station wagon on the first leg of an overland trip that Werner intended to finish at Tierra del Fuego. In March, the couple had parted in Mexico City so that Rosellina could return to Zurich to have the baby.

Dèle and the children met me at La Guardia that evening. When we entered the house in Armonk, the phone was ringing. It was a *Life* Foreign News researcher. "You've heard the awful news?" "Yes," I said, thinking of Werner. She continued, "Do you mind if I ask you some questions about Robert Capa?" I was in a daze. *"Capa?"* The name caught in my throat. "What do you mean, *Capa?*" A brief silence. "Oh, I'm sorry," she answered. "I thought you knew. Bob Capa was killed today in Indochina. He stepped on a land mine and died—

One of Werner Bischof's classic photographs; it was over such a cliff in the Peruvian Andes that his car plunged in May 1954. © WERNER BISCHOF/*Magnum Photos*

America was officially neutral in the Spanish Civil War, which sharply divided public opinion. Thanks to Robert Capa, *Life* presented a fairly sympathetic view of the Spanish Loyalists. This picture of a Loyalist soldier caught at the moment of death, published in the French magazine *Vu* long before *Life*, is one of photography's most enduring images. *Copyright © 1998 Estate of Robert Capa*

instantly." It was too much for one day. It was May 25 in Hanoi, as well as in Zurich, where that day Daniel Werner Bischof was born.

The next morning I met with Julia, Cornell, and Edie Capa to discuss funeral arrangements. Julia was beside herself. What to do? Bob belonged to the world, not to Hungary, not to France, not to America, not to Israel. One could not stop the French from giving him military honors in Hanoi, but there should be no burial in Arlington National Cemetery, as someone had suggested. Bob, the greatest war photographer of the bloodiest century, hated war and scorned its monuments and memorials. Père-Lachaise Cemetery, in Capa's beloved Paris, was considered seriously for a few hours, but there had been too many women in Bob's life since Gerda Taro, who was interred there.

The most common New York solution to this problem for a nonreligious Jew was a funeral home. Julia rebelled; Bob was no common man. I then made a suggestion. I had become a "convinced" Quaker, a member of Purchase Meeting, near Armonk, accepted by the Friends as "one who seeks, not as one who feels that he has found the answers." I had recently attended a Quaker funeral and been impressed by its democracy and simplicity. No priest, no rabbi, no minister. Silence, no music. Just a gathering of friends. I described it to the Capas, and they immediately agreed. The "memorial service," not a funeral, was held the following Sunday afternoon, honoring both Capa and Bischof. It deserves a special place in ecumenical history. Fortunately, the huge French military coffin bearing Capa's remains had not arrived. Fresh-cut flowers were the only decorative element in the severely plain old meetinghouse, modeled on the original one built there in 1727. The place was packed. It is Quaker custom to seat a few senior members up front on the "facing bench." I shared it with the clerk of Purchase Meeting on one side of me, Edward Steichen on the other. The clerk explained the custom: anyone who felt so moved could speak, but si-

Frame number eleven marked the end of Robert Capa's long and glorious career as a photographer, abruptly terminated on May 25, 1954, when he stepped on a land mine while covering France's war in Indochina. When we received the film at Magnum, I ordered that it be printed and distributed in this way, in tribute to a great photographer—and true friend. *Copyright © 1998 Estate of Robert Capa*

lence was also appropriate. Steichen, a mere seventy-five at the time, arose first: "We salute you, Robert Capa and Werner Bischof." We were off. With pauses for silence, there were tributes by friends from everywhere, even a telegram from Ingrid Bergman. Finally, Cornell Capa stood up in the front row. Throwing a prayer shawl over his shoulders, he recited Kaddish. Another moment of silence, and Julia arose. She wailed as if at the grave, flailing her arms in grief.

The old Quaker cemetery at Purchase was running out of room, so I made burial arrangements with the Quaker meeting in Amawalk, thirty miles further upstate. Members of the Capa family and their closest friends assembled there two weeks later to face Capa's coffin. As we gathered at the grave, a young photographer approached. Inge Bondi came to me, cognizant of the intimacy of the occasion, and said, "John, can't you tell him to go away?" I started to and then stopped abruptly. "After all," I said to Inge, "whom are we burying?" It was Dirck Halstead, the eighteen-year-old photographer of the local newspaper. Capa was his hero. Dirck went on to cover the war in Vietnam for United Press International.

For the May 1954 issue of *Infinity*, published by the American Society of

Magazine Photographers, I wrote, "Robert Capa was somewhat careless as a photographer but was carefully dedicated as a man. He participated with courage in almost every great tragedy of his time, and never lost heart nor faith. . . . He died with a camera in his left hand, his story unexpectedly finished. He left behind a thermos of cognac, a few good suits, a bereaved world, and his pictures, among them some of the greatest recorded moments of modern history. He also leaves a legend, for which there is no other description than—Capa."

There was no choice for Magnum but to carry on. We decided to meet in Paris as soon as possible, to discuss the future. We would be joined by Bob's "kid brother," Cornell, who would himself give new meaning to the Capa name and legend in the annals of photojournalism. But the disasters of 1954 were not over for me. Three weeks later, Dèle dropped me at Idlewild Airport for my flight to Paris. As she drove home, she noticed something peculiar: the cars ahead of her appeared to have two license plates. Her double vision was the first symptom of a fatal illness.

An eighteen-year-old named Dirck Halstead took these pictures of Robert Capa's burial in the Quaker cemetery at Amawalk, New York, on June 11, 1954. As he was and remains for many young photographers, Capa was Halstead's hero. © DIRCK HALSTEAD

LIFE

A PENETRATING LOOK AT
THE PEOPLE OF RUSSIA
PHOTOS BY CARTIER-BRESSON

**MILITARY APPRAISAL
AT MOSCOW TROLLEY STOP**

20 CENTS

JANUARY 17, 1955

In late December 1954, I presented Henri Cartier-Bresson's reportage on Russia to Edward K. Thompson, managing editor of *Life* in its greatest days. We agreed on a deal and then Ed asked me, "What do you see for a cover?" I proposed this picture, knowing that the *Life* logotype would fit nicely into the composition. Ed immediately agreed. © HENRI CARTIER-BRESSON/*Magnum Photos.* Life *Magazine Cover © Time Inc.*

18

Decisive Moments

Suddenly we were all middle-aged. On the last day of June 1954, the members of Magnum assembled in the rue de Lisbonne apartment of Henri and Elie Cartier-Bresson to discuss the future. Magnum was no longer the upstart child of its founder, Robert Capa, whose game was to beat the odds on the impossible bet. Now the founder was gone; we were on our own, and it was not much fun. Margot Shore, our Paris bureau chief, was devastated. She tried to express her feelings in a letter: "My belief in Magnum is in great part my belief in Bob. . . . I am not sure that we are strong enough to make up for him, so I suggest that we do not try to. . . . To state it frankly, but not in any kind of defiance, I want to suggest that we leave Bob's chair vacant, for it will stay that way no matter what we can do." There was no argument. According to my handwritten notes, the best surviving record of the meeting, we named no president but three vice presidents. Chim agreed to be vice president for finance, the worst job, with the extra responsibility of drawing up a certificate of incorporation, some bylaws, and a stockholders' agreement—Magnum had never gotten around to such matters. George Rodger agreed to be vice president for Paris operations, even though he lived in England. Cornell Capa, although new to membership, was named vice president for New York. None of these jobs was paid, of course.

The five photographer members (the new VPs plus Henri Cartier-Bresson and Ernst Haas) then voted to offer me, as executive editor, full stockholding equality with themselves by the purchase of ten shares of Class A stock—which had never actually been issued. For this dubious privilege I was to pay $1,000. The stock itself was unimportant; what counted was equality, in principle, with the photographers. However, since they could easily outvote me as a group, whatever authority I had, along with my fancy title, was strictly moral. Therein lay the problem. Capa had ruled by charm and fiat; in effect I had been his deputy. Now we had a company with three heads, who were seldom in the same place at the same time. I believed that we should put ourselves in the hands of a real businessman and proposed that Magnum hire itself a CEO—in effect a boss for me and the staff. I had just the person in mind: the young Schlumberger executive Jean Riboud, whom we all knew as a friend of the Cartier-Bressons. Son of a Lyon banker, Jean had been captured by the Germans in World War II and had spent eighteen months in Buchenwald. He was bilingual, as much at home on Wall Street as on the rue Saint-Dominique. He was already our unpaid, friendly counselor. I tried to persuade him to take on the direction of Magnum as an international enterprise. He declined, but told his brother Marc that he was not only flattered but tempted. Jean rose to become CEO of Schlumberger and a man of influence in both France and America, a confidant of President François Mitterrand. Eventually, by default, Chim emerged as Magnum's president, just as in 1952 George Rodger had briefly taken on the presidential role at a time when Capa was fed up with it. From Paris, Chim went off to his base in Rome's Hotel Inghilterra. His friend Henry Margolis, a Harvard-trained New York businessman who owned, among other things, the gourmet restaurant Chambord, was there on vacation. He agreed to help with Magnum's corporate paperwork, but it took time. Chim did not have the Magnum house in order until the following year. He was then formally elected president.

Cornell Capa, Bob's younger brother by four and a half years, was the welcome newcomer. The "Capa" kids (they never were the Friedmanns, to me) had been raised in a brown-brick apartment house at Városház utca 10, in Budapest. When I finally saw it, visiting Budapest with Cornell in 1989 for a Robert Capa exhibition, it reminded me of 5515 Woodlawn, the house in which I'd grown up in Chicago. Small wonder that we felt like brothers, though raised a world apart. Cornell had joined Bob in Paris in 1936. He was introduced to photography in the bathroom of his hotel on the Left Bank, where he made prints for Bob and Chim and Cartier-Bresson. The following year, Cornell moved to New York with their mother and became a professional lab man, first at the agency Pix, then at *Life*. In 1946, he became a *Life* staff photographer, posted first to Dallas, where he covered "cats-and-dogs" stories, followed by a two-year stint in London, where he grew closer to Bob: "We were no longer just brothers; we were brothers in photography." In 1952, Cornell returned to the United States to cover the presidential campaign of Adlai Stevenson, with whom he became fast friends. Bob's sudden death in 1954 interrupted Cornell's breakthrough study of the education of retarded children, which resulted in a two-part *Life* series and a book, *Retarded Children CAN Be Helped.*

Cornell knew he was always welcome at Magnum, but he also knew it would mean a financial and perhaps professional sacrifice. After the events of May 25, 1954, he knew he had no choice. He was determined to preserve his brother's—and Werner Bischof's—photographic heritage. In so doing, he would help steer Magnum through some difficult times and would eventually create one of the great world institutions of photography, the International Center of Photography, which today occupies two magnificent exhibition and office spaces, in midtown Manhattan and on Fifth Avenue's Museum Mile.

Magnum's most immediate problem in the summer of 1954 was the Paris office. With Bob gone, it lacked dynamic direction. We left George Rodger to cope as best he could. Margot resigned almost immediately, leaving George in despair. "Paris makes no sense at all," he wrote, proposing a shutdown or a move to London. "We must make our decision immediately . . . on the one vital question—to close or not to close." This was extreme, and I hastily suggested that we talk with Charles Rado, the Hungarian founder of the Rapho picture agency, about a merger, to share overhead. Fortunately, this idea went no further. George returned to England, and Chim, Cornell, and Ernst Haas converged on the Pastoria Hotel in late August for an emergency conference with him. But even the mention of Magnum now gave George a violent headache. He turned his governorship of the Paris operations over to Henri, who was off shooting in the USSR. Just as well. Henri was no administrator, but he saved Magnum in its most critical hour. Earlier, his self-assigned coverage of Gandhi's death in January 1948, and his *Life*-assigned coverage of the Chinese Revolution, beginning that December, had won him journalistic recognition and an Overseas Press Club award, even though his methods were unconventional. Thanks to the Gandhi and China stories, and many resulting second sales, Henri's credit with Magnum rose to $5,000. Capa warned him, "If you take it out, we will be bankrupt."

Henri and I did not yet know each other well. I had gotten a sense of his origins when I lunched with him in 1944 at the family apartment on the rue de Lisbonne. But in those war-weary days I would not have guessed that the Cartier-Bresson family had once been served by a butler wearing white gloves, that Henri was required to address his father as *vous*, and that he had been raised by English and Irish nannies.

His heart lay with Surrealism, an affection Bob Capa scoffed at, advising him to "just call yourself a photojournalist." Henri often spoke of his disdain for photography and love of painting but was extremely private about his own work—not to mention critical: he destroyed most of his early paintings. I had heard him speak of himself as a Surrealist but didn't realize that his paintings were anything but—his painting master, André Lhote, was conservative by Cubist standards. Henri simply enjoyed the company of the Surrealists and their revolt against convention. He expressed this revolt in the first years of his seri-

"There is nothing in this world that does not have a decisive moment," said Cardinal de Retz—a phrase that became associated with Henri Cartier-Bresson. Cartier-Bresson set about capturing such moments, as in this 1948 tour of China for Magnum Photos. © *Magnum Photos*

ous photography (1932–1934), in France, Italy, Spain, and Mexico. I remember being shocked when I first saw his pictures of Mexican whores. When Henri showed his photographs to Gertrude Stein, she advised him to go into the family business—thread. Fortunately, he was simply amused. Henri was always uncomfortable with his family name; he signed his early pictures "Carter" or "Cartier." One of his many signatures—I have it on a postcard—was "En rit Ca-Bré etc."

We met again in New York just before Magnum was founded, when Henri and his wife, Elie, were occupying the apartment of a friend of a friend under the Queensboro Bridge. By then I had seen his "posthumous" show of 1947 at the Museum of Modern Art—"posthumous" because Beaumont and Nancy Newhall, who directed MOMA's department of photography in its early years, had lost contact with him during the war and thought him dead. This exhibition carried his career forward to include some of the photographs taken during his swing through America in 1946–1947. I came to know and love that work.

Henri's masterful 1952 compilation, *The Decisive Moment*, set the standard for monographs by photographers. Henri Matisse designed a bold four-color jacket that signaled the book's significance as a work of art. It was lovingly published by Tériade, the Greek connoisseur and founder of the art magazine *Verve*. Just as important as the compilation of 126 black-and-white photographs—half from the Eastern world, half from the West—was the 4,500-

word preface by the photographer himself. On the first page, there is a quotation from cardinal de Retz: "*Il n'y a rien dans ce monde qui n'ait un moment décisif*" ("There is nothing in this world that does not have a decisive moment"). One sentence of Henri's in particular gave me a new appreciation of the profession into which I had haphazardly plunged thirteen years previously: "To me, photography is the simultaneous recognition, in a fraction of a second, of the significance of an event as well as of a precise organization of forms which give that event its proper expression." With *The Decisive Moment* I felt that finally photojournalism had its intellectual raison d'être. Henri challenged photojournalists—including those who *edit* photographs—to take with utmost seriousness a medium that has the possibility of merging Truth with Beauty. The search for "decisive moments" became the preoccupation of photojournalists.

There was great international speculation about the "new look" of the Soviet Union after the death of Josef Stalin on March 5, 1953. Henri and Elie Cartier-Bresson applied for Soviet visas late that year. Henri's objective was to photograph the Soviet peoples, not the forbidden "military objectives" such as railway stations. He and Elie lost no time in getting to Moscow when their visas came through in August 1954. Their working methods differed sharply from those of Capa and Steinbeck, who could never seem to shake their hosts. Henri later explained, in the preface to his 1955 monograph *The People of Moscow:*

> We laid out a plan. My photographic methods are not very common in Russia. Besides, neither my wife nor I speak Russian. We were given an interpreter. Every morning, he came to fetch us at our hotel and took us to wherever we wanted to go. Whenever we needed authorizations, he took care of the matter for us. He was very efficient and helpful. Often, in the street, people, startled by a foreigner bluntly snapping pictures right in their faces, came up to me. As I did not understand them, I stammered the only Russian sentence I had learned: "Tovarich perevodchik suda" (comrade interpreter, come here!). Then I would salute and proceed with my work, while the interpreter explained things. Soon they stopped paying attention to me. . . . I tried to capture a straightforward image of the people going about their daily life, to catch them in their ordinary acts and their human relationships. I fully realize how fragmentary that image is, but so much is certain: it represents my visual discovery faithfully.

Fragmentary or not, Henri's prestige was such that upon his return he was in the enviable position of being courted by three major American magazines—and I took pains to subtly let them each know it. Editor Ted Patrick spoke of doing an entire issue of *Holiday*. Editor Dan Mich saw an opportunity to capture the Cartier-Bresson label for *Look*. Managing editor Ed Thompson of *Life* was taking no chances. On October 8 he wrote directly to Henri at my suggestion, primarily about the treatment of the story: "As I told John, it would be our plan not to try to read anything into it that isn't there. . . . We would follow your captions as closely as possible. . . . Speaking from my standpoint, this could be the high point so far in the relations of LIFE and Magnum."

This made delicious reading to me, as Henri's agent. However, it made my problem only the harder. There could be only one satisfied customer. In the long run Magnum needed all three publications. I flew to Paris in late November. Pierre Gassman's Picto lab had made hundreds of modest 8-by-10-inch prints, and Elie Cartier-Bresson had faithfully captioned them. We spent a couple of days going over the material together—all black and white. Henri had shot some color but couldn't find it. The following Tuesday, I was in Ed Thompson's office at *Life*. I put the entire stack of prints on his big table. Ed proceeded at his own pace, poker-faced. Finally, he looked up and said, "Okay, thirty-five thousand dollars, two parts." I got him up to $40,000 by throwing in *Life*'s international edition. Then Thompson turned to me and asked, "What do you see for a cover?" I was ready for him: "How about this?" I pulled out a vertical of two Russian officers checking out two lovely young women on a Moscow street

Life's managing editor Ed Thompson was a great picture editor—probably the best there ever was. He always worked in his shirtsleeves and usually communicated in a succession of grunts. With him, at left, is *Life*'s deputy art director David Stech (my collaborator on many projects) and national affairs editor Hugh Moffett. ALFRED EISENSTAEDT/Life *Magazine* © *Time Inc.*

corner. There was no need to explain it: the officers symbolized Russian military might, but they were fallibly human. The composition was perfect Cartier-Bresson—with ample room for the *Life* logo at top left. Thompson bought it in an instant.

With *Life* about to hit the stands, I returned to Europe and made the rounds, selling the story in Germany (to *Stern*), Italy (to *Epoca*), England (to *Picture Post*), and of course France (to *Paris Match*). In Norway, Sweden, Finland, Holland, Belgium, and Switzerland similar deals were made by Magnum agents. It was a success beyond Robert Capa's maddest Magnum dreams. Our biggest financial crisis—so far—was past. In April, Henri wrote to me:

> I have been looking for my income tax report I had lost and I found the Russian color. . . . I am so sorry not to have found them earlier but you know French people never throw anything away and during forty years in the same house, a family piles up many treasures. I found at the same time as my Russian color a little box I had lost and which I cared for very much. On the box, my grandmother, before she died in 1932, had written "Petits crayons ne pouvant plus servir à rien" [Little crayons good for nothing]. Please tell this to Ed [Thompson]. I am sure he knows French ways of life. And ask him not to get too mad.

Dèle's condition steadily worsened that fall. Along with the double vision, she was experiencing dizziness, her speech was slightly slurred, and her gait was wobbly. "Is it cancer?" I asked her doctor. "No," he replied, "but some things are worse than cancer." He had decided on tests at the Columbia Presbyterian Medical Center. A few days later Dèle called me at the office. With feigned cheerfulness, she announced, "Guess what? I've got multiple sclerosis." My face must have fallen to my desk. Eve Arnold, who happened to be in the office with me, spontaneously threw her arms around me.

The most notable image of Chim's coverage of the brief 1956 war between Israel and Egypt portrays a running child. Chim (a.k.a. David Seymour), a confirmed bachelor, was ever sensitive to children. © DAVID SEYMOUR/*Magnum Photos*

19

Chim's Fate

W hat's with Magnum?" was the heading for a gossipy newsletter sent to our clients in the spring of 1955. By now there was much to boast about. No fewer than 60 of the 503 pictures in Edward Steichen's "Family of Man" exhibition at the Museum of Modern Art were by Magnum photographers. Books were in preparation by Cornell Capa (*Retarded Children CAN Be Helped*), Henri Cartier-Bresson (*From One China to Another*), Inge Morath (*Fiesta in Pamplona*), and George Rodger (*Le Village des Noubas*). Werner Bischof's *Japan* had been posthumously published. The newsletter went on to report that Ernst Haas had passed up the Bandung Conference in order to "disappear" in Bali; that Marc Riboud had managed to photograph in one of the oldest hammams of Istanbul by hiding a camera under his bath towel; that Erich Hartmann had been made an honorary citizen of Freedom, Oklahoma; that Inge Morath had been first to photograph the collection of Picassos in the home of Picasso's sister, in Barcelona; that Elliott Erwitt had done a photographic "interview" with a celebrated carrier pigeon at Fort Monmouth, New Jersey—under the heading "Memoirs of a V.I.P." (very important pigeon); and so on.

The lighthearted tone of the promotion piece concealed some bitter disappointments. Nevertheless, I was beginning to feel a new and, as it turned out, unwarranted sense of confidence. The biggest advance was the rationalization of Magnum's roster. The weekly bulletin called "Where's Magnum?" had listed the whereabouts of no less than thirty-one photographers, of whom only seventeen were full-time members (that is, stockholders) and associates (hopeful members). Both members and associates were expected to market *all* their photographic work—assignments as well as stock pictures—through Magnum, thus giving Magnum a substantial portion of their income. It required a serious commitment; Magnum guaranteed them nothing, beyond international representation.

We decided to cease active representation of "stringers." We created a category called "contributing photographers," honoring independent photographers of distinction and proven friends of Magnum who had no other agency. That list included Ansel Adams, Philippe Halsman, Dorothea Lange, Russell Lee, Herbert List, and, briefly, Richard Avedon and Edward Weston. Except for Halsman, whose portraits we frequently sold in Europe, it was largely an arrangement of mutual respect. We also agreed, through his son Peter Hunter in The Hague, to list the archives of the great Erich Salomon. His negatives had escaped the Nazis when Salomon perished. We announced these changes in June, and immediately the full-timers felt better. Magnum would now concentrate its efforts on representing *them*. At the 1954 "summit" meeting after the deaths of Capa and Bischof, we had voted membership for the five young Americans—Arnold, Erwitt, Glinn, Hartmann, Stock—in addition to Cornell Capa and one European, Kryn Taconis of the Netherlands.

Kryn was fearless. During World War II, the Germans had bombed his native Rotterdam to bits, commencing five years of occupation that became increasingly brutal. As a photographer's apprentice, he joined the Dutch resistance, forging passports and using his camera to record documents obtained in espionage. His teacher was executed; Kryn was arrested. Released after three months, he obtained bogus papers that enabled him to rescue Allied pilots and Jews from the Gestapo. In the fall of 1944, with northern Holland still under German occupation, he became a member of the Dutch resistance group Ondergedoken Camera (Underground Photographers). With his Rolleiflex hidden in a briefcase and later with a Leica concealed in a paper sack, he documented the final months of Nazi occupation in Amsterdam's "hunger winter" of 1944–1945, when thousands starved. After the war Kryn became a *Time/Life* stringer in Amsterdam. He soon caught the attention of Robert Capa, who invited him to hang around the Magnum Paris office, shooting an occasional story. Kryn was our "flying Dutchman." A Magnum document of December 1955 reported that "Kryn Taconis went from Amsterdam to Geneva for the Conference on Atomic Energy, then to Athens to Paris to Amsterdam to Paris to Marseille to Cairo to Addis Ababa to Khartoum—and has headed for the Belgian Congo."

In 1955, three more Europeans were made members: Marc Riboud from France, Erich Lessing and Inge Morath from Austria. It was Inge who had come to Paris Magnum with Ernst Haas in 1949 at Robert Capa's invitation. As Vienna correspondent for the German picture weekly *Heute,* she had covered many stories but had not thought of taking pictures herself. Capa proposed her to Cartier-Bresson as a researcher, and he was immediately impressed. She spoke English, French, Spanish, Italian, and a little Romanian in addition to her native German. Later she picked up Greek, Russian, and Chinese. The daughter of a distinguished Viennese chemist, Inge had majored in philology at the University of Berlin. She had refused to join the Hitler Youth and was sent to assemble aircraft parts at Berlin's Tempelhof Airport. The airport was bombed regularly, but she survived until war's end, when the gate was blown open and she walked out—all the way home to Austria. By the time she found her parents' house in Salzburg, she had come close to suicide.

Inge studied photography by closely observing Haas and Cartier-Bresson at work. In 1951, in London, she decided to shoot on her own, signing her pictures Egni Tharom. "Everyone thought Egni was a man," Inge has said, "and complained to me about *his* technique. I promised to let *him* know about that!" By 1953, Capa and I decided that Inge was ready for a major *Holiday* assignment and sent her off to Spain. Capa advised her to "get yourself dressed like a lady." She photographed Balenciaga and returned with a new wardrobe. She was elegantly feminine but built like a runner. Once, on location in Mexico with John Huston, she saved the life of war hero Audie Murphy, who was starring in a Huston film. Murphy fell out of a boat while fishing. Hearing his screams, Inge stripped and swam almost half a mile to his rescue, returning to shore with Murphy clutching on to her bra strap. In 1961, Inge arrived in Reno with Cartier-Bresson to photograph the filming of Huston's *The Misfits*. There she met Arthur Miller, the scenarist, whose marriage to Marilyn Monroe was in the process of breaking up. Miller was immediately attracted by this "slender, noble-looking young woman with bobbed hair and a European accent, who seemed both shy and strong at the same time," as he remembers in his memoir, *Timebends.* They married the following year.

Erich Lessing, the other Austrian who became a member in 1955, followed a quite different path. Immigrating to British-mandated Palestine in 1939, Lessing raised fish on a kibbutz and drove a taxi in Tel Aviv before joining the British 6th Airborne Division. Returning to Vienna, he began professional photography as a stringer, first for AP, then for Magnum. In 1954, I made a deal with James "Scotty" Reston, Washington bureau chief of *The New York Times*, for Lessing to join his team covering the Geneva Conference, which was partitioning Vietnam. Lessing was in Budapest for the Russian clampdown in 1956. That bloodbath so disgusted him that he turned from reportage to the production of books of cultural history. There are now dozens, largely in color.

Marc Riboud was the second Frenchman, after Cartier-Bresson, to become a Magnum member. His route was also unconventional. Like his elder brothers Jean and Antoine (now one of France's foremost capitalists), Marc joined the Resistance in World War II. He then studied engineering and worked in a factory, only to find, in 1951, that he really wanted to be a photographer. Encouraged by Henri, he began selling pictures through Magnum. His photo of a painter languidly applying his brush to the Eiffel Tower is an early classic of his oeuvre. Bob Capa took over Marc's journalistic education, sending him to London for a year to improve his English and to make connections.

Like Henri, Riboud composed fast; he also shared with Capa a superb sense of timing. With these attributes he has gone far: innumerable trips to China, Japan, India, to North Vietnam during the conflict, to the Mideast, to Africa, to North and South America. Today he is a contributing photographer, along with most of Magnum's "senior citizens": Cornell Capa, Henri Cartier-Bresson, Hiroshi Hamaya, Erich Hartmann, Sergio Larrain, Erich Lessing, Wayne Miller, and Marilyn Silverstone. They are free to sell independently without losing the Magnum percentage—a privilege the founders of Magnum never envisaged for themselves. The photographic estates of Werner Bischof, Robert Capa, Philippe Halsman, Herbert List, George Rodger, David Seymour, and W. Eugene Smith are represented in the Magnum archives.

In the spring of 1956, Dèle and I paid a visit to Rome, conducted by Chim, our very own Roman emperor. Chim had published *The Vatican* with freelance journalist Ann Carnahan, and seemed to know everyone: the pope's chauffeur, shoemaker, and pharmacist, the gardeners and plainclothesmen, the scholars of the Vatican Library, the cleaners of the carpets in the Sistine Chapel. Pope Pius XII had given him a private photographic audience. With the possible exception of Cartier-Bresson, Chim was the most cultured member of Magnum. He could discuss music with Toscanini and classical art with Bernard Berenson, both of whom he photographed at home. A gourmet and connoisseur of wine, Chim was an enthusiastic consumer of the *dolce vita* of modern Rome. Leonard Lyons, the *New York Post* gossip columnist, came to town while we were there, and we all made a pilgrimage for cocktails to Gina Lollobrigida's villa on the Appian Way.

Chim insisted on referring to Magnum as a "family," somewhat to the distress of the less sentimental Cartier-Bresson. Chim himself was a confirmed bachelor. Nevertheless, he specialized in children, both professionally and personally. He made a big fuss about Magnum children, remembering their birthdays, bringing them presents. The two most favored were Magnum's half orphans, the two Bischof boys. Dèle and I stopped in Zurich for a visit with Rosellina, in the enchanting home that she had made of Werner's studio. She never quite recovered from his loss, but we were warmly introduced to a young photographer, a protégé of Werner's: René Burri. It was not surprising that they later married and established a family of their own, but Burri didn't have an easy time living in Werner's house and shadow. Perhaps not the extraordinary artist that Werner was, Burri was more comfortable with journalism; he was named a Magnum associate in 1956 and became a full member four years later.

When we arrived in London, we found Henri and Elie Cartier-Bresson working on a story for *Holiday*. In the lounge of the Pastoria, Henri and I interviewed a young photographer from New Zealand. His name was Brian Brake, and we found his talent so impressive that we virtually accepted him as an associate on the spot. Brake had such manual dexterity that he could cover a story simultaneously in color and black and white, alternating the two cameras on his chest. His color essay "The Monsoon" ran in leading magazines in the United States (*Life*), England (*The Queen*), France (*Paris Match*), and Italy (*Epoca*), and all four versions were later exhibited at New York's Museum of Modern Art in an exhibition called "The Photo Essay" (an idea I "sold" to John Szarkowski, MOMA's director of photography).

Chim and I had discussed my intention of exploring newspaper syndication as a way to break *Life*'s virtual monopoly on the news picture market. *Time* and *Newsweek* took little initiative in picture coverage in those days. Many a Magnum story went into the wastebasket, so far as America was concerned, because *Life* had its own people on the story. Magnum could place only the crumbs. To augment its own coverage, *Life* would buy single pictures at space rates, $150 a page, with a minimum of $25 or $35 for a small picture. How to crack the newspaper market? I had often discussed this with one of my Armonk neighbors, Thomas N. Schroth, the young managing editor of the Brooklyn *Eagle*, once one of America's great newspapers—Walt Whitman served as editor from 1846 to 1848. Tom was enthusiastic about improving the *Eagle*'s picture display, but before he could do much about it the *Eagle* died. Schroth and I had made up some sample layouts, adaptable to standard newspaper half pages or tabloid spreads. Charges were to be based on circulation, with an average of $75 a week per newspaper. The first reactions from newspapers were good, but Magnum's senior members were quite alarmed. Ernst Haas spoke for the group: "It is time to reconsider where we are, what we want and where we want to go. If we want a PHOTO EMPIRE or a happy little democracy." As it turned out, there were few real takers in the newspaper world. My plan was put on hold.

Forget about newspapers, Chim knew what we really needed: a new office in New York. The Sixty-fourth Street basement was bursting at the seams, and that summer we were flooded, although the files escaped damage. In October, I found a terrific space atop a building, largely occupied by diamond merchants, at 15 West Forty-seventh Street. It was close to our most important customers and had a view in four directions. Best of all, it had a kind of Magnum character—unpretentious, a little funky, wide open. The rent was going to double, and

Chim began to have second thoughts, but finally he consented. We would open there for business, and a new chapter of Magnum's history, on Friday, November 11, 1955.

Nineteen fifty-six began as a good year for Chim. He moved from the Inghilterra to a flat: "Rome is my sentimental base," he wrote me. "My apartment here grows in comfort and is almost a menace to freedom." He persuaded his friend Ingrid Bergman to give him, for *Look,* an exclusive on the family she had created with Roberto Rossellini. Fritz Gruber, director of exhibitions for the biennial Photokina trade fair in Cologne, invited Magnum to put on a group show, its first. Pierre Gassman's Paris lab printed until the last minute. Chim headed a small Magnum delegation for the opening on October 4, proudly escorting Theodor Heuss, first president of the German Federal Republic, and giving interviews to the press. On October 10, Chim had dinner with Ingrid Bergman in Rome. She complained to him bitterly about the *Look* story, saying that they had failed to check the text with her, as she thought they had promised. Chim told me that she was not seriously upset, but he couldn't understand *Look*'s behavior. Unlike *Life,* which gave photographers the status of prima donnas, *Look* paid scant attention to their demands. This, however, was a case of common courtesy. Then Chim was off to Greece.

"Take it easy. We don't need the money." That was the message I cabled to Chim when he told us of his intention to join the Israeli forces that invaded Egypt on October 29, 1956. I was thinking of Robert Capa—of the time I had phoned him in Tokyo to try to dissuade him from joining the French forces in Indochina, shouting, "It's not *our* war!" But this was different. Chim was devoted heart and soul to Israel. His parents had died in the Holocaust; in Israel he and his sister had found their surviving relatives. Chim always tried to make a pilgrimage there for the Holy Days and to report the progress of the young nation annually. One of his most touching pictures showed a proud kibbutznik holding high his firstborn son—the child Chim would never have.

Chim was at Olympia, deep in the Greek Peloponnesus, photographing the archaeologists who were excavating the ancient Olympic stadium, when he got the news of the invasion. On October 31, he wrote from Athens to Gertrude "Trudy" Feliu of Paris Magnum:

> I did not hear the news about Israel until four in the afternoon. My little Olympia story which I found as a lovely excuse to come to Greece suddenly meant nothing. . . . I immediately started arrangements to hire a car and was finally successful. We drove half the night until we reached Athens. . . . The city is full of frus-

Just before leaving Rome for Greece, and then Egypt, where he met his death, Chim had dinner with Ingrid Bergman to discuss the final story he shot of her, for *Look*. She complained about the text but was pleased with the pictures. This is one, showing Ingrid with her son, Robertino Rossellini. © DAVID SEYMOUR/*Magnum Photos*

trated correspondents trying to get to Israel. I have run into many
old friends as soon as I arrived and we were all plotting together. . . .
I would like to be into things. . . . I feel we cannot stay out of world
events if we are to grow as a group in world photography.

On November 5, Britain and France joined Israel in the war on Egypt. It was
one day before the U.S. presidential election, and their move caught Dwight
Eisenhower's administration off guard. In shock, the Americans, in rare collaboration with the Russians, called for a withdrawal of all forces. Frustrated in
his attempts to get to Israel, Chim decided to go to Egypt with the British. Chim
probably did not know that Magnum's Burt Glinn was already in Israel, but the
fact of Burt's being there would not have dissuaded Chim. Chim and I were due
to meet in Paris in November, but on the sixth he wrote me a postcard from the
Ledra Palace Hotel in Nicosia, Cyprus:

> *Dear John,*
> *Sorry for the delay of our meeting, but hope we will meet soon. My best*
> *to Dèle and kids—love.*
>
>

Yours,
DAVID SEYMOUR
>

It was unlike him to sign in any way but "Chim." The message was handwritten, but the signature was printed in block letters, suggesting that he either
conceived of the card as a document or that he was leaving the hotel in such
haste that he asked the concierge to fill in the address and sign it. In any event,
they were his last words to me.

At 2:00 A.M. the next day, November 7, a cease-fire was declared. Thus when
Chim, in a borrowed British army uniform, arrived in Port Said, northern ter-
minus of the Suez Canal, there was little for him to do but photograph soldiers
patrolling the streets. Not much of a story, so when he heard the following Saturday, November 10, that there would be an exchange of wounded with the
Egyptians to the south, he teamed with Jean Roy of *Paris Match* to cover it.
Somehow they obtained a jeep and started off for the town of Suez. Roy
drove—Chim had never learned to—down the causeway that runs across the
marshes between the Suez Canal, on one side, and the Sweet Water (drainage)
Canal on the other. As they reached the final British outpost, an officer warned
them to stop, but Roy gave the "V" sign and roared on. Half a mile further, they
came to the first Egyptians. Again they were ordered to stop; again they drove
on. But only for a moment. As machine-gun fire roared through the air, the
jeep veered into the drainage canal. Both men were found dead in the wreckage.

With Chim in my spare Magnum office at 15 West Forty-seventh Street. The empty champagne bottle on the window sill was a poignant memento of a happier time—a bottle we had no doubt shared, in spirit if not in reality, with Robert Capa and Werner Bischof, whose memorial plaque rests against it. There would be another plaque, all too soon, for Chim. © BURT GLINN/*Magnum Photos*

It was Sunday night in Armonk, and the phone rang insistently. Burt Glinn was calling from Israel, so excited that at first I couldn't make out what he was saying. I thought he was calling about his own pictures. "Calm down," I said, "your Israeli soldier may be on the *Life* cover that closed last night." Burt shouted back, "John, I'm calling to tell you that they got Chim! It's not confirmed yet, but I think Chim is dead!" Two weeks later we buried Chim from the Riverside Chapel in New York. Chim's good friend Henry Margolis spoke with great affection. Thirty-three years later, I would stand in the same spot and pay tribute to Henry, who suffered a massive heart attack at a formal Lincoln Center party with his favorite girl. He died in his tuxedo, at eighty. Chim would have loved that. The shroud that clung to us after Chim's death gradually dissipated. A decade later, his colleague *and* friend, Henri Cartier-Bresson, had this to say: "Chim picked up his camera the way a doctor takes his stethoscope out of his bag, applying his diagnosis to the condition of the heart: his own was vulnerable."

On July 26, 1956, the passenger liners *Stockholm* and *Andrea Doria* collided off Nantucket. The *Andrea Doria* sank, and fifty-one people died. Only Gene Smith was available to cover the story for Magnum, but he was exhausted from making prints of his enormous Pittsburgh project. I agreed to stay with him through the night, at a Hudson River pier, to await survivors. Gene noticed this nun, clutching a teddy bear in anticipation of a child who might, or might not, return. *Copyright © 1998 The Heirs of W. Eugene Smith*

20

The Many Woes of
W. Eugene Smith

I thought I knew Gene Smith. Hadn't we worked happily together on the eve of World War II? We had gone off to war in opposite directions, but I shared his passionate belief in the idiocy of war and his frustration at the way it had been presented in the press. When Gene's first postwar *Life* essays appeared, they hit me as a revelation of photojournalism in depth. Each reflected the standards I wanted to set for the *Journal*'s "How America Lives." In "Country Doctor" (1948), Gene lived with his subject for weeks, "fading into the wallpaper" to record the daily trauma embodied in the practice of Dr. Ernest Ceriani of Kremmling, Colorado. In "Nurse Midwife" (1951), Gene found a heroine in Maude Callen, a South Carolina midwife. It was the first time a black person had been featured by *Life* in such a way. Readers sent thousands of dollars to build Maude a new clinic. "Spanish Village" (1951), designed by *Life*'s Bernard Quint, was hailed as the greatest of all *Life*'s photo-essays. Gene resigned his *Life* contract on November 2, 1954, as the magazine closed his twelve-page photo-essay on Albert Schweitzer, "A Man of Mercy." The massive project had consumed Gene for almost a year, and he felt that the published layout did not do his effort justice: "I would have preferred silence," he said. Harry Luce wrote to Gene to express his regret, adding that he hoped Gene's pictures "will still be available, although from the other side of the counter."

The moment I heard the news, I thought of Gene for Magnum. I was excited at the prospect. I talked up the idea with Cornell Capa and Ernst Haas, but I had no idea how disturbed Gene had become. I did not know that he had been admitted to Bellevue Hospital for psychiatric treatment following his return from "The Spanish Village" in 1950, which delayed its publication to 1951.

Gene then quit the *Life* staff for a contract that required him to produce only three stories a year; he actually produced only one of importance in 1952, "Chaplin at Work," and one in 1953, "The Reign of Chemistry." I did not realize that he had been, consciously or unconsciously, seeking an excuse to quit *Life* entirely. Schweitzer was but the pretext. I knew he was having an affair with photographer-writer Margery Lewis, but I did not know that she had secretly given birth to his son, Kevin Eugene Smith, while he was off with Schweitzer in 1954. Meanwhile, he had failed to support his own family—his wife, Carmen, and four children. He was combining heavy drinking with amphetamines.

Life was the only magazine in the world capable of supporting Gene's leisurely rate of performance and his expensive habits—he invariably worked with an assistant and the very best of equipment. It was, I realized too late, foolhardy of Magnum to commit itself to sustaining Gene Smith and his burdens, both real and imaginary. To compound our problem, the first deal I made for Gene was the worst I have ever made for any photographer. Gene's first customer actually appeared on the scene even before Gene joined us. I knew Stefan Lorant's reputation as the innovative but tricky Hungarian who had edited no fewer than four photographic magazines. The anti-Nazi views of his *Münchner Illustrierte Zeitung* had won him six months in a German concentration camp in 1933; only the intervention of the Hungarian government had gotten him out. Taking refuge in England, he had founded *Weekly Illustrated* in 1934, *Lilliput* in 1937, and *Picture Post* in 1938. Winston Churchill then suggested that he do a book explaining America to Englishmen. Introduced to Harry Luce by Joseph P. Kennedy, then the American ambassador to the Court of St. James's, he visited Time Inc. and returned to England with hundreds of pictures. The next year he emigrated to the United States for good. Settling in Lenox, Massachusetts, Lorant turned to editing photographic books rather than magazines. When we met, Lorant had just been commissioned by the Allegheny Conference to do an illustrated book to celebrate Pittsburgh's bicentennial. He wanted Gene Smith to shoot a picture essay on contemporary Pittsburgh as the book's centerpiece. "Unfortunately," Lorant explained to me, his budget did not "permit" him to pay more than $1,200, plus $500 for expenses, but all he needed was book rights; the second rights—which would stay with the photographer—would be invaluable. As for expenses, Gene could live on the bottom floor of a house a Pittsburgh executive had loaned to Lorant. It even had a darkroom. Gene was almost eager to accept—he was going to show *Life*. I should have known better, but I agreed to the deal—verbally. Gene went off to Pittsburgh with enough equipment, and phonograph records, to stay a year—Lorant had figured on two to three weeks.

When I returned from Europe in June 1955, the news from Pittsburgh was

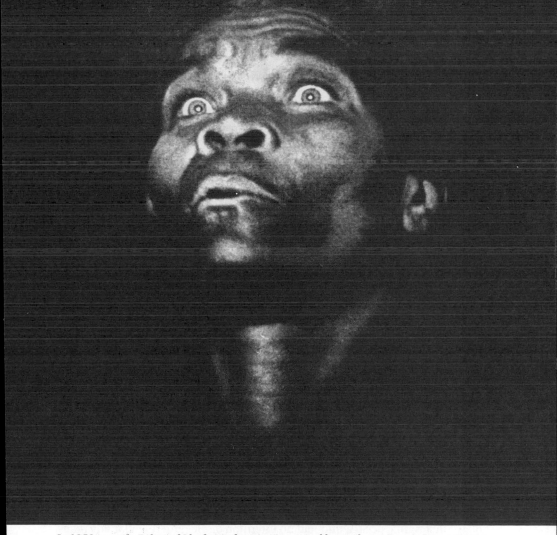

In 1953 my wife, Dèle, and I had visited a primitive mental hospital near Port au Prince, Haiti, a veritable snake pit. When I heard that a modern mental health clinic would be established there, I asked the sponsors to assign Gene Smith to tell the story, before and after. "Before," of course, made the stronger pictures. This one Gene called "Mad Eyes." *Copyright © 1998 The Heirs of W. Eugene Smith*

bad. Gene had already been there for three months, with little to show for it. His films of the first two months had been stolen from his station wagon. He was starting over. I went to see him in Pittsburgh and found a perplexed Stefan Lorant. Unfortunately, I had brought along copies of the unsigned contract. Lorant asked if I would sign. Reasoning that I had given my word and my word was my bond, I signed. The implications of this were far more serious than I could have imagined. Gene finally returned from Pittsburgh in August with 11,000 negatives. Rather than make master prints, his common practice, he decided to make "proof prints," 5 by 7 inches, of a large percentage. The problem was that he tried to make each one a master print in miniature, and he was soon exhausted. One morning he called me from the darkroom of his house in Croton-on-Hudson, obviously on the verge of breakdown. I said I would try to find him an assistant. Luckily enough, a young man named James Karales, a graduate of Ohio University's well-known Department of Photography, came to Magnum after lunch that day to show me his portfolio. I wasn't much interested in his pictures, but when he told me he had made the prints himself, I asked him if he would like to work in the darkroom with Gene Smith for a couple of weeks. His pay would be, perhaps, fifty dollars a week. "When do I start?" he asked eagerly. A seasoned commuter, I pulled a New York Central timetable out of my pocket and asked, "Can you make the 3:53 to Croton?" Gene met him at the station that afternoon. Karales stayed two years, living as one of the family—which occasionally meant going hungry.

The next problem was where to sell Gene's mammoth photo-essay. We couldn't very well go to *Life;* Gene wanted to "show them" he could survive without Time Inc. During his stay in Pittsburgh, we had been forced to turn down an assignment offered Gene by *The Saturday Evening Post* on radio announcer Arthur Godfrey. Later we had to turn down *Collier's*—a "peace" essay for Christmas. Neither had the slightest interest in Pittsburgh. Of the "big four" large-format mass magazines, that left only *Look.*

By this time, Smith and Karales had filled both the dining room and living room of the big house in Croton with proof prints—thousands of them, tacked up on easels. They were so impressive en masse that I decided to invite prospective customers to Croton. *Look*'s art director, Allen Hurlburt, and managing editor, William Arthur, came first; they reported back favorably to editor Dan Mich. We even agreed on a price, $20,000. It all became moot, however, when Mich asked Lorant to write the text. Lorant was furious, insisting that he had bought first rights, period, and had no intention of yielding them for *any* magazine piece. Mich, understandably, withdrew *Look*'s offer. By now Smith had tied up virtually all of Magnum's capital; there was no way out until we somehow sold Pittsburgh. I consulted Howard Squadron, Magnum's lawyer, who filed suit against Lorant. Lorant filed a countersuit. Gene also took the unprecedented step of registering his personal copyright with the Library of Congress on three huge volumes of contact prints—11,000 images—under the title "A City Experienced: Pittsburgh, Pa." At this, Lorant agreed to negotiate. In a five-hour meeting, attorneys for both sides came to an understanding that Gene could sell one magazine essay and three ads prior to book publication. My signature on the contract had cost us almost a year.

Now we could only go crawling back to *Life*, whose editors, bless them, didn't rub it in. I went to Robert Elson, the deputy managing editor whose "arbitrary" closure of the Schweitzer story had caused Gene to resign. After checking with Ed Thompson, Elson authorized a $2,500 down payment. That was in July. In October, *Life* was still waiting to see the pictures. It was obvious that Gene's concept of the story was very vague. He described it as "an experience that is Pittsburgh." Smith wanted to bring in his own layouts. Thompson refused to look at anything but the photographs and assigned deputy art director Bernard Quint, who had done the famous "Spanish Village" essay, to make a layout. Smith worked with Quint, but when Thompson asked Gene if he approved the layout, he only mumbled something that sounded critical and walked out. Thompson interpreted this as rejection. I only wish I had been there. No further payment was made. Finally, in 1958, after an international *Popular Photography* poll voted Smith one of "the world's ten greatest photographers," Bruce Downes, who edited both "*Pop*" and a sister publication, *Photography Annual*, agreed to run Smith's layout of thirty-two pages—later increased to thirty-eight—in the *Annual* exactly as Gene wanted. The fee was fifty dollars a page, including text—the usual rate for a magazine aimed at amateurs. Gene insisted that the essay be called "Labyrinthian Walk." Indeed it was. Gene was utterly depressed when he saw the final result, far from *Life*'s size and quality. "Pittsburgh is dead," he wrote to one friend, and to Ansel Adams: "The presentation is the witness . . . and there it lies, a failure." The textbook in self-destructiveness was written, in the red ink of his own blood, by W. Eugene Smith himself.

Pittsburgh was so all-consuming that Gene could do little else in his first three Magnum years. *Ladies' Home Journal* sent him to photograph a black professor in the South, an assignment that constituted most of his $2,582.78 magazine income for the year 1955. In 1956, when the Italian liner *Andrea Doria* sank off Nantucket after colliding with the Swedish liner *Stockholm*, I got Gene to work with me through the night to cover the arrival of survivors at Pier 88 in New York. Gene made a number of good pictures and one classic—a young nun, a woman of spectral beauty, holds her fingers gently to her lips in an expression of utter anxiety; in her other hand she grips a teddy bear, intended for one of the surviving children of the disaster. To my dismay, *Life* rejected the picture.

Gene's greatest success during his years with Magnum was one neither he nor Magnum had much to do with—credit goes to Edward Steichen for selecting Gene's backyard photograph, which he called "The Walk to Paradise Garden," of Gene's children Patrick and Juanita as the final image of "The Family of Man." Taken in 1946, it had been rejected by *Life*, where Wayne Miller found it buried in a file. It has since become what art historians call an "icon" of the twentieth century. Perhaps because the faces of the children are unseen, people see them as their own, toddling into the future. Magnum records show that we sold twelve prints of it, made by Gene himself from the copy negative, for fifty dollars each, in 1955. Today such prints sell for thousands of dollars.

Gene's real needs were immense. His advances from Magnum amounted to a dole that finally added up to $7,000, more than Magnum's original capital. We couldn't do more as a company, but we did join Gene in begging from friends. The Smiths' housekeeper, Jasmine "Jas" Twyman, who lived with her daughter in the Croton house, went out to do day work in other people's houses to earn money for food—for the Smiths as well as herself. One Christmas, Louise Lewis, the black matriarch who was nobly helping us out in Armonk, cooked two big dinners. One I took over the hills to Croton. Gene was not there—he could no longer face his family problems and had moved into a loft on Sixth Avenue, in the wholesale flower district. In stark awareness of his desperate situation, Gene wrote to me on January 25, 1958, "I have been a misfortune to Magnum from the day of being part of Magnum, and I am now in a far worse position than I was at the beginning to be anything but a handicap to Magnum. My failure with Magnum has been so devastatingly monumental, twisting so dangerously about both our necks, that I believe there is no other course than resignation." I persuaded Gene to stay on until the end of that year, hoping to recoup the money he owed Magnum. That spring, sitting next to me on the commuter train, a young Armonk neighbor and philanthropist named John Heyman told me that he was soon bound for Haiti with Dr. Nathan Kline, a prominent New York psychiatrist. Kline had persuaded some drug companies to fund a modern mental health clinic in Port-au-Prince to replace a "snake pit" that was one of the world's most primitive mental institutions.

I jumped. I knew exactly the place he was talking about. In January 1953, after leaving the *Journal* and before starting at Magnum, Dèle and I had vacationed in Haiti. We had made friends there with De Witt Peters, the American who had founded the Centre d'Art, for the promotion of Haitian primitive art. Through him we met several of Haiti's leading painters and also a man, straight out of Graham Greene's *The Comedians*, named "Doc" Reser. He had come to Haiti as a U.S. Marine during the long-lasting U.S. occupation (1915–1934) and had stayed on. One Sunday afternoon, Peters drove us out of Port-au-Prince and down a dusty country road to the modest frame house where Reser lived with a Haitian woman. Reser invited us to "see something" nearby. We drove a mile or so, then turned into a wooded area where there were barracks, scattered like cow barns, with adjacent corrals. Soon we saw that the animals they enclosed, living on the bare dirt and excrement, were silent men and women, dressed in rags. "This is Haiti's home for the insane," said Reser. He had visited it for years, doing what he could to soothe the suffering of the inmates and to stir public sympathy. I described my visit there to John Heyman and then told him about Gene Smith. In no time he agreed to hire Gene to document Kline's project. Gene went twice to Haiti, once for the "Before" (the "snake pit"), once for the "After" (the new clinic)—although of course it was not as simple as that. He produced some stark images, including one he called simply "Mad Eyes."

I went along with Gene for the second tour, staying with him at the Olafson, the rather seedy but charming hotel made memorable by Graham Greene in *The Comedians.* It had come into the hands of Roger Coster, a French photographer who had been a Magnum stringer; he refused to charge us rent. We covered the dedication of the new clinic, followed by a reception at the Maison Blanche given by President "Papa Doc" Duvalier. Was it an odd sensation to drink champagne with Haiti's dictator? Was it the most improbable cocktail party I have ever attended? Yes to both.

When John F. Kennedy became president in 1961, Cornell Capa talked the White House into giving Magnum access to the new administration for a picture paperback, *Let Us Begin*. Cornell, shooting one day at the White House, took a look outside and saw the First Mother proudly pushing John-John across the South Lawn. *Copyright © 1998 Cornell Capa*

Fidel Castro, binoculars in hand, patrols the beach following the Bay of Pigs. This photo did not appear in *Let Us Begin*. © BOB HENRIQUES/ *Magnum Photos*

21

Camelot and Cuba

It was said of Molly Thayer that "she knows everyone." She did. Born in Southampton, New York, the town that looks down on all other Long Island communities, Mary "Molly" Van Rensselaer Cogswell was a debutante of the twenties who made a fortunate marriage to a gentleman named Sigourney Thayer. Unfortunately, he died young. As a widow, Molly augmented her income through various jobs in journalism. She owned one of those slim, lovely town houses that line the streets of Georgetown in Washington, D.C. Hers was right across from that of columnist Joseph Alsop. Magnum's Elliott Erwitt met Molly in 1958 when *Vogue* asked him to shoot what "People Are Talking About" in Washington. Molly, at *Vogue*'s request, made the arrangements. He was so impressed by her efficiency that he talked me into signing her up as "our Washington correspondent."

One fine October day in 1960 I shuttled to Washington on some *National Geographic* business for Magnum and went by Molly's for coffee. She occasionally wrote for the women's pages of *The Washington Post* (it was before the era of "Style"). John F. Kennedy's presidential campaign advisers had decided that Jacqueline Kennedy should give a press conference just for women reporters. To show what they thought of the idea, the *Post* refused to send a regular staff member; instead it sent Molly, a stringer, whose subsequent story thrilled Mrs. Kennedy to the extent that she wrote a note to Molly promising an "incredible scoop" if her husband won. My eyes lit up with dollar signs when Molly told me. I called my former boss Mary Bass at *Ladies' Home Journal* and told her I had something extremely important to discuss. She and Bruce Gould saw me almost immediately. He smiled when he read the note. "John, you can tell Mrs.

Thayer that we would be *very* much interested in having Mrs. Kennedy's authorized biography, including her picture albums." He added, "And *you* know
that we would be prepared to pay top price for it."

On Wednesday morning, November 9, John F. Kennedy awakened in his
beach house in Hyannis Port, Massachusetts, to learn that he had defeated
Richard Nixon for the presidency. The very first call of congratulations taken
by Mrs. Kennedy came from Molly Thayer, who had been given the private
number. Jackie was brief and businesslike, promising that Molly would hear
from her as soon as she returned to Washington. That Sunday evening, true to
her word, a Secret Service agent came to the Thayer door—the Kennedys lived
just eight blocks away—to drop off a big bundle, packed with family scrap-
books. A treasure trove, and all of it exclusive.

My job was to select the photographs and supervise the layouts. Upon seeing
Molly's first draft and the rough layouts, the Goulds decided to run the story in
three parts, with the first part appearing in the February issue. It would hit the
stands on January 20, Inauguration Day. That issue was supposed to close December 10, so we had little time. Thanks to Jackie's strictures—she insisted on
seeing final copy—I felt especially confident of our position. I sent Bruce Gould
a three-page outline of the terms. There was no argument. My asking price for
the entire package was $100,000—a record-breaking deal for the time. After
paying expenses, the money was divided between Molly Thayer, as author, and
Magnum, as agent. The Kennedys got nothing—except another boost in their
popularity.

Mrs. Kennedy gave birth to "John-John" on November 24 but never lost
sight of her *Journal* deadline. On December 10, she wrote to Molly that the
President-elect had requested that the piece say something complimentary
about Charles De Gaulle, the prickly French president. Layouts went back and
forth for Jackie's comments and corrections, which Molly relayed to me in
cryptic notes. The first installment was now ten days overdue. It would *have* to
go to press in the third week of December. Molly sent the "final" draft to Palm
Beach, where Jackie had now joined her husband to await the inauguration.
On Sunday morning, December 20, Molly called to say that Jackie, Jack, *and*
Bobby Kennedy had just called from Palm Beach, delighted with her piece and
asking only minor corrections. The principal one—demanded by Jack and not
by Jackie—was to censor part of an incident where Jackie, aged six, was tossed
off her pony in a Southampton horse show and promptly got up and swatted
the pony. Jack wanted to play down Jackie's temper.

Cornell Capa covered the Kennedy campaign in 1960 and soon made friends
with the candidate, just as he had with Adlai Stevenson in 1952 and 1956. A
week after Kennedy's inauguration, we met with press secretary Pierre

Salinger at the White House with a proposition—the brainchild of Cornell and his friend Richard Grossman, personal assistant to Richard Simon of Simon and Schuster. Magnum would do a quick paperback picture book on the first hundred days of the Kennedy administration, to be entitled *Let Us Begin.*

Eight Magnum photographers immediately went to work worldwide—the idea was to illustrate both foreign and domestic challenges to the new administration. Cornell himself chose to shoot the White House, finding fresh perspectives in the Oval Office and catching Jackie as she pushed John-John's carriage through the grounds. Simon and Schuster lined up name writers. The photography went relatively well, but we were all too aware that the success of our book would depend a lot on the success of Kennedy's first hundred days. On April 21, day 92, I took the 7:00 A.M. shuttle with Cornell to report to Salinger. I fastened my seat belt and took a look at *The New York Times.* A five-column headline read: KENNEDY SAYS U.S. WON'T ALLOW COMMUNISM TO TAKE OVER CUBA; DOES NOT BAR UNILATERAL MOVE. It gave me a sinking feeling. Cuban exiles had landed at the Bay of Pigs four days before. Most Americans were surprised; not Fidel Castro. At the White House the mood was grim. I had prepared a little joke for Salinger, which I now gave him hesitantly. Elliott Erwitt had been commissioned by the office of New York governor Nelson Rockefeller, who had his eye on the next presidential election, to make some pictures of the governor as a man of the people. In one such exercise, Rockefeller managed to corral a small crowd of the curious on a sidewalk near his Albany office. In looking at Elliott's contact sheet, I noticed that he had photographed the scene not once but three times. In the first frame there was a little black dog to one side, looking up toward Rockefeller, who was busily working the crowd. In the second frame, the dog was strolling toward a tree. In the third, he was lifting his leg. I handed Salinger the three pictures in sequence, saying, "Here's a contribution to the 1964 reelection campaign." He roared with delight, jumped out of his chair, and took off. Several minutes later he returned, saying, "The boss hasn't had such a good laugh since we came here." On this day the White House realized that the landing at the Bay of Pigs was a total failure. John Kennedy's first hundred days—later we learned that he abhorred that concept from the beginning—had turned into a disaster. Our Magnum book did somewhat better, selling more than 100,000 copies.

Unlike most of the press, Magnum had tried hard to bring the CIA-backed Cuban exile force to public attention. In 1959 we had begun distributing the work of Andrew St. George, a Hungarian-born American who had served in U.S. Army Intelligence in World War II and spoke good Spanish. A commuter from Dobbs Ferry with a wife and child, he appeared to be anything but a revolutionary. Nevertheless, he managed to join Fidel Castro's invasion in the Sierra Maestra in 1959, and his jeep followed Castro's Cadillac all the way to

These pictures may have provided President Kennedy with his only laugh during the Bay of Pigs crisis. Elliott Erwitt took this sequence at one of Nelson Rockefeller's stump speeches in Albany, New York—a warmup for a presidential run he was planning in 1964. I noted the dog's reaction to Rockefeller's oratory and had prints made for my visit to Kennedy's press secretary, Pierre Salinger, who jumped at the chance to lighten his boss's dark mood. It worked. © ELLIOTT ERWITT/*Magnum Photos*

Havana. St. George's pictures were published in *Look* and then *Life.* Thereafter he scored one scoop after another in Latin America.

On October 28, 1960, ten days before Kennedy's election, I had cabled Magnum's Paris office, explaining the story being sent to them:

CUBAN REBELS EXSTGEORGE. SIGNIFICANT POINT OF STORY THAT AN INVASION OF CUBA IS ACTUALLY BEING PREPARED BY ANTICASTRO GROUPS. LATIN VOLUNTEERS—YANKEE ADVENTURERS, SPIES, ARMS SMUGGLERS, DISREPUTABLE BOATMEN, VETERAN REVOLUTIONARIES OF EVERY HUE SWARM THROUGH MIAMI BY HUNDREDS. OUR TAKES FOUR AND FIVE SHOW A TYPICAL SEMICLANDESTINE RECRUITMENT CENTER IN MIAMI WITH HALFNAKED RECRUITS LOUNGING AMONG MATTRESSES ALSO GROUP OF INVASION OFFICERS, VETERANS OF FOUR DIFFERENT LATAM ARMIES ATTENDING BLACKBOARD BRIEFING ETC. . . . ALSO EXCLUSIVE SHOTS OF U.S. AND CUBAN SUICIDE VOLUNTEERS PREPARING TO SPEARHEAD INVASION. . . . THIS REMAINS EXCLUSIVE DESPITE PRESS ASSOCIATION ATTEMPTS OBTAIN STORY AND HAS UTMOST POLITICAL SIGNIFICANCE.

We got almost nowhere in placing this and subsequent similar stories. In American journalism, I was beginning to learn that it often doesn't pay to be "too far out in front." Realizing this, I showed the pictures to John Radosta, then picture editor of *The New York Times.* I asked no special price. If the *Times* would only publish it, others would follow. Radosta didn't let me into the newsroom, receiving me in a third-floor cubbyhole, but it was obvious that he at least consulted the Foreign Desk. In twenty minutes he came back with a curt answer: "Our people know all about this. We're watching it."

The *Times* was indeed watching. Tad Szulc, covering the Caribbean for the *Times* out of Miami, was one of the few correspondents who knew as much as St. George. On April 6, 1961, he filed a two-column story saying that the invasion of Cuba was "imminent." The *Times* buried the story following top-level discussions—the final decision was made by publisher Orvil Dryfoos after consulting Washington bureau chief James Reston, who was under pressure from the White House.

It would take five years for the *Times* to confess this particular sin. In a speech in Minneapolis in 1966, managing editor Clifton Daniel publicly regretted the *Times*'s decision. Even John Kennedy had come to regret it. The story of Daniel's 4,000-word speech was reprinted under the headline KENNEDY LATER WISHED *TIMES* HAD PRINTED ALL IT KNEW. Magnum could have provided the pictures.

These rubber stamps, with some of the most famous names in photography, bear witness to the durability of Magnum Photos, which celebrated its fifieth anniversary in 1997. © ALEX WEBB/*Magnum Photos*

22

Departure

I n 1990, the duke of Edinburgh was given a private preview of Magnum's "40th Anniversary" exhibition a few hours before it opened at London's Hayward Gallery. His guides were Henri Cartier-Bresson and Burt Glinn, then Magnum's chairman and president. As he left, Prince Philip turned to Glinn for an explanation of how an organization of such diverse individuals managed itself. Burt flippantly replied that nobody really knew. Whereupon Prince Philip said, "It sounds to me like a perambulating disaster."

He was not far off. The miracle is that Magnum has outlasted most of its major clients. The weekly *Life* expired in 1972 after thirty-six years; *Look, Collier's,* and *The Saturday Evening Post* were already gone. These were the big four of the "golden age" of American magazine publishing, devoted to the mass audience advertisers love. But advertisers, like lovers, are fickle. They deserted the mass magazines for television, which delivered an audience of astounding numbers. First to go were the two magazines best known for fiction and articles, *Collier's* and the *Post.* The photojournalism of *Life* and *Look* had hurt them both. In the fifties at *Collier's,* and in the sixties at *The Saturday Evening Post,* new editorial regimes tried valiantly to don the cloak of photojournalism. We at Magnum began to profit from the change, but it was too late. I recall being invited to the *Collier's* office on Fifth Avenue for a drink on the magazine's last day, shortly before Christmas 1956. The holiday season is always crucial in publishing. It's either make (there were Christmas bonuses at Time Inc.) or break—*Life* would fold just in time for Christmas 1972. Gardner "Mike" Cowles had folded *Look* a year earlier.

On the night of March 18, 1960, a party was held in the office of *Life*'s managing editor, Ed Thompson, to mark the move from the "old" Time & Life Building on Rockefeller Plaza to the present one, the forty-eight-story structure opposite Radio City Music Hall. The party was memorable even by Thompson's standards. His big oak layout tables were covered with confetti and bottles; someone had carved EISIE in one of the cork bulletin boards for no particular reason; and in the deputy managing editor's office someone had grease-penciled "Burt Glinn is the Cornell Capa of *Popular Photography* and John Morris is the Willy Loman of Magnum"—which made little sense except to the drunk who wrote it. Burt and I could have done without the attention. This party marked the end of an era. What few then knew was that *Life*, for the second year in a row, had lost money, thanks to the high cost of inflating its circulation amid falling ad revenues. The next year, Harry Luce, taking what I regard as bad advice, decided to change managing editors. Thompson was out, or rather kicked upstairs. George Hunt, his successor, asked me to lunch, confiding to me that he was firing picture editor Ray Mackland. But instead of asking *me* to take over, he asked my opinion of Dick Pollard. I recommended him, feeling like John Alden touting Miles Standish for the hand of Priscilla Mullens.

In England, too, the traditional picture magazines failed and floundered—*Picture Post, Illustrated, Illustrated London News.* On the Continent, picture magazines fared somewhat better, but only because it took longer for television news to catch on, costs were lower, and Europeans were more habituated to reading than watching. Magnum was founded at a time when those great picture magazines were alive and well. They provided the springboard for Magnum's plunge into covering the world in pictures.

How did Magnum survive when they foundered? First of all, Magnum had an esprit that is the very essence of photojournalism. It began with Robert Capa. Burt Glinn once said, "Capa reflected a lifestyle editors aspired to." No argument. It was manifest in Capa's understated courage—he gambled his life and treasure as fearlessly in Rockefeller Center as he had in Normandy. Capa's style rubbed off, for better and sometimes for worse, on many of us in Magnum. At the weekly *Life*, to me the greatest of all picture magazines, this was implicitly acknowledged by the fellowship accorded to Magnum people on all levels. The Magnum spirit—the French call it "*mystique*"—also affected other magazines. Eve Arnold and Burt Glinn were favorites at *Esquire,* Brian Brake at *National Geographic. Holiday,* under the leadership of editor Ted Patrick, art director Frank Zachary, and picture editor Louis Mercier, often turned over entire issues to Magnum to illustrate. Henri Cartier-Bresson, Elliott Erwitt, and Burt Glinn were their favorites.

The highly competitive fashion magazines were a special case, since no Magnum photographers were known for fashion. Carmel Snow, editor of *Harper's Bazaar,* had a high regard for Cartier-Bresson, and this was echoed by her celebrated art director, Alexey Brodovitch. Once they tried Henri on a fashion assignment. Once was enough. Henri is almost incapable of posing a picture. Alexander Liberman, the art director of Condé Nast magazines, had known the work of Capa, Cartier, and Chim ever since he had edited *Vu* in prewar Paris, but he did not play pictures of the real world as Snow and Brodovitch did.

A Magnum photographer had the right to refuse any assignment offered to him. I didn't dispute this, but it didn't make my life any easier. I was the buffer between the magazines and the photographers and often caught in the middle. I thought we had an obligation to cover the news, not just make pleasing pictures. I admired Cartier-Bresson for refusing to let his pictures of Russia, China, and Poland be used as propaganda in the Cold War. Henri would rubber-stamp his prints: THIS PHOTOGRAPH CAN BE REPRODUCED ONLY WITH THE ACCOMPANYING CAPTION OR WITH TEXT STRICTLY IN THE SPIRIT OF ITS CAPTION. He was also known for insisting that his pictures not be cropped—he always shot the full 35-millimeter frame—but he relaxed this requirement if it interfered with good layout.

Fortunately, there was usually a Magnum photographer who would respond to the journalistic challenge at hand. When President Eisenhower sent troops to Little Rock to enforce school desegregation in 1957, Burt Glinn volunteered, at a time when *Life*'s reporters were being beaten up. In 1961, when freedom riders were attacked in Montgomery, Alabama, I persuaded Magnum's Bruce Davidson to fly there with me—I thought he needed company. When we arrived the city was under curfew, enforced by National Guardsmen with live ammunition. I had to leave on the third day. Davidson stayed on, riding the bus to Jackson and making a classic photo of a Guardsman sitting behind a young black girl, his bayoneted rifle separating them. That bus was shot at three times. Bruce had joined us in 1957, becoming a member two years later. He had a way of stalking his subjects, moving like a cat, that produced wonderful results.

My biggest challenge was to find support for a group news project. In 1957, five Magnum photographers, in response to European demand, jointly covered the visit of Queen Elizabeth and her consort, Philip, to the United States. We processed, edited, and shipped the story on a daily basis during the entire week. I hired Lee Jones, the tall and stately picture editor who had just quit her job at *This Week*, to assist. On the queen's final day in New York, Cornell Capa sailed with her past the Statue of Liberty; Ernst Haas, mounted on a weapons carrier, rode with her parade up Broadway. Burt Glinn shot down from 1 Wall Street, and Gene Smith worked the street, capturing the Sanitation Department's sweepers in formation. Dennis Stock awaited her at City Hall. The photographers then leapfrogged to get her at the Waldorf-Astoria Hotel, the United Nations, the Empire State Building, Rockefeller Center (with Haas secreted in a beauty salon), back to a Waldorf banquet, then to Idlewild Airport. Great fun.

This exercise in news coverage, perhaps the most elaborate in Magnum's history with the exception of Nikita Khrushchev's visit two years later, is scarcely mentioned in Magnum's own chronicles. It was an *editors'* tour de force, perhaps more satisfying to Lee Jones and me, and to Michel Chevalier, who had just become our Paris bureau chief, than to the photographers.

Khrushchev's 1959 visit to America was a severe test of Magnum as a news organization. In this case seven photographers were accredited for various parts of the eight-day transcontinental tour, and five others participated. We distributed sixty pictures. The expenses were heavy, but the project eventually made a little money. Cartier-Bresson, our in-house critic, was far from satisfied, writing, "I looked carefully at all the pictures. . . . Let me tell you my opinion: under-editing, as far as quality and story is concerned; half of the pictures would have been quite enough." Henri was right, *and* he was wrong. No doubt he recalled his own assignment for *Ce Soir* to cover the coronation of King George VI in 1936, when he had made three memorable pictures, all showing the crowds in Trafalgar Square. Someone else had had to shoot the king. Burt

One of Magnum's most ambitious news projects was coverage of Nikita Khrushchev's 1959 visit to the United States. Henri Cartier-Bresson, our in-house critic, thought the pictures lacked "depth," but this one of the Soviet leader regarding the Lincoln Memorial is especially memorable.
© BURT GLINN/*Magnum Photos*

Glinn made a Khrushchev picture just as memorable: Nikita photographed from behind, gazing upon the statue of Abraham Lincoln at the Lincoln Memorial in Washington. *Life* used it—turned on its side—across two full pages. It somehow made hollow Khrushchev's boast "We will bury you."

I took great satisfaction in the fact that Magnum was truly international. At a time, for example, when Americans were forbidden to travel to Communist China, Magnum had two photographers there at one time: Frenchman Marc Riboud and New Zealander Brian Brake. Our Jewish members were somewhat privileged in Israel, our Aryans in Arab countries (Magnum later acquired an Iranian, Abbas, and currently has members of a dozen nationalities). Only once, in my eight years with Magnum, did we have a serious internal conflict rooted in national differences. It arose in 1957, when a story by our Dutch member Kryn Taconis was suppressed by the Paris office. Kryn never had it easy in Magnum. In the summer of 1957, he decided to gamble his life and his fortune, such as it was, on a "big one." In Cairo he contacted agents of the Algerian Front de Libération National and arranged to spend two weeks on patrol inside Algeria with rebels of the Front's First Battalion. The FLN's guerrillas were then pinning down half a million French soldiers. From a French standpoint, any contact with the rebels was tantamount to collusion. The French press was largely subservient. There was no official censorship, but "sensitive" stories were cleared with the Ministry of Defense and ways were found to crack down on "dissident" journalists—taxes, for instance, might suddenly become a problem.

Kryn gave us scant warning of his intentions, but we realized that Magnum's Paris office should have little if anything to do with the story. On Monday, September 2, I got word that Kryn had returned from Algeria and was back in Amsterdam. I met him there that night. Together we edited his contact sheets, selecting thirty-four prints. The story was disappointing. There was no action. But it did show the rebels as human beings, not as the "terrorists" pictured by the French. My plan was to hand-carry the story to Paris, where I would decide on a method of attribution and distribution. But Tuesday afternoon Cartier-Bresson called to warn me *not* to bring prints with me. I did arrange for Imre Rona of ABC Press, Magnum's Hungarian-born Dutch agent, to mail a set of prints to the Paris *Life* office. Henri met me at Le Bourget on Wednesday; we picked up Trudy Feliu and went straight into conference with Jean Riboud. We took the precaution of talking outdoors. We considered offering the story as the work of "a Dutch journalist." On Sunday, we decided to proceed with European distribution from Amsterdam. In Germany, *Stern* passed but the picture weekly *Quick* bought, the only major sale. There were sales in Holland and Norway; some interest was shown by *Epoca* in Milan. On Monday I lunched with Jean Riboud in Paris and told him it was hard to sell such a story anonymously. He said he felt such a decision should be the photographer's, at *his* own risk. We discussed this with Henri, and it was my impression that he agreed. I went on to Zurich to attend the opening of a Bischof exhibition. That night, I found a message at my hotel: Henri had called from Paris, demanding that the story be entirely withdrawn and all sales canceled. I rushed back to Paris. It developed that Michel Chevalier, on the job only three days, had finally seen the actual story—the prints I had been forbidden to hand-carry. He felt the story was too innocuous to be worth the risk to the Paris office.

I should have resigned then and there. If it stood for anything, Magnum stood for the free expression of its members. An innocuous story should present even less of a threat than a powerful one, I argued. But the French members of Magnum were now unanimous. I insisted that only Kryn could withdraw the story. He was summoned to Paris. Faced with the strong emotions of his French confreres, he submitted to the kill with a claim for compensation, later settled at $2,500.

The main reason Magnum survived even though the picture magazines did not was that by the mid-fifties, first in New York, then in Paris, Magnum had many clients for "corporate" work and a few for all-out advertising. The more enlightened companies gave us loose guidelines. Schlumberger, for example, simply wanted documentation of its international operations for its house organs. The editorial requirements of Standard Oil's slick magazine *The Lamp*, which gave major assignments to Bischof, Rodger, Cartier-Bresson, and others, seemed no different from those of *Fortune*. In retrospect, however, it can be seen that in the postwar period the big oil and auto companies changed the face of America, corrupting city councils, state legislatures, and Congress to publicly subsidize highways, ripping cities asunder, and violating virgin lands. Some of the damage has been repaired, but America's railroads, whose lobby was impotent and which also faced indirect public subsidy for the airlines, are probably ruined forever. Magnum played its modest part in this, as did Roy Stryker's Standard Oil photographers.

Relations between Magnum and the motion picture industry, although personal and complex, were the most fruitful of all. Capa literally gambled his way into the business, beginning with John Huston's *Moulin Rouge* in 1952; Huston employed Magnum photographers ever after. Chim's Old World sophistication appealed to director Anatole Litvak (*Act of Love*) and producer Mike Todd (*Around the World in Eighty Days*). Ernst Haas appealed not only to directors such as Huston, Howard Hawks, and William Wyler but to their leading ladies as well.

In 1960, John Huston filmed *The Misfits*, a story based on Nevada's grisly traffic in wild horses, written by Arthur Miller and starring Clark Gable, Marilyn Monroe, and Montgomery Clift. Negotiations were handled by Lee Jones. An expert judge of pictures and people, Lee knew and got exactly what she wanted, despite the fact that everyone who talked to her felt that Lee fully agreed with him, or her. She made a deal with *The Misfits*' producers for Magnum photographers to cover the production exclusively. No fewer than six did, at various times. Monroe, as usual, demanded the right to approve the photos to be released. This did not sit well with Cartier-Bresson. I consoled him, saying, "Let's face it, you have encountered one of the century's most formidable women, a character cast from Zola; in her little way she has had you too!"

Cornell Capa was the Magnum photographer who best understood the necessity for building a truly professional organization, both in New York and abroad. His election in 1957 as acting president after Chim's death marked a turning point: the news even made *The New York Times*'s financial pages. We also appeared as guests, as a group, on NBC's morning *Home Show*, emceed by Arlene Francis. The studio provided a trapeze for Henri to sit on, swinging above the rest of us. It was his theory that this would make him less conspicuous!

My position in Magnum had been strengthened by the Kennedy/Thayer coup, but Magnum and I were getting weary of each other. It had now been eight years. Things came to a head at the 1961 members' meetings in August, perhaps the most passionate in Magnum's emotional history. At an angry session in Cornell's apartment on Fifth Avenue, the members voted, as I stepped out of the room, that I could be removed by the executive committee at any time. Afterward, I walked silently up Fifth Avenue with Henri, from the Capas' apartment at Thirty-first Street to the Magnum office on Forty-seventh Street, refusing to speak to him, although my anger was not directed at him personally. Magnum and I formally parted in January 1962. Elliott Erwitt, now president, began his report to members and staff as follows: "This year let us look at Magnum rationally and intelligently. Let us make no mistake about that mystical Magnum which we usually hear about from others and sometimes talk ourselves into believing and sometimes wish existed. That Magnum is dead." I felt somewhat differently. My final report to Magnum only hinted at what I had learned in the fifteen years since that first magnum of champagne at the Vandiverts'. It concluded, "The events of last August were enough to break my heart. Fortunately the wounds have healed—I understand you better than you understand me. . . . It has been a fantastic fifteen years together."

The Washington Post welcomed innovation, and for my brief tour there as graphics editor I made the most of it, running horses in color along the top of the front page, for example, and experimenting with picture selection, size, and placement. My greatest coup, however, was arming the staff photographers with unlimited rolls of film and new cameras. HORSES: JACK ROTTIER/*The Washington Post*

23

To the *Post*

year before my departure from Magnum, I had attended the annual convention in Washington, D.C., of the American Society of Newspaper Editors. I was selling for Magnum. Salesmen, except for a handful from the most powerful syndicates, were not welcome at such meetings, but many editors were curious about Magnum. Their warm response to our coverage of the Kennedy administration's first hundred days encouraged us to launch, in June 1961, the Magnum News Service, a monthly packet of pictures and picture stories for newspapers. When I left Magnum a year later, it became a joint venture between me and Magnum. I did the editing and selling; Magnum and I were to share the profits. I was naïve enough to think there would be some. I soon learned the hard facts of daily newspaper life. Most papers thought in terms of picture quantity, not quality. And speed: it was the first picture, not the best, that got used. After eight months the Magnum News Service boasted "twenty-four subscriber newspapers with a circulation of eight million in North America, and distribution to twelve foreign countries." What I didn't reveal was that the clients were getting the service for as little as fifty dollars a month apiece.

I was determined to find a way to syndicate pictures profitably. The idea for an "Independent Picture Service" came to me in the shower one morning in April 1963. IPS would offer pictures by means of a regular publication, a kind of "contact sheet," selected from the work of *all* freelance photographers, not just Magnum's, from which editors could order the pictures they wanted. It could be printed and mailed at low cost. Small papers could pay as little as five dollars for each picture ordered. Wouldn't that be the way to broaden the market? The first four-page "IPS Contact Sheet" went out on June 24. Postcard orders, for a seven-picture story on "New York's Red School House" and eleven singles, totaled only $405. Subsequent issues pulled little better. Failing to successfully syndicate picture stories with brief text, I turned to the syndication of text pieces illustrated by pictures, the more conventional system. One of these was by a young Swedish journalist named Leo Lönnbrink. He had bet his fellow journalists in Göteborg that he could freelance his way around the world, starting with $200 in cash, a rucksack, and no credit cards. He was subsequently jailed in Angola, kicked out of Katanga (now Shaba, Congo) for trying to investigate the death of U.N. Secretary General Dag Hammarskjold, and expelled from Rhodesia. He somehow got to India and, hitchhiking across Burma, Thailand, Laos, and Cambodia, reached Vietnam. Lönnbrink flew with an American Special Forces unit to the "strategic hamlet" of Long Fu. With his camera under his shirt, he photographed South Vietnamese secret police interrogating two Vietcong suspects. I headlined the story "Torture in the Name of Freedom." Only a handful of U.S. newspapers, among them the *New York Herald Tribune*, cautiously published the story. An assistant managing editor of *The Washington Post* bought the story but then asked to "renege," saying that "the photographs are a little too risky for us to use. I hope you understand our position." I didn't and could barely contain my scorn.

On several occasions I did make page one. In November 1963, Magnum's Marc Riboud introduced me to French journalist Jean Daniel, then foreign editor of *L'Express*. They were headed for Washington and Havana. The next day Daniel interviewed President Kennedy, who talked at length about Cuba and told Daniel he wished to see him upon his return from Havana. The president wanted to avoid another communications vacuum such as the one that had occurred during the Cuban missile crisis.

On November 19, Castro came to Daniel's Havana hotel room at 10:00 P.M. They talked until four in the morning—so long that Castro's bodyguard is seen sound asleep in Marc Riboud's photograph of the scene. Castro said to Daniel, "I think that Kennedy is sincere. . . . But I believe that a President of the United States is never truly free." Two days later, November 22, Castro invited Daniel and Riboud to lunch at his home at Varadero Beach. About 1:30, the telephone rang. Cuban president Osvaldo Dorticos was calling to tell Castro that President Kennedy had been shot. At that moment it was unclear whether he would survive. Two hours later came the news of Kennedy's death. Castro said, "Everything is changed. Everything is going to change. . . . Kennedy was an enemy to whom one had become adjusted. This is a very serious matter, very serious." Jean Daniel's story, with Riboud's pictures, made front pages in New York, Chicago, Miami, San Francisco, and many other cities, grossing almost $2,000. *The Washington Post* bought it but buried it inside.

A Vietnamese peasant accused of spying for the Viet Cong is strung up by his wrists and interrogated by a member of the South Vietnamese secret police. This picture was one of a number of serious news photographs distributed through the short-lived Independent Picture Service and its weekly newsletter *IPS Contact Sheet.* © LEO LÖNNBRINK

There were more exclusives. On January 27, 1964, Edgar Snow, my old friend from the Jack Goodman group of the anti-McCarthy days, cabled from Paris to offer an exclusive "fivehour newspacked interview" with Chou En-lai. In ten more cables I worked out a deal for IPS distribution. Snow and the Chinese premier had a long history together. Chou En-lai was the first important Chinese Communist Edgar Snow had encountered when he crossed the Red lines in 1936, carrying a letter of introduction to Mao Tse-tung written in invisible ink. Chou was then in command of an east front Red Army in a tiny "cave village" north of Yenan. Chou greeted Snow in English: "I am in command here. My name is Chou En-lai. . . . It does not matter to us that you are not a Communist. You can write about anything you see." Snow met Mao three days later. His was one of the great scoops of the twentieth century, still as readable as ever in 1937's *Red Star over China*. Snow's 1964 interview with Chou, at the Chinese embassy in Conakry, Guinea, made the front page of *The New York Times* and *The Washington Post*, but his evenhanded report was too tame for most newspapers. In March, I sent Snow a check for his share of the profits: $587.50. This was no way to make money.

I decided to take one more gamble. On January 27, 1964, I announced "AN IPS EXTRA—The Exclusive Account in the Words of the Man Who Killed Lee Harvey Oswald: MY STORY by Jack Ruby with William Read Woodfield." Ruby's account came to me via Lawrence Schiller, a former *Life* and *Saturday Evening Post* photographer. Schiller has since hustled his way to media success as a packager of various hot book deals, notably with Norman Mailer and most notoriously on both sides of the O. J. Simpson case in *I Want to Tell You* "by" O. J. Simpson, and his own exposé of the defense, *American Tragedy*. The Ruby package sold to seventeen newspapers, grossing about $8,000. Despite the story's credibility, however, I had nagging doubts as to whether I had done the right thing to circulate such a self-serving document just before the Ruby trial. It was time to take stock. On March 16, we mailed a candid "Note to Editors: Here's the latest issue of *IPS Contact Sheet*. It could also be one of the last. We find ourselves in the position of a Broadway play which opened to good notices, but has not fully caught on at the box office." That "Contact Sheet," number 27, was indeed the last.

In April 1964, I again attended the convention of the American Society of Newspaper Editors. At the final party, hosted by the *Los Angeles Times* in Washington, D.C., I was confronted by two friends from *The Washington Post*. It was not by accident. Editor Russell Wiggins and managing editor Alfred Friendly took me aside: "We hear things aren't going so well. Would you like to come to work for us?" And so I found myself assistant managing editor (graphics) of *The Washington Post*. Friendly offered me $20,000 a year, roughly twice the salary of his reporters, and although it was no more than I had finally earned at Magnum and at my bankrupt IPS, I gladly accepted. My position was an entirely new one at the *Post*—and for that matter at any American newspaper of that time. My assignment was nothing less than to improve the look and visual content of the paper. I was to supervise the so-called picture desk (then consisting of a single picture editor whose job was primarily to caption the pictures selected for him by the news editors), the Art Department (whose three "artists" spent their time retouching photos, doing charts, and making up the daily weather map), and the sixteen staff photographers, including one "inside man" and their boss, chief photographer Hugh Miller. "I don't know what you're going to do about Hugh," Friendly confided to me. "He's kind of an institution." Miller had worked for the *Post* seemingly forever. He had begun in the 1920s as a shooter in the school of flash powder and chewed cigars. As manager of the *Post* photo staff, he was a legendary tightwad, barking out an assignment: "Fire at Thirteenth and F. Here's a roll." Miller rated assignments by the number of rolls of film they might require. He purchased film in hundred-foot reels. Photographers were required to save their used cartridges so that the "inside man" could reload them. Thus the photographers never knew how many frames they could count on, and many times the end frames were fogged. Nor did Miller believe in spoiling his men by buying them the latest "gadgets." Those who freelanced on the side surmounted this by buying their own equipment, but the others made do with what they were given. I discovered that Charles Del Vecchio, a former president of the White House News Photographers Association, was shooting with just one old camera body and one lens—and not through choice, like Cartier-Bresson, whose personal style required only one Leica and a 50-millimeter lens. Del Vecchio hated Miller to the point where he refused to "ask for any favors," such as a new camera. The three-man Art Department used equally obsolete methods, systematically retouching photos until they were almost unrecognizable in the paper.

On my first day, Monday, June 1, 1964, Al Friendly introduced me to deputy managing editor Ben Gilbert and asked him to break me in. Gilbert was the ultimate Washington insider and relished the petty politics of a metropolitan area that included portions of Maryland and Virginia in addition to the then disenfranchised District of Columbia. The area was beginning to take its name from the Beltway, the interstate highway that circled the capital. Unlike *The New York Times*, the *Post* drew readers of all classes. Fifth of the five Washington dailies when banker Eugene Meyer had bought it at auction in 1933, it was now first of the three survivors. The afternoon Scripps-Howard tabloid *Daily News* was about to expire. Only the Noyes family's *Evening Star* and *Sunday Star* continued to fight hard for readers and advertisers. When the *Star* bought color presses for its brand-new plant in Southeast Washington, the *Post* felt it had to do likewise.

Few other major American newspapers were then using ROP color (run of paper, as opposed to a magazine section), and in no other city were there two competitive papers doing so regularly. Ben Gilbert told me I must be ready with color for page one every Thursday (the food advertisers' day) and Sunday, and any other day that color advertising would support the cost of the special inks. On Sunday mornings, when the *Star* and *Post* went "head to head," we were directly competitive.

The *Post* permitted experimentation. I once persuaded Gilbert to run a shallow eight-column color picture of wild ponies romping by the sea *over* the *Post*'s page-one logotype. Another time we displayed, fourteen inches tall, a color picture of Communist China's first atomic bomb blast, copied from *China Pictorial*, the regime's English-language magazine. We also ran a color photo from the Bureau of Mines, showing the yellowish pollution caused by acidic runoff in a mountain stream. I was an attendee of the 3:30 news conference in Friendly's office, where space was allocated to the various news sections: City, National, Foreign. As I found later at *The New York Times*, pictures had no separate space budget. Representatives from Promotion and Circulation also attended these meetings in an effort to better guess how to sell the next day's paper—which might bear little resemblance to the one that had been discussed. Major news has a habit of occurring at awkward hours. I soon discovered the power of the night editor to turn a dream layout into a nightmare. A picture I had sent down for five columns might be reduced to a virtually unreadable three.

On Thursdays, I joined a handful of key editors along with cartoonist Herblock for a lunch with publisher Katharine Graham in her top-floor private dining room. In those days, Mrs. Graham was just beginning to establish what would become a major presence both at the *Post* and within the permanent Washington power structure, having just succeeded her late husband, Philip Graham, as head of the company. In 1946, Eugene Meyer had turned control of the *Post* over to his son-in-law, a brilliant young lawyer who had clerked for Supreme Court Justice Stanley Reed. Katharine devoted herself to raising their children. In the next seventeen years, Phil Graham labored to turn the Washington Post Company into one of the great success stories of American publishing. In 1948, he bought control of radio station WTOP, the CBS Washington affiliate, and a succession of wily purchases followed, including that of *Newsweek* in 1961. But by this time Phil Graham was suffering from manic depression. On August 3, 1963, he killed himself after a long bout of mania. When I joined the *Post* in June 1964, Kay Graham had been its chief operating executive for only a matter of months. I could not be sure that she would remember me, but at the first Thursday luncheon she offered her hand cordially, saying, "Are you the *famous* John Morris?" We had been contemporaries at the University of Chicago, and she was kidding me about our contrasting roles there—I had been a highly visible (or very noisy) student editor, and she, one year behind me, had stuck to her studies. At the Thursday luncheons, however, I kept my mouth shut and listened. It was fascinating to hear the casual discussion of news and editorial policy. Kay modestly put forth her own views as questions: "Al, don't you think Rocky is gaining on Goldwater?" Under Phil Graham the *Post* had come to play a major political role behind the scenes. He was largely credited with persuading John Kennedy to accept Lyndon Johnson as his vice presidential running mate at the Democratic Convention in Los Angeles in 1960. The paper bore an obvious sympathy for the Johnson administration, and the editors were greatly concerned about the reporting of certain delicate issues, such as the time one of Johnson's aides was arrested for making advances in the men's room of the Washington YMCA. The *Post* was, of course, no less cautious in its reporting of Watergate ten years later—a fact that gets submerged in the larger truth that the *Post*'s reporting toppled the Nixon administration.

In some ways *The Washington Post* in 1964 was still a provincial newspaper. We had about two and a half foreign correspondents, and no domestic bureaus except for a token one in the *Newsweek* building in New York. David Halberstam attributed to a *Post* reporter the crack that the paper "will cover any international conference that there is, as long as it is in the first taxi zone." For both national and foreign picture news, we depended on AP and UPI. We rarely made picture assignments outside the Washington area, and the management was alarmed when I began purchasing an occasional Magnum or Black Star picture for twenty-five dollars each. Freelancers were offered ten dollars. There was only one full-time picture librarian in the "morgue," as newspapers call their reference libraries. I discovered to my dismay that the *Post* had not even been sending staff photographers to the White House, except on social occasions when the women's pages required coverage for the late editions. I was determined to change that.

My first and easiest task was to inspire the staff photographers. I became their hero almost overnight when I told Hugh Miller to buy film in boxes and to hand it out ten or twenty rolls at a time. He couldn't argue. The next move was to get the photographers properly equipped. We settled on a minimum of two camera bodies and four lenses per man, and I battled the requisition through the business office. Miller had been assigning photographers largely on the basis of rotation—next man up—with mixed results. I set out to find out what each man (there were no women) could do if challenged. My very first week, the City Desk came up with a story by the *Post*'s "gardening counselor" on the sad state of groundskeeping around the Capitol—not the likeliest subject for lively pictures. I told Miller I wanted to go out with the photographer. He gave me James McNamara, a veteran who was not known for prizewinning pictures. We walked the grounds together, soon finding an abundance of weeds through which to frame the Capitol dome, even a little poison ivy. I sold one picture for page one and three more for an inside layout. McNamara, with some personal attention, was a new man. Not only that, Congress appropriated an extra $75,000 for groundskeeping; the next year the *Post* expert found the outlook from Capitol Hill much improved.

I found that the staff was much better than it had been rated. Their common denominator was service in the military—seven had made sergeant. Their average age was forty-four. Only one was a college graduate, although several had attended college. That didn't bother me if they could feel and see pictures and possessed basic street smarts. We had two young stars, Dick Darcey and Wally McNamee, who could handle the toughest of news assignments. As our horizons expanded, we sent Darcey to Selma, Alabama, to cover a tense freedom march on the state capital. Governor George Wallace had refused to protect the marchers. President Johnson replied by federalizing the Alabama National Guard. Emboldened by the Selma junket, we sent McNamee, an ex-Marine, all the way to Vietnam—to my knowledge the first foreign assignment for a *Washington Post* photographer.

The Washington scene was congenial for photography. Two blocks from the *Post*, with the Russian embassy halfway between, *National Geographic* was beginning to compete with *Life* for the title of number one American photographic magazine. The two wire services, AP and UPI, each maintained large photo bureaus. The Washington bureaus of *Time, Newsweek,* and *The New York Times* had staff photographers, and the third news weekly, *U.S. News & World Report,* was headquartered on the edge of Georgetown. Skilled photographers and picture editors were working at the U.S. Information Agency and the White House, where Lyndon Johnson gave unrestricted access to photographer Yoichi Okamoto. Virtually all these resident photographers belonged to the White House News Photographers Association, then the nation's most powerful group of photojournalists. Their annual banquet, at cherry blossom time, attracted leaders of the photographic industry from around the country, and the list of honored guests usually began with the president of the United States. The WHNPA operated as a powerful clique, officially determining the distribution of photo passes for national political conventions as well as for inaugurations and other Washington events. Unofficially, it enforced the taboos of the times: for example, a photographer who had dared photograph the leg braces of Franklin Roosevelt would immediately have been expelled. The WHNPA represented the status quo, going along with the restrictions that had long been imposed on the picture press in the courts and Congrcss and by the executive branch of government. I had some ideas about changing all that. I was quickly voted into membership, but I could see it was going to be an uphill battle.

My big test was soon to come: covering the inauguration of Lyndon Johnson on January 20, 1965. He had been elected in a landslide, and the country was in a mood for celebration, fourteen months after the assassination of John F.

Kennedy. The *Post* decided to go all out, and I was put in charge of the inaugural pages, along with copy editor Morris Rosenberg. First we had to produce a twenty-page special section on Inauguration Day, labeled "The Great Society," after Johnson's campaign theme. For a scene-setter in the main news section, I sent staff photographer Darcey up in a helicopter to photograph the city covered in snow. He persuaded his pilot to fly into the forbidden zone. The resulting scene, stretching from the reviewing stand on Pennsylvania Avenue, past the White House and the Ellipse and far beyond to Washington National Airport, came out pale blue in the light of dawn, as the streetlights flickered yellow. The color was so subtle that I had a hard time selling it to Ben Gilbert, but after I told him that "it will look just like Wedgwood china," he finally authorized a huge cut, five columns by fourteen inches. The next morning, Ben Gilbert presented me with a Wedgwood ashtray, compliments of his wife. "When my wife opened the paper this morning," Ben explained, "she shouted, 'Ben, it's just like Wedgwood!' "

Ben Bradlee and Katharine Graham did not laugh when they realized the implications of my abrupt dismissal from *The Washington Post* in August 1965, thanks to office politics: I wound up with a comparable position at their competitor, *The New York Times*. I love this happy picture of the two of them. *Courtesy*, The Washington Post

Jobless at Forty-nine

Two months into my job at the *Post* the Pentagon reported that an American destroyer, the *Maddox*, had been fired upon by North Vietnamese patrol boats in the Tonkin Gulf on Sunday, August 2, 1964. In the twenty-minute skirmish, with no American casualties, a retaliatory air strike from the carrier *Ticonderoga* had sunk one of the North Vietnamese boats and damaged the others. Our task, with the information available, was to ensure that the *Post*'s front page would look as boldly historic as that of our only acknowledged rival, *The New York Times*. There was precious little to work with to illustrate Sunday's big "attack"—just the crude maps and file pictures of the ships and their commanders released by the Pentagon. This was an act of provocation welcomed by some members of Lyndon Johnson's administration. Hawkish U.S. experts, in both the White House and the Pentagon, saw little hope for victory by South Vietnam without direct U.S. intervention, primarily through the use of airpower. They proposed to "punish North Vietnam" by blockading Haiphong harbor and bombing ninety-four specific "military objectives." This amounted to an act of war and would require a supporting resolution from Congress. One was duly drafted in late May 1964, but it was withheld for fear of congressional opposition.

There were no correspondents with the *Maddox* and *Ticonderoga* forces—or with the other side, for that matter—and *The Washington Post*, like the rest of the press, was content to present the story as the White House and Pentagon told it, gross exaggerations and omissions intact. The public was quite unaware of what had secretly been taking place behind the scenes. By 1964, there were fifteen thousand American "advisers" in Vietnam, but the Pentagon sought no publicity for them—especially for the fact that they were fighting, and occasionally dying, alongside their Vietnamese trainees. The first pictures of American *combatants* in Vietnam were taken by the gutsy American freelancer Dickey Chapelle and published in *National Geographic*, of all places, in November 1962. She later died on one of the first all-American patrols in Vietnam, when the Marine in front of her triggered a booby trap. Dickey was the first American woman reporter ever killed in action. I tried, with little success, to distribute Dickey's pictures through IPS, just as I syndicated the story by Leo Lönnbrink, in which (unseen) Americans stood by while their Vietnamese "colleagues" performed the torture.

By 1964, CIA-trained South Vietnamese commandos were repeatedly raiding the North—just as those from the North were raiding the South. The U.S. Navy was conducting electronic surveillance of North Vietnam, code-named "DeSoto" patrols, from within "international waters"—as defined by the United States. On August 2, the destroyer *Maddox* was on such an operation. Two high-speed patrol boats manned by South Vietnamese commandos were nearby, returning from a raid on an island near Vinh, one of North Vietnam's busiest ports. Thus the "attack" on the *Maddox* could easily have been considered defensive from North Vietnam's viewpoint.

From no standpoint was I proud of the *Post*'s performance during that crucial week. We began on Monday, August 3, with this front page:

Despite a plea for instant retaliation from General Maxwell Taylor, who had recently replaced Henry Cabot Lodge as American ambassador in Saigon, the administration's response on Monday was confined to sending the destroyer *Turner Joy* and the carrier *Constellation* to the scene. Not surprisingly, there were no live pictures. On Tuesday, we diverted our readers with a striking but totally irrelevant picture of a new exhibit at the Smithsonian:

On Tuesday, August 4, the Pentagon's hawks were rewarded with news of a second "attack" on the *Maddox*. History has since shown that nothing much really happened, since there was no damage and there were no casualties. In fact, six hours after the first report, the ship's commander radioed, "Review of action makes many reported contacts and torpedoes fired appear doubtful. Freak weather effects on radar and overeager sonarmen may have accounted for many reports. No actual visual sightings by Maddox. Suggest complete evaluation before any further action taken." But the president had already been overheard to say, presumably to Secretary of Defense Robert McNamara, "I not only want those patrol boats that attacked the *Maddox* destroyed, I want everything in that harbor destroyed; I want the whole works destroyed. I want to give them a real dose." He summoned the National Security Council at 6:15 P.M., congressional leaders at 6:45 P.M. He told them he would submit a resolution requesting congressional "support for U.S. combat operations in Southeast Asia should they prove necessary." At 7:22 P.M., the carrier *Ticonderoga* received authorization to bomb two bases for North Vietnamese patrol boats and a supporting oil depot. A second carrier, the *Constellation*, got its orders a few minutes later. Planes were heading toward their targets even as President Johnson spoke to the nation shortly before midnight. For Wednesday's paper there was plenty of action to report but still no pictures.

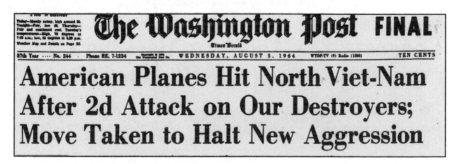

By Thursday the "conflict," which was in actuality one-sided, completely dominated the paper. In New York, Ambassador Adlai Stevenson explained our action to the United Nations. In Washington, Secretary of Defense McNamara briefed the press. The most significant picture taken Wednesday was by Yoichi Okamoto, the White House photographer. It showed the president twisting the arm of Senator William Fulbright, chairman of the Senate Foreign Relations Committee—but it was held back by the White House press office. The *Post* editorialized, "President Johnson has earned the gratitude of the free world." Columnist Walter Lippmann cautiously went along. The District of Columbia's National Guardsmen went off on summer maneuvers, the *Post* reported, "with their sense of purpose renewed." A crude map ran on page one:

The *Post*'s banner on Friday virtually gave Congress an ultimatum:

On Saturday morning, the *Post* triumphantly recorded the almost unanimous vote of confidence as both Senate and House passed the "Tonkin Gulf resolution," which served as a blank check for further military action. Only two senators, Ernest Gruening of Alaska and Wayne Morse of Oregon, opposed; the House's one "nay" was cast by Congressman Adam Clayton Powell of Harlem. Since photographers were then prohibited from photographing congressional debates, the *Post* settled for an unconsciously ironic photograph of twin monkeys on page one. I offered it to the editors with a straight face:

By Sunday morning's paper, things were back to "normal," as the president returned to his ranch in Texas and attention focused on another war—this time a real one. In contrast to the Tonkin Gulf, the wire services covered this incident with live pictures from the start.

Turkish Jets Hit Cyprus As Greeks Take Towns

Interestingly, *The New York Times* played the news of that week quite differently. News of the original Sunday incident appeared as a normal lead story, in one column, with an adjacent map and photo of a Navy press conference. Only on Wednesday, August 5, the day that has since been adopted as the official starting date of the Vietnam War, did the story take over page one, with the banner U.S. PLANES ATTACK NORTH VIETNAM BASES. On Saturday, the news of Friday's Senate passage of the Tonkin Gulf resolution did not even make the lead story, which was JOHNSON ANTIPOVERTY BILL APPROVED IN HOUSE, 228–190, BUT FOES BALK FINAL VOTE. The war, the longest in America's history, was never declared.

It was now time for the weekly newsmagazines to take over. Extreme as the *Post* had been, the weeklies' belligerence was worse. *Time* portrayed "the Communist intruders" boldly speeding toward the destroyers, firing with "automatic weapons." *Life* had the American ships "under continuous torpedo attack," and *Newsweek* told of "U.S. jets diving, strafing, flattening out . . . and diving again," concluding that "it was time for American might to strike back." I was discovering the role of *The Washington Post*, the breakfast reading of the nation's capital, in creating congressional consent. The American people were deceived by President Johnson—as they had been by President Kennedy—into supporting a war that proved to be unwise and unwinnable. By uncritically presenting the administration's case for American involvement in Vietnam, and by not properly pursuing an investigative role as the independent "fourth estate" of government, *The Washington Post* was a party to that deception.

Following the Tonkin Gulf resolution, Lyndon Johnson was content to keep Vietnam in the background until after the presidential election on November 3. His massive victory over Barry Goldwater freed his hand; ironically, he had accused the senator of wanting to lead the country to war. In February 1965, following attacks on American military installations, President Johnson authorized air attacks on North Vietnam. By coincidence, Kay Graham and *Newsweek* editor Osborn "Oz" Elliott were in Saigon that month on a round-the-world tour. They were given full VIP treatment. When Kay returned to Washington, it was obvious to us in the newsroom that the publisher fully agreed with Russell Wiggins's editorial support for the war effort. Lyndon Johnson told Wiggins that the *Post*'s editorials were worth two divisions to him.

Soon after Katharine Graham returned from Vietnam, something happened at the F Street Club, a few blocks from the White House, that would profoundly affect my future. Not only had Mrs. Graham returned more convinced than ever that the war must and could be won; she returned with a resolve to shake up the editorial side of *The Washington Post*. After consulting columnist Walter Lippmann and Scotty Reston of *The New York Times*, who declined the job for himself, she invited the blue-blooded, ballsy Ben Bradlee, Washington bureau chief of *Newsweek*, to lunch. She asked whether he'd be interested in moving to the *Post*. Bradlee's now-celebrated answer: "If Al Friendly's job ever opened up, I'd give my left one for it." In early July Katharine Graham announced that Bradlee would join the *Post* as an assistant managing editor. Her intention was obvious: that he would replace managing editor Al Friendly and perhaps also displace editor Russ Wiggins, but no dates were set.

Her move had a secondary effect that I doubt Kay fully anticipated. Ben Gilbert, having worked up from reporter and city editor to deputy managing editor, had long hoped that he would eventually succeed Friendly. Now it was clear that he would not, and he took the blow physically, ending up in the hospital with an ulcer. When he returned to work, his anger was manifest and I received the brunt of it. We had previously worked together smoothly, but he now scorned every proposal I made. "Terrible! Do it over!" he bellowed in response to a page-one color proof I brought him the afternoon of August 18. I felt I had had enough of his outbursts and told him what I thought of such behavior. "It's you or me," he replied. "You're fired!" I soon discovered that he meant it. I went to Al Friendly and told him what had happened. Far from being sympathetic, he seemed embarrassed, refusing to discuss the matter. My next stop was Wiggins. But as editor of the editorial page, Wiggins told me that he didn't want "to get mixed up in the affairs of the newsroom." I had one last chance: Kay Graham. She received me promptly, alone in the large living room of her house in Georgetown. I had assembled my work of the past year—a radical transformation of the *Post*'s pictorial content and thus of the look of the whole paper itself. For more than an hour, she pored through my presentation, page by page, occasionally making a comment. Then she closed the bundle, turned and shook her head. "I'm sorry, Johnny," she said, "but we've hurt Ben Gilbert as much as we're going to hurt him. I'm afraid it's good-bye." And so, three months short of my forty-ninth birthday, my brief tour of duty at *The Washington Post* came to an end.

25

To the *Times*

Decades earlier, I had accepted the fact that I was entering a mercurial business, and I knew there would be time for taking stock. That time was now. After her long and valiant fight with multiple sclerosis, Dèle had died in 1964. I had married Marjorie "Midge" Smith, the assistant to the headmaster of Woodstock Country School in Vermont, where I had enrolled my three children. Midge brought to the marriage two boys, Kirk and Oliver, whom she had raised without their father. We bid Washington good-bye and returned to New York.

While casting about for the next suitable position, I took on a project that had been a dream of Dorothea Lange, who had become a good friend. She had proposed the creation of a new national photographic archive, an updated version of the Farm Security Administration project. Just before her death she asked me to head the project, with blessings from Edward Steichen and others. Unfortunately, we failed to raise the funds necessary for such an endeavor—the Ford Foundation said no on the same day Dorothea died—and that was that. I next occupied myself with a book project that *Life*'s Dick Pollard had purchased for Time-Life Books—he had bought all rights to the historic file of color photographs taken by Hugo Jaeger, a photographer on the staff of Heinrich Hoff-

Number 229 West Forty-third Street, headquarters of *The New York Times*, remains the most prestigious address in newspaper publishing. Many a head of state has dined here with the publisher on the top floor. The whole building hums with activity. *Courtesy*, The New York Times

mann, Adolf Hitler's official photographer. Jaeger had taken color, although he
was supposed to be shooting only in black and white. He had squirreled away
his color pictures, literally underground, for twenty years, until he felt that he
could safely sell them without being charged with either larceny or war crimes.
His pictures presented a remarkably candid and often unflattering portrait of
Hitler, his henchmen, and their ladies. Few candid color pictures of any kind
were taken before World War II, and no color file chronicled the history of that
period so systematically on such a high level. There were about two thousand
color transparencies, taken from 1937 to 1940, and a thousand black-and-
white stereo pictures. On May 1, 1966, I returned to the staff of Time Inc., this
time with the full research and design support of the Books Division staff. I
worked directly under Time-Life Books editor in chief Maitland Edey and had a
private office on the thirty-second floor of the "new" Time & Life Building in
Rockefeller Center, with a job paying three times as much as the one I had resigned twenty years previously. I was back home. By midwinter, layouts were
done and I had begun writing, but opportunity was determined to prevent me
from finishing the book.

On March 3, 1967—I remember the date because later that afternoon I attended a memorial service for Henry R. Luce, who had died in Phoenix three
days before—Emanuel "Manny" Freedman, an assistant managing editor at
The New York Times, took me to lunch at Sardi's. He had invited me on the pretext of "a consultation" about the selection of a new *Times* picture editor. I was
delighted by the opportunity to help place one of my friends in such a good job.
I named several. To my dismay, Manny replied, "We know all those guys. They
either don't want us or we don't want them."

Then he came to the point: "What about you?"

"Manny," I said with a laugh, "you don't want me. I was *fired* by *The Washington Post*."

"Yeah, but we know what happened. We checked it out."

I protested that I had an important book to finish, but the following week I
found myself across the table from Clifton Daniel. It was my first time in the
managing editor's huge office overlooking West Forty-third Street. Daniel was
a small, animated man, made to seem smaller by his enormous desk. He was
Margaret Truman's husband, the former president's son-in-law; the Daniels'
wedding portrait had made the cover of *Life*. We had met once before.

"What do you think of the way we play pictures?" Daniel asked across a vast
expanse of desk.

"I think it stinks," I answered.

"So do I."

We were off to a friendly discussion that continued a full hour. A few days
passed, and Manny Freedman called to say he wanted me to talk to Harrison

Salisbury and A. M. "Abe" Rosenthal, both assistant managing editors, and executive editor Turner Catledge. Things were getting serious. I tried to stall so that I could finish the Hitler book, but Daniel said it was now or never. I agreed to start at the *Times* on May 29, 1967. The Hitler book was never completed.

Theodore M. Bernstein was the one assistant managing editor of *The New York Times* who had *not* been asked to interview me for the job of picture editor. The significance of this initially escaped me. For fifteen years Ted Bernstein and his assistants, collectively called the "bull pen," had decided the daily content and makeup of the *Times*. They had final say over all stories, headlines, and graphics that originated with the desks: Foreign, National, Metropolitan, even Sports, Women's, Financial—and Pictures. Authors of the authoritative *New York Times Style Book*, they were the arbiters of grammar, taste, and equity—and what passed for political correctness in those days. They could even question editorials and columns, but seldom did. The Bernstein gang arrived in the afternoon and worked into the night, finally dismissing the staff, toward 3:00 A.M., by saying "Good night."

All this was about to change. I was to be one of change's instruments, and Clifton Daniel, a "morning-after" managing editor, was determined to accomplish it with as little bloodshed as possible. I was told to "observe" for as long as I liked. My first day on the job, May 29, 1967, I sat alongside John Radosta at the head of the Picture Desk, located near Forty-third Street in the huge third-floor newsroom. The newsroom was roughly the size of a football field, extending all the way to Forty-fourth Street, where it overlooked Shubert Alley. News executives and their assistants sat under the Forty-third Street windows. They could look straight to their left into the managing editor's office, so large that it permitted him to hold private conversations without bothering to close the door. Visibility is an asset on newspapers; even top editors must appear to be easily accessible. Most *Times* editors, even those few who also have private offices, sit in the open, but invisible walls separate them from those who have no serious business. Reporters, too, learn to lose themselves to their phones or keyboards, unaware of the immediate world. Things have improved, but the newsroom in 1967 was little different from the one Russell Baker had found when he came from Baltimore in 1954, with dozens of desks "aligned in rows as neatly as a military graveyard," as he remembers it in his autobiography.

Along Forty-third Street the hierarchy extended east from Daniel to the four assistant managing editors: Manny Freedman, Abe Rosenthal, Harrison Salisbury, and Ted Bernstein, who had a small glassed-in office. Just outside it were the news editors of the bull pen. Next, for the convenience of the news editors, came the Picture Desk, actually six small desks shoved together covering an area about the size of a billiard table. It was better equipped to handle words than pictures. Wirephoto machines were at hand, but there were no photographers in sight: they worked out of the "studio" on the ninth floor, and their prints were delivered by lab men. The Art Department, which precisely cropped and if necessary retouched the pictures selected, was on the eighth floor. The picture archives were also on eight. Photos were engraved on the fifth floor, in a process that had changed little since the nineteenth century. A dumbwaiter delivered the resulting zinc cuts to the fourth-floor composing room. All very complicated.

At four o'clock I followed Radosta into the managing editor's office for the daily "page-one" conference. As a nonparticipant, I sat to one side, along with the publisher and representatives from Circulation, Promotion, and the Times News Service. Editors from each of the news desks briefly reported the stories they considered worthy of page one. There was little surprise; written summaries had already been distributed to all concerned. On this particular Monday, foreign news dominated. War threatened in the Middle East. Egyptian president Gamal Abdel Nasser had closed the Strait of Tiran, blocking Israel's access to the Red Sea. The U.N. Security Council was deadlocked; Jerusalem reported a skirmish near Gaza. *Times* correspondent John Finney reported from Washington that the State Department was trying behind the scenes to work out a deal that would keep the peace. There were two stories from Rome: the pope had named twenty-seven new cardinals, and de Gaulle had arrived for a meeting of European Community leaders. Saigon reported that Vietcong frogmen had bombed a hotel in Hue, killing five. The National Desk could offer only the regular Monday decisions of the U.S. Supreme Court, plus the appointment of newscaster John Daly to head the Voice of America. The Metropolitan Desk had even less: the salary demands to be made by New York City teachers and a loosening of rent controls by the John Lindsay administration. Financial had little and Sports passed: only such sports events as the World Series, the Kentucky Derby, and the Super Bowl were likely to rate page one of the *Times*. I noted that Radosta made no effort to sell any particular pictures for page one. Later in the day I would see why.

For the next two hours, the job of the Picture Desk was to choose and "move" (slug and size and send by tube to the Art Department) pictures that somehow matched the verbal report that would fill the next day's ninety-six-page paper. This required constant consultation with the various news desks ("Is this guy in the story?") and with the Makeup Desk, which laid out the inside pages. Financial, Sports, and Women's handled their own pictures. The makeup men, who worked on the inside pages from "scratches"—miniature pages that showed the placement of ads—were friendly but firm: "No, John, I can only give you a two-column—make it about five inches deep. Can't you see it has to sit over this ad?" Even so, some of the "moved" pictures would end up as "overset," unused in the first edition.

At 6:30, I was invited into Ted Bernstein's office as an observer at the most crucial meeting of the day, the *actual* page-one conference. I did not realize at the time what an extraordinary privilege it was, as ordinarily the picture editor, like the heads of the other desks, was not welcome. When Harrison Salisbury, as assistant managing editor, once invited himself to that meeting, the result was a furious handwritten protest from Bernstein to Daniel, saying "It was almost as if he were a spy and we [the bull pen editors] the ones being spied upon."

The front page of *The New York Times* was a tribunal that daily passed judgment on the conduct of the world. Statesmen analyzed it to see how the world was doing, candidates to see whether they were losing or gaining ground. Page one quantified both triumph and disaster. An unrecognized instrument of triage, it evaluated matters of human concern, deciding which merited attention and which, by omission, were unworthy. Page one's balance was as delicate as that of a performer on the high wire. Restraint and responsibility were the key words. The *Times* was, and still is, the antithesis of oversimplified tabloid journalism.

At Ted Bernstein's *Times*, news developments were measured almost mathematically in terms of the headline size they deserved. On a "normal" news day, the largest head permitted for any story was an "A head," then composed from thirty-point Latin Antique Extra Condensed, with banks and crossline in twelve-point News Gothic. That day, John Finney's Washington-datelined story was chosen to lead the paper of May 30, 1967, in the right-hand column:

> *U.S. SAID TO WEIGH*
> *A PLAN FOR ENDING*
> *AQABA BLOCKADE*
> *Initial Step Would Open Gulf*
> *At Once to All Shipping but*
> *Israeli-flag Vessels*

The two related stories were just as carefully weighed and played. Next in importance, with an "R head," was the United Nations–datelined story: "Mideast 'Breathing Spell' Supported by U.S. in U.N." Well below it, under a "Z head," was the Jerusalem-datelined story, "Israeli and Egyptian Units Exchange Fire near Gaza."

Thus the *Times* front page was informative, conscientious, and unprovocative. In the tabloids the play would have been reversed, with the Gaza skirmish getting a screaming headline. Perhaps I should say, "In the tabloids *in those days*"—today's tabloid editors are largely unconcerned with foreign news, and the screaming headlines go to local murders and sex scandals.

Bernstein and his colleagues, news editor Lewis "Lew" Jordan and late man

Thomas Daffron, next had to deal with the day's other stories and the pictures. It was Daffron's job to finally put the paper to bed, at three in the morning. Bernstein thought of pictures mainly as a means of breaking up his beloved type. His usual practice was to have one picture at the top of the page, one at the bottom, and sometimes not even that. When the word had gotten around that I was taking the *Times* job, one of my friends had cracked, "Becoming the picture editor of *The New York Times* is like becoming the recreation director at Forest Lawn."

Radosta had little to offer that day for page one and nothing at all to illustrate the lead story. War preparations were far advanced in Israel and Egypt, but censorship was in force and the wire services were not accustomed to taking pictures until battle actually commenced. So on Monday, May 29, Ted Bernstein settled for a three-column Associated Press picture, showing French president de Gaulle saluting an honor guard in Rome, at the top of the page. Its chief virtue was that it separated the foreign report from the national, one of whose three Supreme Court stories made the "off lead," under an "A head" in column one. A United Press picture of John Daly joking at USIA's Washington press conference ran at the bottom of the page.

With the page-one dummy drawn, Bernstein turned his attention to the "second front," or the front of the second section, its bottom half invariably occupied by the News Summary and Index. The top was thought to require pictures, usually local in nature. John Radosta was invited to the second-front conference, and he came prepared with the "scenes" that Bernstein preferred. Ted quickly chose two unrelated pictures, a four-column of Brooklynites protesting nocturnal noise at the Fort Greene Meat Market and a three-column of an eighteenth-century Dutch farmhouse in upstate Kinderhook, newly restored because of some association with Washington Irving. That left room for four other Metropolitan stories and two shorts. Ted was pleased.

Putting on his coat promptly at 7:30, Bernstein turned to me: "Would you like to come along?" It was a singular invitation. Night after night, the captain of the ship, he dined alone at "the Greek's," a restaurant called the Pantheon on Eighth Avenue. He indulged himself in just one martini, very dry. He was a chain-smoker, a vice that was to prove fatal. We did not talk about that night's paper but were content to probe each other's past. It was obvious that Daniel had given me a buildup. I needed no buildup on Ted, for around the city it was said that Bernstein was the man who *actually* put out the *Times*. That talk would soon change. I found him delightfully open and unpretentious but oddly provincial in a curious way. He had never gone anywhere, had probably never reported a story; he had lived only behind a desk. Nevertheless, he was extremely well informed and his instincts were decent. I would learn that he had opposed Reston and the Kennedy White House in suppressing the Bay of Pigs story in 1961, only to be overruled by the publisher.

At nine, we were back. It was time to go "upstairs." A tiny elevator, holding three at a time, would take us to the blue-collar world on the floor above, the noisy fourth-floor composing room. There, thanks to my experience on *The Daily Maroon* decades earlier, I felt somewhat at home. There were dozens of Linotypes and what seemed like an acre of printers' stones. Each stone, a waist-high metal table, held one or two chases, rectangular metal frames the size of a page. Printers had been working all afternoon with the Advertising Department's makeup men to place the ads inside them. Now the News Department's makeup men faced the printers across the forms, translating the "scratches" into cold-type reality. Bernstein and Jordan, shirtsleeves rolled up, hovered over page one, closest to the elevator. They had to read it upside down. An expert printer, wearing an apron, stood on the other side of the form, following their verbal instructions. Printers had the advantage of looking at the page right side up but had to read right to left. None of us newspeople was permitted to so much as *touch* a cut or a slug of type. That was the prerogative of the printers, written into their archaic contract. I never got used to that; the gulf between blue-collar craftsman and white-collar editor seemed idiotic and unnecessary. Weren't we putting out a newspaper together?

Already many early pages had closed, under the guidance of the makeup men. As they "went down" (to the stereotypers for plate making), the page numbers were marked off on an electric scoreboard. Page one was normally the last to close, and its deadline was precise: 9:15. The closing is now *two hours later,* but that's small change compared with the revolutionary conversion to cold type and pasteup—which today have given way to electronic page makeup. The composing room I have just described no longer exists.

We descended to the newsroom three by three to find the copy desks reading proofs of the important pages. About 9:40, the first papers were brought up from the press room by Samuel Solovitz, a career copyboy. A few minutes later, in Bernstein's office, the bull pen would go through the main news pages together, one page at a time, partly for correction but mostly for fitting. Inevitably there would be "overset"—stories, or pieces of stories, that had been crowded out. How could they be shoehorned into the late city edition, the showpiece paper and the "edition of record," which would close at midnight? The city edition, after all, was but a proof. It was the job of the assistant picture editor who worked late to try to reinstate favorite pictures that hadn't made it into the first edition. He would also be called upon to "cover," with a one-column cut of "someone in the story," a page that looked barren.

Soon after I started work, I received a memo from A. O. Sulzberger inviting me to the "publisher's luncheon" on Tuesday, June 20. This was a daily affair that the paper's top executives were obliged to attend. The guests were carefully selected according to the *Times*'s varied interests. Many a president and head of state had preceded me. Daniel had introduced me to Arthur Ochs "Punch"

Sulzberger, the young publisher, but this was my first real contact with this formidable family, rulers of the *Times* since 1896, when Adolph Ochs, Punch's
maternal grandfather, had bought the unprofitable newspaper for $75,000.
Punch's father, Arthur Hays Sulzberger, had married Ochs's daughter, Iphi-
gene, and taken over as publisher upon Ochs's death in 1935. The Sulzbergers
had three daughters, followed by a son who was called by his childhood nickname "Punch"—one sister was named Judith, or Judy. The oldest daughter,
Marian, made a fortunate marriage in 1941 to a successful stockbroker named
Orvil Dryfoos. He reluctantly came to work at the *Times* and did so well that in
1961 his ailing father-in-law named him publisher. Then, in 1963, he suddenly died of a heart attack and Punch was named publisher. Like Katharine
Graham, he had never expected to be publisher, although he had worked his
way around the building. Also like Katharine, he showed amazing aptitude for
the job once he had it. He was open and friendly, but I usually dealt with him in-
directly.

When I entered the publisher's fourteenth-floor dining room, I was astonished to find Arthur Hays Sulzberger at the table, sitting in a wheelchair, Iphi-
gene across from him. It was like meeting an ailing king—barely functioning at
seventy-five—and his lively consort. I was introduced as the new picture editor
and had the pleasure of telling him, "Mr. Sulzberger, I am very honored to be
here at last. I applied for this job exactly twenty-one years ago."

At the end of my first week of "observation," I felt I had learned what I
needed to learn from John Radosta, who was moving on to cover auto racing
for Sports. I had never greatly admired John's skills as a picture editor, although he had introduced 35-millimeter cameras, as well as contact sheets for
editing—a revolution in the *Times* newsroom. On Monday, June 5, 1967, the
world awakened to full-scale war in the Middle East. It was day one of what
turned out to be the Six-Day War. The *Times* responded with distinction: coordinated by foreign editor Seymour Topping, eight bylined dispatches told the
story on page one; three full pages were cleared inside, for jumps and six more
staff bylines, including a "Talk of Tel Aviv" from Scotty Reston, who had arrived from Cairo via Athens an hour after the war began. The only dateline
missing was Damascus: Thomas Brady had been arrested before he could file.
A summary and three-column map dominated page one under a three-line
banner in 48-point Century bold italic caps:

ISRAELI AND ARAB FORCES BATTLING;
BOTH CLAIM LAND AND AIR VICTORIES;
CEASE-FIRE EFFORTS STALLED IN U.N.

Impatient to handle the big news myself—even though few pictures were
coming through—I told Daniel that I was ready to take over and took Radosta's

seat at the overcrowded Picture Desk. I noticed that a water cooler blocked easy access to the wirephoto machines. It seemed a simple matter to move it a few feet to line up with one of the columns that punctuate the open floor. No sooner had the desk clerk accomplished this than I heard a roar: "Fuck you, Morris!" Abe Rosenthal came charging at me. We had unwittingly moved the cooler so that it blocked his view of the newsroom.

A picture that speaks volumes about the enormous difference in style between *New York Times* managing editor Clifton Daniel (*right*) and his successor, A. M. Rosenthal. *Courtesy,* The New York Times

26

A Table at Sardi's

T he challenge to the new *Times* picture editor was obvious. It was to match the scope of *The New York Times*'s reporting, and the depth of its editing, with comparable quality in the picture report. In covering the Six-Day War, for example, we had no pictures we could call exclusively our own. Day and night, we received by wirephoto the full service of Associated Press and United Press International. Every eight to ten minutes, a fresh picture would roll into view on a fax monitor or a print would plop from a wirephoto receiver. Direct phone lines connected us to the AP picture desk in Rockefeller Center and the UPI picture desk in the New York Daily News Building. We made constant demands, but there was no way "the wires" could "match" the many exclusives filed by *Times* correspondents and still meet the routine demands of their more provincial newspaper clients—who insisted, for example, that every major-league ball game be covered with at least one picture.

We had to begin in our own backyard. Following the cease-fire that ended the Six-Day War, world attention turned to New York as heads of state arrived for a U.N. General Assembly session of special importance. Among them was Soviet premier Aleksei Kosygin. On Thursday evening, June 22, at 6:45, just half an hour before the normal engraving deadline for the first edition, the White House announced a "summit conference" for the following day at the home of the president of Glassboro State College in southern New Jersey. Glassboro! Where is *that*? Whoever heard of Glassboro State College? Certainly not our picture files, nor those of the two wire services. It was impossible to find a picture of the conference site, in a rural area halfway between New York and Washington, for the first edition. Perhaps impossible even for the Late City? It was a good three-hour drive from New York. I noticed, however, that it was only about forty miles from Wilmington, across the Delaware River. Bill Snead, an alumnus of Rich Clarkson's great picture newspaper, the Topeka *Capital Journal*, was now chief photographer for the Wilmington papers. Told of the news, he was only too eager to go and shoot, for his paper as well as ours. Arriving in Glassboro at dusk, he made a mood shot of the college president's house, alight with summit preparations. Returning to Wilmington, he transmitted it in ample time for our late city edition. It was my first page-one "Special for *The New York Times.*"

The next problem was the summit itself. The Metropolitan Desk assigned fifteen reporters. We shared the rental of a helicopter to cover the Kosygin motorcade from the air, with an unexpected dividend: as Kosygin's limousine turned off the New Jersey Turnpike and passed a farm on Route 322, a white horse galloped up to greet the Soviet premier. I whooped for joy when I saw the frame on the contact sheet and spread the picture across eight columns on an inside page of the first edition—the bull pen, of course, cut it back to six. Never would the *Times*, unlike *The Washington Post*, put such a picture on page one— not even today.

The *Times*'s staff photographers were just as varied as those I had found at the *Post* and just as hungry for recognition. The average age of the thirteen daily staffers was forty-four—not exactly youngsters in such an active profession—but the oldest, Ernie Sisto, was at sixty-three one of the best. In 1945, when a twelve-ton Air Force bomber had crashed into the seventy-eighth and seventy-ninth floors of the Empire State Building, Ernie had put his name into the annals of press photography by making a picture of the wreckage from the parapet just above, persuading two rival photographers to hold him by his legs. Ernie could still be counted upon to bring back a picture of the one play that told the story of the ball game. The youngest photographer on the staff was breathless Barton Silverman, who spoke nonstop Brooklynese. At Brooklyn College, Silverman found that his studies were interfering with his career. He answered a help wanted ad: "Large New York newspaper needs photo-lab technician; good working conditions; must be willing to run errands." Like his hero Ernie Sisto, Silverman soon specialized in sports. He swam out to sea to cover water surfers; he caught a downhill skier while skiing himself; he camouflaged himself into the course of the Watkins Glen Grand Prix to get a telephoto view of the racers' wheels seemingly rolling over him; he climbed the mast of a yawl for a layout on sailing. He was inexhaustible, irrepressible. As a reward, I sent him to the University of Missouri Workshop, the first *Times* photographer to go. It was relaxing to have him out of town for a week.

Whereas magazine photographers often have the luxury of shooting frame after frame until they get it right, shooters for newspapers have to call their clicks. Neal Boenzi, whose talent had already brought him a string of merit raises by the time I arrived, was such a photographer, editing situations with his eyes. He would reduce Weather to a three-picture sequence of a cop helping a young woman cross a slushy street. He summarized "Life and Death in the City" in two pictures: a newborn girl in the arms of her mother and a "stiff" laid out, feet first, at the morgue. When it came to tackling the problems of complex feature stories, no photographer was better than Edward Hausner. He had been invited to join the *Times* by Arthur Hays Sulzberger, who had seen him in action as an Army photographer overseas. Jack Manning, the one photographer with extensive outside experience, was also very versatile. He had studied at the Photo League and done magazine photography through Pix. Manning had been taken on by John Radosta in the early sixties. Radosta had also added Barton Silverman, promoted from the lab, and Don Hogan Charles. Charles, an African American, photographed the city's black ghettos with great empathy. He summed up the close proximity of Manhattan's rich and poor in one picture: a smartly dressed young white woman walking her dog past a black matron carrying a bag of groceries on Park Avenue where it entered Harlem.

In the greatest understatement of my hiring process, Clifton Daniel had told me, "You will find a number of people concerned with art and layout in the building. They are not in your jurisdiction, but make the most of them." I started with Joseph Schultz, whose title was something like "Director of the Art Department, The New York Times Company." He reported directly to the publisher. His domain was subdivided into *New York Times Magazine* layout, newspaper layout (mostly for Sunday sections), and maps and charts. He also controlled the ninth-floor New York Times Studio through his protégée Shirley Baig. It serviced the newspaper and did commercial studio portraits for anyone who wanted to pay the price. The other Art Department at 229 West Forty-third Street would profoundly change the course of American newspaper design. It was in the head and hands of Louis Silverstein, art director for *Times* Promotion. His sophisticated *Times* ads in *The New Yorker* had already attracted attention. In July 1967, Lou and I worked together on a hush-hush *Times* project for an afternoon paper intended to fill the gap left by the demise of the *World Journal Tribune*. It was to be edited by Abe Rosenthal. Only four weeks into my job, Clifton Daniel had called me in to say, "I hate to do this to you, but Abe has asked to borrow you for several weeks."

It soon became clear that words, not pictures, would come first. Silverstein, devoted to white space, had frequent clashes with Abe, who was devoted to filling it up, but each learned to respect the other. Two dummy issues were printed, but the project was soon canceled—it was feared it would hurt the *Times* itself. Copies are scarce—the Gray Lady had no desire to publicize an abortion. Silverstein was soon elevated from Promotion to corporate art director. From that time on, Abe Rosenthal called on him whenever the *Times* sought graphic innovation. That meant plenty of work when, less than a decade later, the *Times* went to six columns and a four-section paper, each with its own designer. Silverstein was the founding evangelist of the Society for Newspaper Design, which spread his gospel throughout the land.

With some relief I returned in August to the more mundane demands of the daily. Clifton Daniel's intention was to wrest control of the "second front" away from the bull pen. They had already begun to accept the inevitable by giving me larger pictures but clung to the A heads and column rules so typical of conservative *Times* makeup. As soon as I had a small bank of good stories, I went to George Cowan, the senior designer of the eighth floor. A Londoner from the East End, born George Cohen, Cowan happily worked both sides of the Jewish-Irish axis that dominated Forty-third Street. The week of September 8, we worked up several layouts. Managing editor Daniel was away. His intention was to look at them the following Monday and, if satisfied, to issue a written directive giving responsibility for the second front to Arthur Gelb for story content and to me for pictures and layout.

On Sunday, September 14, Lawrence "Larry" Hauck, the bull pen's weekend editor, went to the Picture Desk as usual, asking, "What have you got for the second front?" Unwittingly, the weekend picture editor brought him the new layouts. Hauck saw one on "The Talk of Buffalo" by a young reporter named Sydney H. Schanberg, with pictures by Eddie Hausner. The layout was horizontal, just one story above the fold, no column rules. "Looks good to me," Hauck said, "I'll run it"—which he did, in the paper of Monday, September 15, 1967. Thus, accidentally/on purpose, was accomplished one of the biggest changes in makeup of *The New York Times* in all its history. Daniel's directive proved unnecessary. We were off and running. Gelb and I were given full control of the second front. Two or three times a day, I would see him striding toward me, a few sheets of copy paper in hand, to ask, "How good are the pictures with this story?" Normally he accepted my picture judgment without question, but if I resisted and he was really keen on the story, he would throw an arm around me with an air of conspiracy: "You know, *there's a lot of interest in this story*," hinting that *someone*, perhaps Rosenthal or even the publisher, had a stake in it.

For the next six years, six days a week, Arthur Gelb and I controlled the best showplace in New York. Arthur's curiosity and enthusiasm were almost childlike. The second front was our playpen. We could run almost any kind of story if the copy was charming and the pictures looked fresh. In retrospect, my favorites seem to have concerned children. Science writer Jane Brody discovered that "Children Scribble the Same the World Over"—an echo of the *Ladies'*

TUESDAY, SEPTEMBER 24, 1968

The New York Times

L +∘∘   49

Life and...

...Death in the City: One Day's 665 Dramas

Patrolmen Thomas Snyder, left, and Michael Regney with Lorenzo Tucker, morgue side, in Manhattan Medical Examiner's office with cardiac victim

Mrs. Mercedes Torres had a daughter, Maritza, as her first-born, at St. Vincent's Hospital

Weather Reports Caught Off Base

My first big task as *Times* picture editor was to transform the front of the second section of the daily paper, known as the Second Front, into a display page. This one is by *Times* star staff photographer Neal Boenzi. In two pictures, he symbolized the vital statistics of one day in New York, as reported by Tom Buckley. NEAL BOENZI/The New York Times

Home Journal's "People Are People." Reporter Lacey Fosburgh wrote about "Child Poets." We ran their poems beneath sensitive portraits by Don Charles. Photographer William Sauro, who joined the *Times* after the *World Journal Tribune* folded, accompanied reporter Richard Lyons to a school that had been hit by German measles. Reporter Michael Kaufman and photographer Lee Romero told the story of an adventurous Harlem ten-year-old so eloquently that in 1973 their story became a book, *Rooftops & Alleys.* Reporter Joseph Treaster covered a rock festival in Connecticut with Bart Silverman. The participants thought nothing of appearing nude in front of the camera and set some kind of *Times* precedent when a bare-assed boy was shown striding across the foreground in a five-column picture.

Most of the ideas came from Gelb and his staff, but I got in some of my own, often concerning photographers. One was on Cornell Capa's first "Concerned Photographer" show at the Riverside Museum, forerunner of his International Center of Photography. Others chronicled Edward Steichen's ninetieth birthday party at the Plaza Hotel and a meeting arranged by historian Beaumont

Newhall at Rochester's George Eastman House of pioneer photographer Felix Man and editor-historian Stefan Lorant, my former foe. The strongest of my second fronts was by Bart Silverman, on the slaughter of baby seals in the Gulf of Saint Lawrence. Bart skillfully summarized the story in three pictures: a baby seal is clubbed; the adult seals watch; the hunters drag their boatloads home across the ice. The story caused an uproar.

The new approach soon spread to other pages. In the fall of 1967, Gelb gave reporter J. Anthony Lukas three weeks to research the background of a young woman named Linda Fitzpatrick. She had grown up in a proper suburban home only to become a radical terrorist who blew herself up with her own bomb. George Cowan did the layout; the story won a Pulitzer Prize. Soon reporters were aiming their stories for the second front, pleading with the Picture Desk for favored photographers, later dropping by my desk to get inspiration from the pictures and writing their stories to them—not unlike the practice at *Life*.

People were beginning to take notice. Said a commentator on WCBS radio: "You look at the good gray *New York Times* today, and it's not so gray. They've gone to pictures." I had waited twenty-one years, but I was beginning to feel as though I owned a small piece of the place. On Forty-fourth Street, the *Times* backed up to Sardi's, the traditional restaurant of the theater district. Sardi's regulars knew that the *Times*'s back stairs led down to a newsprint loading dock from which one could easily skitter into the restaurant. Sardi's was the place to hear the latest *Times* gossip. Vincent Sardi's welcome was proportional to one's status in the theater—or at *The New York Times*. I soon found that I had no trouble getting a table at any hour of the day or evening.

Semi-anonymous guardians of the newspaper's accuracy, balance, and integrity: Members of the *New York Times* bull pen pose on an occasion long forgotten, wearing *Times* printers' aprons. Headed by news editor Lewis Jordan (*seated*), I knew them as (*left to right*) Chick Butsikares, Larry Hauck, Bob Crandall, and Tom Daffron—who was most often the designated "late man." Tom put the paper to bed by calling out "Good night!" at 3:00 A.M. *Courtesy*, The New York Times

Nothing, in my judgment, was too good for *New York Times* staff photographers and picture desk personnel. I would occasionally lure them to staff meetings with dinner in an executive dining room or, in this case, by taking over Abe Rosenthal's big office. ERNEST SISTO/The New York Times

The New York Times

VOL. CXVII...No. 40,186   NEW YORK, FRIDAY, FEBRUARY 2, 1968   10 CENTS

PRESIDENT ASKS PAY-PRICE CURBS AND RISE IN TAX

INFLATION FEARED

Economic Report Says Failure to Act Risks a 'Feverish Boom'

Text of Johnson's Economic Report, Pages 20 and 21.

By EDWIN L. DALE Jr.

NIXON ANNOUNCES FOR PRESIDENCY

Discloses Plans in a Letter to New Hampshire Voters —Opens Drive Today

By ROBERT B. SEMPLE Jr.

Richard M. Nixon in official campaign photograph.

HOUSE, 382-4, VOTES HELD TO CONSUMER

LINDSAY REDUCES OUTLAY OF FUNDS FOR NEW SCHOOLS

Cites Unused Backlog as He Submits a 'Tight' Capital Budget of $996-Million

Excerpts from capital budget appear on Page 22.

By RICHARD E. MOONEY

M'NAMARA SAYS SOVIET DOUBLED ITS ICBM'S IN '67

But Secretary, in Farewell Report, Tells Congress U.S. Force Is Bigger

Excerpts from the McNamara report are on Page 16.

By WILLIAM BEECHER

STREET CLASHES GO ON IN VIETNAM, FOE STILL HOLDS PARTS OF CITIES; JOHNSON PLEDGES NEVER TO YIELD

GUERRILLA DIES: Brig. Gen. Nguyen Ngoc Loan, national police chief, executes man identified as a Vietcong terrorist in Saigon. Man wore civilian dress and had a pistol. A picture sequence of the execution is on Page 12.

A RESOLUTE STAND

President Won't Halt Bombing—Predicts Khesanh Victory

By MAX FRANKEL

HIS FAMILY SLAIN BY VIETCONG: A South Vietnamese

ENEMY TOLL SOARS

Offensive Is Running 'Out of Steam,' Says Westmoreland

By CHARLES MOHR

A shocking picture came over the wire on the afternoon of February 1, 1968. Taken by Eddie Adams of AP, it showed the summary execution of a Vietnamese civilian by the chief of South Vietnam's national police. I took it to the early news conference, arguing that the only question was not whether to use it, but how big? EDDIE ADAMS/AP/The New York Times

27

The Guns of '68

Is anyone taking any notice?" cried Don McCullin, the noted English photographer, in the title of the passionate book he published after covering his seventh war. It is the question that haunts every thoughtful photojournalist. In the spring of 1967, just before I joined the *Times*, my wife, Midge, edited a book of photographs contrasting war (in Vietnam) and peace (at home). It was called *And/Or*—war and/or peace. The cover contrasted Elliott Erwitt's photo of his wife, Lucienne, playing with their firstborn baby and Dang Van Phuoc's photo of a Vietnamese mother shielding her baby from sniper fire. The book's worthy but futile aim was to shock the American public into calling for a halt in hostilities. I wrote the preface.

Book dummy in hand, Midge first got the endorsement of Edward Steichen, retired at eighty-eight, on one of his periodic visits to curator Grace Mayer's office at the Museum of Modern Art. Midge then shuttled to Washington and went straight to the office of Arkansas senator William Fulbright, who by then regretted rushing the 1964 Tonkin Gulf resolution through the Senate. Fulbright promptly endorsed the book. Leaving his office, Midge stepped into an elevator and found herself face-to-face with Senator Robert F. Kennedy. Holding out the dummy, she stammered, "Senator, may I show you something?" He stepped off the elevator, saying, "Please come along to my office." There he flipped through the pages and asked Midge, "What can I do to help?" She asked for an endorsement. The senator had been an early supporter of the Vietnam War, declaring on a visit to Saigon in 1962, "We are going to win." By 1967, however, he was having second thoughts. In ten minutes a secretary returned with Kennedy's statement for the book jacket. The book did well, but the war intensified.

I had been hired as a *Times* editor just before *And/Or* would appear, so I asked Clifton Daniel if there was any reason why I should take my name off the preface. He replied as though I need not have asked. *The New York Times* was *not* the hawkish *Washington Post.* The *Times* had been the first American newspaper to establish a Saigon bureau, in 1962, sending there a hard-nosed reporter, David Halberstam. Along with Neil Sheehan of UPI and Malcolm Browne and Peter Arnett of AP, Halberstam embarrassed the Kennedy administration by reporting the facts about the failure of the South Vietnamese army and its American "advisers" to win the war against the Vietcong. Just a month before he was assassinated, President Kennedy suggested to Punch Sulzberger and Turner Catledge (then managing editor), at a White House meeting, that Halberstam be transferred: "You weren't by any chance thinking of sending him to Paris or Rome or London?" Kennedy asked. Sulzberger refused to take the hint; Halberstam won a 1964 Pulitzer for his reporting from Vietnam. Nevertheless, the *Times*'s news columns, like those of *The Washington Post,* presented the Johnson administration's misleading account of the 1964 Tonkin Gulf incident and seriously underplayed its significance. *Times* editorials were more critical. While at first endorsing the Tonkin Gulf resolution, editorial page editor John Oakes soon caught on. A *Times* editorial on September 23, 1964, headlined "The Gulf of Tonkin Mystery," denounced "bureaucratic confusion and secretiveness." By 1965, Scotty Reston, along with *Times* editorials, was questioning the President's credibility. In his memoir *Deadline,* Reston revealed how Lyndon Johnson called him to the White House and "gave me the works," saying, "Why don't you get on the team?" Reston told Johnson that he thought he was trying to save face, whereupon: "He stood up and showed me to the door. 'I'm not trying to save face,' he said, 'I'm trying to save my ass.' " When in 1967 Harrison Salisbury of the *Times* reported from Hanoi on the civilians killed by American bombing raids, *The Washington Post* carped that his reporting amounted to a new enemy weapon—as "clearly conceived" as the Vietcong's "poison-tipped bamboo spikes."

Shortly before the four o'clock news conference on Thursday, February 1, 1968, a startling picture came over the AP wire from Saigon. It was Eddie Adams's now-famous photo of the summary execution of a Vietcong suspect by General Nguyen Ngoc Loan, chief of the South Vietnamese national police. It was taken at the moment Loan pulled the trigger of his revolver, a scant six inches from the head of his victim, who stands helplessly, hands tied behind his back, wearing the plaid sport shirt of a civilian. One could sense, but not see, the impact of the bullet; the man's face is slightly distorted, cringing in anticipation of death. I proposed it for page one to all the assembled editors so that it could not be ignored at the later makeup session. Thus there was no dispute about *whether* to use it, just a discussion of *how*. Ted Bernstein, determined that the brutality manifested by America's ally be put into perspective, agreed to run the Adams picture large, but offset with a picture of a child slain by the Vietcong, which conveniently came through from AP at about the same time. London's *Daily Telegraph* exactly duplicated our layout the following morning. We went them one better by also running, on an inside page, the photos of the victim that Adams took just before and after.

Eddie's picture followed by thirty-six hours the Vietcong's all-out attack on American installations in South Vietnam, the infamous "Tet offensive." Four thousand men descended on Saigon alone. Militarily, the attacks were soon repulsed, but the Adams picture, more than any single image to come out of the Vietnam War, led people to question whether it was a war worth winning.

Six weeks later, a U.S. infantry company slaughtered more than one hundred civilians in the village of My Lai. The incident would not be revealed for a year, but in early 1968 it became clear that President Johnson himself was becoming disillusioned with the war. He was also losing his grip on the electorate. On March 12, Senator Eugene McCarthy, running as an antiwar candidate, almost defeated Johnson in the New Hampshire primary. Five days later, although reluctant to split the peace vote, Senator Robert F. Kennedy announced his candidacy for president.

On April 1, 1968, the *Times*'s banner headline read: JOHNSON SAYS HE WON'T RUN; HALTS NORTH VIETNAM RAIDS; BIDS HANOI JOIN PEACE MOVES. Momentarily there seemed hope for peace, but only four days later the banner read: MARTIN LUTHER KING IS SLAIN IN MEMPHIS. It was Thursday, April 4, and we were closing the first edition. A few minutes after 7:00 P.M., Earl Caldwell called the National Desk from Memphis. Caldwell was one of the *Times*'s growing staff of black reporters. He was in Memphis to cover Reverend Dr. Martin Luther King Jr.'s attempt to organize support for a strike by 1,300 Memphis sanitation workers. Earl had taken a room just below that of Dr. King in the Lorraine Motel and heard shots. Stepping out of his room, Caldwell saw King lying in a pool of blood on the balcony above. There seemed little hope that he would live. The *Times* was caught unprepared. An "advance obit" of at least one full page of text and pictures should have been ready on a man as distinguished as the Nobel Prize–winning civil rights leader, but he was only thirty-nine, in good health, and constantly in the news. The standing obit had not kept pace with him; it was totally inadequate. Only two pictures were engraved in metal. I called for the entire King picture file, seeking *the* portrait for page one. King died at 8:05 P.M., and we were well past the engraving deadline for the nine o'clock close. In the commotion, freelance photographer Ben Fernandez came to my desk with his recent picture of the King family. We rushed it into the city edition. For the late city, I chose a picture that moved that night on the AP wire. It

The assassination of Dr. Martin Luther King, Jr., in Memphis, occurring just before the first edition closed on April 4, 1968, caught us without a proper obituary. For the late city edition I chose this portrait, which came over the AP wire that evening.
AP/The New York Times

THE REV. DR. MARTIN LUTHER KING Jr.

showed a King I had never seen before—hand to chin, eyes closed, pensive and prayerful. It has since become a classic.

Now the country was really in turmoil. It became dangerous for photographers, especially white photographers, to cover events. The *Times* headlined the next day: ARMY TROOPS IN CAPITAL AS NEGROES RIOT; GUARD SENT INTO CHICAGO, DETROIT, BOSTON; JOHNSON ASKS A JOINT SESSION OF CONGRESS. Lyndon Johnson did not name a successor for the 1968 Democratic nomination, but his choice was obvious: Vice President Hubert Humphrey, who had not openly opposed Johnson's war. With Johnson's withdrawal, Humphrey almost automatically became a candidate, but not in time to file for the June 4 California primary. The stage was set for confrontation between McCarthy and Kennedy in California. I was invited to speak to a convention of California press photographers later that week. Midge and I decided to witness the last days of the primary. On primary election night, we dined early with *Times* reporters, who had nothing to do until the returns came in, then spent an hour at the somewhat dispirited McCarthy headquarters at the Beverly Hilton. We knew the action would be at Kennedy headquarters in the Hotel Ambassador. Making our way to the Ambassador ballroom, we passed a pantry where reporters awaited the candidate. At about 11:30, there was a roar as California Democratic state chairman Jesse Unruh introduced Senator Kennedy as "the next president of the United States." Almost everyone there believed he would be. The senator thanked his supporters and concluded, "On to Chicago, and let's win there!" Midge and I climbed onto a camera case for a better view as Kennedy disappeared through a service door to the pantry. The crowd roared for more. Then we heard several small pops over the din. Hundreds of balloons had escaped from their streamers and were clinging to the ceiling. We looked up. At that moment the crowd noise mounted a full decibel. Women were shrieking. Just behind us a television producer shouted, "Let's move!" Pressing forward, I saw a woman who had passed out cold on a table, blood staining her party gown. She had fled the pantry and fainted. At first I thought it was Ethel Kennedy, who had just appeared on the stage with her husband. Stephen Smith, the Kennedys' brother-in-law and Bobby Kennedy's campaign manager, jumped to the podium. Without explanation, he ordered that the room be cleared. We realized that something awful had just happened behind the pantry door. Security men now barred the way. I gave Midge a dime and told her to phone the local *New York Times* bureau. I guessed that *Times* reporter Wallace Turner, assigned to Kennedy, would be too busy just now to keep the bureau informed. He would certainly be calling New York direct. I then made my way backstage, grabbed a house phone, and persuaded the operator to get me through to *Times* rewrite in New York. I held the line for three hours while dictating my first—and only—*Times* page-one story, a "sidebar" to set the scene. It made only the final final edition, held two hours later than normal.

Press photographers immediately plunged into the pantry and recorded the painful scene. There was Boris Yaro of the *Los Angeles Times*, whose picture reached the world via the AP wire; there was David Hume Kennerly, whom I had met just that afternoon in the UPI office; there was Harry Benson, shooting for *People*, who felt his duty compelled him to record the distraught Ethel Kennedy; and there was Bill Eppridge, who had been covering the Kennedy campaign for *Life*.

The wounds of 1968 would not heal. Following the "King riots," unrest spread to the nation's campuses. At Columbia, Berkeley, Chicago, and other universities, students defied authority. The only hope for fresh leadership and a new political direction seemed to lie that summer in the national conventions of the two political parties. The *Times* had always sent a big team of reporters and editors to the Republican and Democratic Conventions but only one photographer—George Tames, working for *The New York Times Magazine* and its leisurely deadlines. I was determined to change that. We could count on the two wire services to cover the spectacle of the convention floor. My aim was to photore-

My one and only page one byline story in *The New York Times*—I had not been hired as a reporter—gave an account of the tragic scene in the ballroom of the Hotel Ambassador in Los Angeles, where I heard the last words spoken by Senator Robert F. Kennedy before he walked off the podium to his assassination. This final Late City edition was held two hours beyond normal press time. UPI/ The New York Times

port the workings of the conventions behind the scenes on a daily basis, the way that only the weekly *Life* had done in the past. I also wanted to record the spectacle with exclusive views that would not appear in other newspapers. For the Republican Convention in Miami on August 5 to 9, I was authorized to send two photographers from the daily staff. AP agreed to handle our special transmissions, as they did for other member newspapers. The *Times* team totaled about fifty, working from two centers: the gaudy Riviera Room in the Fontainebleau Hotel, convention headquarters; and the backstage press room at Convention Hall, where we custom-built a 456-square-foot photo workroom. The convention proved to be anticlimactic. Richard Nixon, making what Scotty Reston called "the greatest comeback since Lazarus," had the nomination virtually sewed up. New York governor Nelson Rockefeller had vacillated too long. There was only one faint hope for "Rocky"—an unholy alliance with California governor Ronald Reagan, who occupied the exact opposite end of the party's political spectrum. By combining forces, and with the help of half a dozen "favorite sons," they might deny Nixon a majority on the first ballot and deadlock the convention. Then it could be a free-for-all. Richard Nixon's carefully constructed machine took him to victory on the first ballot Wednesday night. The only interesting question left was who would be chosen to run for vice president. Midway through the balloting for the presidential nomination, floor pages carried notes from Nixon to a very select group of party leaders, asking them to meet "as soon as possible after the end of the balloting" in his suite atop the Hilton Plaza.

An oral invitation to this meeting had already been extended by Nixon to just one journalist. It was photographer David Douglas Duncan, who was doing five-minute still-picture spots every night for NBC. Duncan and Nixon had met in the southwest Pacific. Nixon, a Navy supply officer, had helped Lieutenant Duncan of the U.S. Marines get fresh gear when he returned from a nasty mission behind Japanese lines on Bougainville. Duncan, alone, photographed this extraordinary meeting in the early hours of the morning. It actually deadlocked, but by Thursday noon Richard Nixon had put over the nomination of Maryland governor Spiro Agnew, his first choice all along. At about 7:00 P.M., I was on the convention floor, preparing for the final session, when I ran into Duncan. "How would *The New York Times* like an exclusive picture of the meeting in Nixon's penthouse that chose Agnew?" he asked, exaggerating only slightly. He showed me the big prints of the pictures he was just about to put on the NBC network.

I jumped: "How soon can I have an eight by ten to transmit to New York?"

"See me at eight o'clock," Dave said.

"How much?"

"I'll give you a bargain. One grand."

I thought it well worth the price, especially for page one, and called Clifton Daniel in New York. Every other morning paper would run a picture of Nixon's acceptance speech, already seen on television. I knew it was too late for the first edition, but Daniel promised to consider it for the late city edition. We wired the photo. Two hours later Daniel called back: "Sorry, it would mean a total remake, not only for page one but for the jump pages." *The New York Times* was not quite ready for such an adventure in photojournalism.

I returned from Miami dispirited, although numerically our little team had scored well. Of ninety-seven Republican Convention pictures run that week, forty-six were made by *Times* staff photographers. No *Times* photographer, however, would have an inside track with Richard Nixon, the next president of the United States. He once confided to George Tames, "I have to admit, I do hate that goddamn unfair *New York Times*!" On to Chicago and the Democratic Convention, but there were to be no winners chosen there—only losers. *The New York Times*'s jet flew us into Midway Airport just four days before the Democratic Convention opened on August 26. I was returning to the stockyards, scene of the dramatic 1952 conventions, which I had covered for the *Ladies' Home Journal*, but the big story this time was in the downtown streets. Thousands of young people were converging on the city, determined to make their voices heard. What had begun as an antiwar movement was now, out of sheer frustration, becoming an antiestablishment movement of many components: civil rights workers, poor people's advocates, pacifists, Communists, anarchists, Maoists, hippies, and Yippies. Their intent was to send a shock wave through the convention, but their specific goals were contradictory and confused. The *Times* augmented its team of political experts with a "riot squad" of young reporters, equipped with helmets and gas masks, who operated by two-way radio from the publisher's station wagon. I rented a trailer and parked it in the press area at the stockyards, where we processed and edited the film shot by five *Times* photographers—Neal Boenzi, Don Charles, and Barton Silverman had been added to Miami's Sauro and Tames.

Harrison Salisbury, in charge of the Chicago operation, soon found himself in serious conflict with the editors in New York over the stories from our own riot squad. Abe Rosenthal, now an associate managing editor responsible for

The story was in the streets at the 1968 Democratic convention in Chicago. Protestors of all kinds tried to disrupt the gathering, and the Chicago police went berserk—everyone was fair game for their truncheons, including members of the press. Despite his feistiness, the *Times*'s Barton Silverman and his three cameras were no match for six big cops. "John, I'm in the slammer! Get me out!" Silverman screamed over the phone on August 28. *Copyright* © FRED W. MCDARRAH

the makeup of the paper, had no sympathy with the protesters. Their obscene slogans were certainly not fit to print—nor, for that matter, was the response of the police, whose standard cry was "Get the fuckin' photographer!" The police wanted no documentation of their heavy-handed methods. It was the police, more than the dissidents, who were out of control. The climax came on Wednesday, August 28, as seven thousand protesters gathered in Grant Park. Arrests began and the police were pelted with rocks and bottles. They began shoving the crowd up against the hotel, finally pushing people through the plate glass window of the Hilton's Haymarket Lounge. A little after 9:00 P.M., I received a call from Barton Silverman, who had been manhandled and arrested by the police while photographing the scene: "John, I'm in the slammer! You've got to get me out! Call Punch! Call somebody! *Do something!*" But before I could do anything, Silverman was out.

The convention was upset, but the outcome was unaffected. It was Humphrey on the first ballot. Months later, a report by the National Commission on the Causes and Prevention of Violence documented what is probably the most massive abuse of police power in American history. There was one piece of good news: no one was killed. However, of three hundred newsmen covering the parks and streets of Chicago that week, more than sixty-five were "involved in incidents resulting in injury to themselves, damage to their equipment, or their arrest." *Times* photographer Silverman is shown on the report's cover, as he resisted arrest. Silverman's picture of a policeman swinging his billy club—at him—is the report's strongest single illustration of police brutality. Those pictures were not published by *The New York Times*, for an ironic reason: the *Times* does not reveal its own involvement in making the news.

When it came to live pictures of the 1969 moon landing, newspapers were helpless until the astronauts returned with film. We relied on often murky images from television. Walter Cronkite of CBS returned the favor, holding up a copy of the *Times* for his nationwide audience. *NYT Pictures*

28

Abe in Orbit

One day soon after I began at the *Times,* Clifton Daniel invited me to lunch at the Century Club, just down Forty-third Street toward Grand Central. The Century is the home of New York intellectuals who have Arrived. On the stairs we encountered former *Times* reporter Gay Talese, then working hard on his book *The Kingdom and the Power.* Even now it is the most useful guide to the first three generations of politics on *The New York Times.* Talese learned that I was one of the group of half a dozen editors who met each morning with Scotty Reston, and he was curious. Reston had agreed to come to New York from Washington in 1968 to resolve a power struggle that had begun over control of the Washington bureau. Reston was temporarily named executive editor and placed in charge of both the daily and Sunday papers—and also of Clifton Daniel and Abe Rosenthal, Daniel's challenger. I was but a bystander in the power struggle, but I had my own plan for the *Times*'s Washington bureau. There were normally as many or more stories from Washington on page one of the *Times* as there were from all other world capitals combined. I wanted to illustrate them with *Times* photos. The 1968 party conventions had proved that we could do our own thing: of 122 pictures used from the Democrats' fracas in Chicago, 90 were by *Times* photographers. On December 7, New York's top editors were invited to a housewarming in the sixty-man Washington bureau's new quarters on L Street, N.W. I had insisted that the new bureau have a small darkroom with facilities for developing, printing, and transmitting pictures. I also had my eye on the remarkably well-connected George Tames, who for twenty-two years had been the sole photographer in the *Times*'s Washington bureau, working exclusively for the *Times*'s Sunday department. Tames was

Washington born and bred, the son of Greek immigrants who lived in the slums that used to surround Capitol Hill. In the course of his career he would come to know and photograph eleven presidents, from Franklin Roosevelt to Bill Clinton. More important, they knew *him*, as did virtually every senator who served during the forty-eight years of Tames's career. George was a Washington insider, a storyteller and prankster, the court jester of Congress. He and his Marine sergeant wife had five children. Tames's favorite president was Harry Truman, the first president to treat photographers as the professional equal of reporters, giving them a room of their own in the West Wing of the White House. In gratitude, the photographers organized the "One More Club" and made Truman its first and only president; the club dissolved upon Eisenhower's election, as "Ike" was stiff and inaccessible to photographers. Once when Tames was assigned to photograph him, Tames followed Eisenhower to a Pentagon men's room and made an appointment while they stood at the urinals. John Kennedy was just the opposite, lending himself and his family to many photo "exclusives." He called the shots, however. He tried never to be photographed wearing glasses, feeling they destroyed his youthful image. Lyndon Johnson was equally tough, decreeing that he be photographed in left rather than right profile.

The first big test of the new Washington bureau facilities and philosophy came with the Nixon inauguration. I chose six photographers and spotted them around town. So much film would have clogged the little darkroom, so we decided to courier the morning take on the swearing-in ceremonies back to New York at lunchtime. I was the courier, in "command" of the company jet, which was standing by at Dulles. Early that morning, I went with George Tames to photograph Hubert and Muriel Humphrey in their apartment in Southwest Washington, as they prepared for their painful rendezvous with Defeat at the east front of the Capitol. Seldom has an incumbent vice president lost an election. It was an exclusive that Humphrey would give only to his "old buddy George"—many times they had clowned together. Now I sensed that both were fighting back tears. I was almost embarrassed that I had asked to come along.

I was now working for Reston, Daniel, and Rosenthal. It seemed the paper had two managing editors. It was Rosenthal, however, who was planning the future of the newspaper. In the late sixties, the profit margins of *The New York Times*, never substantial, began to slip. Until then, news department heads had simply spent "what was required" to get the news. Strict budgets were introduced in 1968, and *Times* executives began a series of suburban "retreats" to assess the future. The "News Committee" was chaired by Rosenthal. I was invited to its session of October 11–12 at a campuslike conference center in Tarrytown, New York. Rosenthal argued that the *Times* could live within its present news space. He held out the prospect of "creating a better paper instead of just a bigger one," mentioning areas such as science and technology and cultural news that needed development. The aim was to make "the presentation of news not only more attractive but more rational, drawing readers through the whole paper." I found his ideas exciting. In contrast with my abrupt career at *The Washington Post*, things seemed to be going well.

In the spring of 1969, the *Times*'s third-floor newsroom burst through into the adjacent Paramount building. This enabled us, at last, to create a modern photo lab next to the expanded picture desk. Behind the desk we built a long work counter, covering slotted storage bins for pictures in current use, and backed up by a fifteen-foot metallic "picture wall." There, using tiny magnets (instead of the conventional corkboard and thumbtacks), we could literally "throw" up glossy prints of pictures tentatively chosen through the afternoon. Editors from the other desks could readily see what we were planning. Comparisons were easily made as later pictures came in for the same or other stories. For each picture finally chosen and sent off to the Art Department and engravers, we made a photocopy. The photocopies, taking the place of the originals, then went onto the wall to give us a constantly updated overview of the pictures going into the first edition.

Pale photocopies of the day's catch were displayed on the *Times*'s magnetic "picture wall" (*background*), a system invented by *National Geographic* and adopted widely by newspapers. But the wall is already a relic; today, picture editing at most major publications happens almost entirely on computer screens. *Courtesy*, The New York Times

The new facilities were barely in place when on Sunday afternoon, July 20, 1969, *Apollo* 11 approached the moon. Abe Rosenthal had been after us for months to plan for the event. I'll never forget the Sunday night of the moon landing. Since the *only* source of news pictures would be the transmissions to the television screen, I arranged, for purposes of making the most of that dismal quality, to station photographers in front of half a dozen different sets in our own building and also at the headquarters of the three networks.

The headlines for that night's front page had been written days in advance, set in 60-point type, the *Times'* largest, and photographically enlarged to the equivalent of 96 points. At 9:30 P.M., following the landing but before the astronauts emerged from their lunar module, the first edition proclaimed:

MEN LAND ON MOON

At 10:58, after astronaut Neil Armstrong touched the moon's surface, the presses were halted for a "postscript":

MAN WALKS ON MOON

By the time the late city edition went to press at 12:46 A.M., Armstrong had been joined by his copilot, Colonel Edwin E. Aldrin, Jr., and the headline was changed to read:

MEN WALK ON MOON

By this time, there were television pictures of the two astronauts operating on the moon's surface and raising a flag. We made up a fresh front page and a picture page; the presses rolled. Downstairs in the *Times* mail room there was bedlam as papers were grabbed as they came off the presses. Next day the final edition had to be reprinted not once but twice.

There was more moon to come. On Friday, July 25, the astronauts returned to earth, to be greeted by President Nixon on the carrier *Hornet*, soon after they landed 250 miles from Johnston Island in the central Pacific. The next day, while they were feted in Hawaii, I flew to Houston to join *Times* photographer Gary Settle to cover their return to the National Aeronautics and Space Administration. In the Sunday paper, I had one of my few bylined stories in the *Times*, leading, "Just as a nervous amateur worries whether his snapshot of the bride and groom will turn out, NASA officials confessed today that they had jitters over the nine rolls of still photographs and thirteen reels of movies shot by the crew of Apollo 11." My primary purpose in Houston was to pick up copies of the moon color films as fast as possible. Rosenthal had decided to do a color newsmagazine supplement, the first in *Times* history, for the following Sun-

Aboard the *Times* company jet, science editor Henry "Hank" Lieberman (*right*) and I prepared a sixteen-page special Sunday color section while flying from Houston to New Jersey's Teterboro Airport with the first moon pictures taken by astronauts. I worked with a light box and Moviola, while art director George Cowan (*with pipe*) and his assistant made layouts at the other end of the plane. It was a color first for the *Times*, conceived by Abe Rosenthal. GARY SETTLE/The New York Times

day's paper. On Tuesday, Henry "Hank" Lieberman, science news coordinator, flew to Houston in the *Times*'s jet, along with George Cowan of the Art Department and a production expert. They had equipped the small cabin with a light box, a Moviola for viewing 8-millimeter film, and layout equipment. Tuesday afternoon at NASA, waiting in line with the wire services and newsmagazines, I got my set of color dupes and a piece of film. We took off. By the time we crossed the Mississippi, Cowan and I had roughed out a sixteen-page magazine; Lieberman was writing to our layouts at top speed. Then, a bad weather break: the Teterboro, New Jersey, airport was fogged in; we had insufficient fuel to hover over it; we had to land at Dulles outside Washington and await Teterboro clearance.

Around 3:00 A.M., we finally made it to Teterboro and rushed by limousine into town. A special room had been set aside for us at a Manhattan office of Alco Gravure, engravers for the special section. We found a nervous Rosenthal and an anxious Walter Mattson, the *Times*'s young executive in charge of production. He was counting every minute and we were already three hours late. Within an hour, Rosenthal had gone over everything Lieberman had brought and gave the okay. Finally we could relax. Abe threw his arm around me, saying, "Man! Maybe we should be running color every day!" I celebrated with him, concealing my true feelings, thinking of my color headaches at *The Washington Post*.

The following day, Abe sent around a memo: "You all met the occasion. It may be one small step for man but it is one big leap for *The New York Times*."

A. M. Rosenthal was in orbit.

James "Scotty" Reston of the *Times*, a two-time Pulitzer Prize winner, just happened to be on Martha's Vineyard, tending to the affairs of his own *Vineyard Gazette*, when Senator Ted Kennedy's car went off a bridge on the nearby island of Chappaquiddick, taking a young woman to her death. © JACK D. HUBBARD

29

Special Transmissions

In the summer of 1969, *The New York Times* officially became Abe Rosenthal's baby. On July 31, Punch Sulzberger announced: "James Reston, who came from Washington to New York at my request to serve as Executive Editor . . . will return to Washington." Clifton Daniel would become "Associate Editor, with a group of new duties." A. M. Rosenthal would become managing editor and Seymour Topping an assistant managing editor. Abe's rivals had left the newsroom, Harrison Salisbury to start the Op-Ed page; Ted Bernstein simply got out of the way. Not long after, Abe would speak lovingly at Ted's funeral. No new executive editor was named. Having been hired by Daniel, I should have been alarmed at this development, but I wasn't. While Daniel's style was opposite to Rosenthal's, their objectives for the paper seemed identical. Abe appeared to be just as interested in improving picture play as Cliff and more likely to accomplish it. The man I would really miss, though I didn't realize it at the time, was Scotty Reston. We had not worked closely together, but I had always admired his low-key style. There was the Saturday morning in July 1969 when I happened to be working the Picture Desk on my day off. The phone rang, "John? It's Reston . . . Scotty. I'm calling from Edgartown, Martha's Vineyard. Ted Kennedy seems to have run off a bridge near here, on Chappaquiddick Island. His car has been found in the water, and there may be somebody in it—not Kennedy. I found a photographer who made some pictures. I think we're ahead of the wires. How do you want them sent?" A big story, soon to become a scandal of immense political proportions, had interrupted the weekend of the *Times*'s executive editor—who also happened to own and publish the weekly *Vineyard Gazette*. A woman who lived near the bridge had called him that morning at the *Gazette* to say there had been a bad accident and she thought Ted Kennedy was involved. Scotty had gone straight to the police station and learned that the police chief was in conference with Kennedy. He had sent a note to the senator suggesting that they meet afterward at Reston's house in the next block. "Of course he didn't," Reston remembered in his memoir. "I never made that silly journalistic mistake again." Reston then went about alerting the National Desk, calling me and filing his story. A Kennedy secretary had drowned in the car. The incident filled Scotty with sadness. When Edward Kennedy had first run for the Senate in 1962, Reston had written in the *Times* that "one Kennedy is a triumph, two Kennedys at the same time are a miracle, but three could easily be regarded by many voters as an invasion." Reston had come to believe, after the loss of both Jack and Bobby, that Ted just might make the best president of the three. Now it could never be.

Another editor whom I instinctively respected was Gene Roberts, the national editor. I was not alone in my high regard for him—and this was many years before Roberts would experience a Second Coming, appointed managing editor of the *Times* after an absence of twenty-two years! A soft-spoken small-town North Carolinian, Roberts had come up in journalism the hard way. He was on his fourth paper, the *Detroit Free Press*, when Harrison Salisbury hired him to cover the South for the *Times*. In 1968, when the Vietnam War was at its worst, he headed the Saigon bureau, and he came to New York in 1969 to take over the National Desk. There he steadily beefed up the roving national staff, hiring gifted writer/reporters away from other newspapers. His staff dubbed him "the frog" for the way his face retracted to ponder a question, opening wide when he had the answer. Roberts was determined to get proper illustration and display for the stories turned in by his talented reporters, so he was a natural ally when I decided to try to hire Gary Settle from the Chicago *Daily News*. Settle was one of the remarkable string of photographers trained by Rich Clarkson on the Topeka *Capital Journal;* he won contests with great regularity. But with two boys in school, Gary and his wife had no desire to move to New York, so we agreed that he should operate out of the Chicago bureau. Settle's beat became the United States. One day, he might be working with a Denver-based correspondent on a story of ranch life in New Mexico, followed by a flight low over the Grand Canyon with a science writer. The following week he might be in South Carolina, riding a newly desegregated school bus; or in Indiana, walking the tracks with a congressional committee investigating a train wreck. When time permitted, Settle would return to Chicago to process and transmit his pictures; otherwise, he would transmit from the nearest friendly newspaper office or wire service bureau.

Gene Roberts helped me get a picture of the My Lai massacre into the *Times*. There was no press coverage of the March 16, 1968, slaughter of Vietnamese villagers by American troops, but Seymour Hersh of a small syndicate called Dispatch News Service finally broke the story on November 13, 1969. A week later, the Cleveland *Plain Dealer* published photos taken by a former Army photographer named Ron Haeberle. He claimed they had been taken with his "personal" camera and were therefore his own property. Haeberle had been giving slide shows to civic groups around Cleveland that had included a few of the massacre pictures. Apparently, there had been little reaction among the attendees. When Hersh's story broke, Haeberle decided it was time to make some money, using his hometown paper as a showcase. With *Plain Dealer* reporter Joe Eszterhas, later to become one of Hollywood's highest-paid screenwriters, Haeberle flew to New York. The next morning, Gene Roberts and I collared the two entrepreneurs at the Gotham Hotel. We wanted only one picture, to document the story, but we had not decided whether we had to pay for it, much less how much to offer. Haeberle's pictures were arguably government property. I was certain that *Life* was interested in the color, but my friend Dick Pollard, then the picture editor, wasn't talking. I guessed that *Life* was unlikely to pay more than $25,000 (in fact, it paid $20,000). Roberts and I sounded out Haeberle and Eszterhas on the price of one picture for the *Times*. They hinted at $5,000, but we made no firm offer. They went off to conclude their deal with *Life*. In late morning, we received word that London papers, copying the photos from the *Plain Dealer*, were going ahead without payment, ignoring the copyright. The *New York Post* followed, in its early-afternoon edition. Rosenthal decreed that it would now be ridiculous for the *Times* to pay. We would publish "as a matter of public interest." The next day, November 22, the *Times* ran one My Lai picture on page three—downplayed to avoid sensationalism. The reaction was not what I had expected. Readers seemed as much incensed by our publication of the picture as by the atrocity itself. Newspapers that played the pictures big were condemned for being "un-American"—the Washington *Star* even had complaints of obscenity because some of the child corpses were naked.

President Nixon had ordered the secret bombing of Cambodia in March 1969 in an attempt to cut off Vietcong supply lines. The strategy proved ineffective, so, without consulting Congress, Nixon ordered American forces to join South Vietnamese in an invasion of Cambodia, announcing it on television after the fact. The news rekindled the campus antiwar movement. On May 4, National Guardsmen killed four student protesters at Kent State University in Ohio. A photograph made by twenty-one-year-old journalism student John Filo showed a girl screaming in anguish over the body of a fallen student. "I didn't react visually," Filo has been quoted as saying. "This girl came up and knelt over the body and let out a God-awful scream that made me click the camera."

The picture reached the Associated Press wire by way of a small Ohio daily. *The New York Times* used it, three columns wide, at the top of page one. Newspapers everywhere ran the picture, and NBC's Huntley-Brinkley *Report* held the image on the screen for seven seconds, in silence. Now the nation's campuses really blew. Two-thirds of the colleges in New England closed, and Governor Ronald Reagan shut the 121 colleges of the California state system for fear of bloodshed.

The Kent State picture, like Eddie Adams's Saigon execution, was another of the images that changed the American public's perception of the war. One was still to come: the 1972 picture by AP's Huynh Cong "Nick" Ut of a little Vietnamese girl running naked from a napalm bombing. I recommended it for page one and recall how relieved news editor Jordan was that the girl was too young to have pubic hair and thus required no retouching.

In 1971, Secretary of State Henry Kissinger continued practicing "secret" diplomacy while Richard Nixon waged "secret" war. In February, South Vietnamese forces made "incursions" into Laos with American support. On February 21, *Life*'s Larry Burrows, in his ninth year of covering hostilities in Vietnam, talked his way onto a South Vietnamese helicopter to get a ride into Laos with three other photographers. They were shot down. When the news came, I thought back to London on the morning of Thursday, June 8, 1944. Larry, with the rest of us in *Life*'s London bureau, had just completed a fifty-two-hour stretch, starting early that Tuesday when we had gotten the news of the D-day landings. Larry lived far away by Underground and was afraid he'd fall asleep on the way home. I persuaded him to come home with me to the flat on Upper Wimpole Street. Frank Scherschel was away, of course. I pointed to Frank's empty bed. But there was no way Larry was going to sleep in that bed. It belonged only to Frank, a real *Life* photographer. Larry lay down on the floor and fell asleep. He was but a humble apprentice, one of the teenagers who worked in the darkroom when I arrived. He hoped to go into the Royal Navy at eighteen but instead was drafted to work in the coal mines. When he got the notice, he said to us philosophically, "I guess it won't be different from working in the darkroom."

No *Times* correspondent or photographer was killed in covering Vietnam. Other journalists were less fortunate. Forty-six were killed in that long conflict, including at least a dozen photographers. Gilles Caron of the Gamma agency and Kyoichi Sawada and Sean Flynn of UPI "disappeared" in Cambodia, never to return. On January 15, 1970, we published a full page of combat pictures from Vietnam by Don McCullin, then working for London's *Sunday Times.* On June 4 Don was severely wounded by mortar fire only ten miles from Phnom Penh.

In April 1971, as the war in Southeast Asia continued without cease, Abe

Rosenthal called me into his office one day to say "I'm going to borrow Renato Perez from your desk for a few weeks. I can't tell you what he's going to be doing." Renato, a Chilean who had come to New York as a student, edited foreign pictures. His several languages included Russian. Perez was assigned to the secret *Times* task force that had just begun work in a suite at the New York Hilton, editing the documents that became known as "The Pentagon Papers." In 1967, Secretary of Defense Robert McNamara, troubled by the stalemate in the Vietnam War, had commissioned a thorough study of its origins by the "Vietnam History Task Force." The study had been completed in 1969 but never released. Neil Sheehan of the *Times*'s Washington bureau obtained copies of the documents from Daniel Ellsberg, one of the authors. Renato's task was to illustrate them. He was given carte blanche to remove pictures—usually late at night—from the *Times* files. Sometime during the week of June 8, Renato returned to the desk as quietly as he had left. I noticed that he seemed crestfallen. On Saturday afternoon, June 12, as the first installment of "The Pentagon Papers" was going to press, I learned why: Punch Sulzberger had decided to give the documents only six pages daily rather than the twelve the editors had requested. That left virtually no room for pictures. As a result, the solid pages of type were uninviting and unreadable. Publication of the "Papers" became almost a nonevent, in terms of affecting the course of the Vietnam War. It was, however, a proud moment for *The New York Times*, whose courage in defying the government was noted around the world as a victory for freedom of the press.

I knew I would never make the *Times* a picture newspaper, but I was determined to show that more and better pictures would bring new readers to our world report. This meant coaxing the thirty-odd foreign correspondents to take responsibility for getting pictures to accompany their feature stories. My foremost ally was *Times* Saigon correspondent Gloria Emerson, whom I had first known when she covered the Paris collections. She was the most sophisticated of all *Times* correspondents about pictures and photographers, and the most demanding. Coverage of the Vietnam War became her obsession. She saw it in the most basic human terms: "The war began like this: one man died, then another, then one more, then the man next to that man. The dying was one by one."

Gloria was a class act, as much at ease when hitching a ride on a Honda as striding down the rue Saint-Honoré, but she did have a tendency to take one over. I loved Gloria for her letters. Some excerpts from 1970:

Saigon, March 8: "I have at last found a good photographer. . . . He is a bit too much on opium but never mind."

Saigon, March 11: "I'm going to be very cross if you don't personally look at the soldiers pix taken by my French photographer."

My favorite *New York Times* correspondent when it came to pictures, Gloria Emerson was passionate about the choice of photographers and about which pictures ran. Gloria had enough flair for two. *Courtesy,* The New York Times

Saigon, June 4: "Glad that Whittaker pix of wounded worked out, so he will not almost have died in vain (his plane was shot at)."

Phnom Penh, June 11: "Walked to Reuters to file copy—it's about midnight—and two boys on Honda stole my handbag almost breaking my arm in the process. . . . I am now keyless, passportless, creditcard-less, addressbook-less, etc. Oh God."

Hong Kong, November 5: "I do wish we would run pictures that told the story even if it makes people sick at breakfast."

Commenting on these letters, Gloria Emerson now writes from Princeton: "I remember nearly all of the photographs of the suffering I sent to you, they are wedged somewhere in my mind, and that is part of the trouble. You want amnesia most of all and it has been denied me."

In the larger *Times* bureaus there was usually sufficient staff to suffer our requests. A long succession of bureau chiefs in Paris, London, Bonn, Rome, Jerusalem, Moscow, Tokyo, and, above all, Saigon, aided by semianonymous desk persons, were enormously supportive. Where possible, I helped them find qualified photographer "stringers"—occasionally one of my old friends from Magnum. One of the first of these was Henri Cartier-Bresson. On November 9, 1970, at the age of eighty, Charles de Gaulle died at home in Colombey-les-Deux-Églises. We asked Henri to cover the funeral. He chose to shoot the faces of the ordinary *citoyens* of the village as they watched de Gaulle's passing cortege. AP's Paris bureau transmitted direct to a receiver in our New York darkroom. The result was a strip of three shallow pictures that ran across the bottom of the jump page. Such results with picture transmission encouraged us to make further news assignments abroad. In Paris, freelance photographer Jean-Luce Hure covered the collections with fashion writer Bernadine Morris. In London our most frequent stringer was Neil Libbert, whom I first met when I noticed a man with a camera looking lost in front of New York's Chelsea Hotel. In Israel, Micha Bar-Am became a stringer in 1968 and worked closely with a succession of *Times* correspondents. In the 1973 Suez war, Micha advanced so fast with Israeli forces that a group of Egyptian soldiers surrendered to him. The more remote *Times*men carried cameras with varying degrees of enthusiasm and/or resentment. Malcolm Browne, who as AP's Saigon bureau chief made the memorable 1963 picture of a burning Buddhist monk, wrote from Buenos Aires in response to my plea, "I'll be happy to start shooting again." But at the same time, James Feron wrote from Warsaw, "Using a camera is one of the quickest ways to get in trouble around here," and Raymond Anderson from Cairo, "At best, cameras are regarded with suspicion here." David Binder, venturing into East Berlin to cover an East Bloc summit meeting, cabled, "The Warsaw Pact is anti-photo, a stance I fully approve."

The 1971 Overseas Press Club award for "Best Newspaper or Wire Service Photo Reporting from Abroad" went to *The New York Times* "for excellence in general photographic coverage from abroad." In June of that year, at a banquet in Pittsburgh, I received, along with *Life*'s Alfred Eisenstaedt, the Joseph A. Sprague Memorial Award of the National Press Photographers Association, "the highest honor in the field of photojournalism."

It was downhill from there.

Somewhat naïvely, I was enjoying the excitement of working for Rosenthal. Of all the editors I had ever known, he was the most demanding. But he was also approachable, and I didn't hesitate to argue with him. Sometimes I argued for things that Rosenthal was not particularly interested in, such as giving wire service photographers the same kind of credit we gave staffers. He didn't buy it.

Rosenthal was under intense pressure to hold down costs, and I'm afraid I was not of much help. I paid little attention to efficiency studies such as the one that discovered "Caption writers are idle an average of 41.6% of the time." I kept pressing for more, not less, staff, pointing out that the New York *Daily News* had more than twice as many photographers and used far fewer display pictures. My budget, for a department of more than forty, was about $1.3 million a year. In April 1972, I argued for deepening and broadening our picture coverage. Abe's answer, several months later, was to ask me to *reduce* staff. I

At the end of the Bangladesh war of independence from Pakistan in 1971, Bengali soldiers displayed some Bihari prisoners at the Dacca racetrack. Soon the gathering turned into a slaughter. Some photographers left the scene, hoping to quiet things down. Michel Laurent and Horst Faas of AP stayed to the end, and managed to get their pictures past the censors. We ran one in *The New York Times*. Prime Minister Indira Gandhi later told Marc Riboud that the publication of these pictures shocked the Indian government into giving stern orders to the troops: no more such atrocities (at least not in front of journalists). The 1971 Overseas Press Club award went to *The New York Times* "for excellence in general photographic coverage from abroad." MICHEL LAURENT/AP

Managing editor Abe
Rosenthal participated
fully in the choice of pictures. I typically presented
them to him at the 6:30
page one conference in
his office. He usually went
with my recommenda-
tions, but not always.
Courtesy, The New York
Times

managed to cut expenses, but by the following March it became obvious that
Abe was far from satisfied. One noon he called me in and told me that I was
through. I was stunned. I asked for some reasons. Abe said something about
my news judgment, that I wasn't sufficiently forceful, that we just didn't com-
municate. He added some nice things, but I could see that they didn't matter.
His mind was made up, although he told me he had no one else in mind for my
job. It was his decision, not the publisher's, he said, but Punch had been informed. I would have several months to quietly look for another job and could
then "resign." He added, "Buckingham may have something for you in the
News Service."

Back in 1969, I had proposed a New York Times Picture Service. The idea
had been welcomed by Rob Roy Buckingham, a small man with an easy smile
and the appropriate nickname "Buck." A former UPI reporter and a crack
salesman, he had built the News Service into a profitable subsidiary—it had
been conceived as a means of unloading onto other publishers some of the expense of maintaining the *Times*'s far-flung staff, and it worked. I figured that
the same principle could be applied to underwriting expanded picture coverage.

On May 17, 1973, "a new facility, NYT PICTURES," was announced by Sydney Gruson as senior vice president of the *Times* for subsidiary operations.
"Headed by John G. Morris, picture editor of the *Times* since 1967," it would
"serve the picture needs of worldwide media." It sounded like such big business
that even *The Wall Street Journal* ran the story.

Our first international scoop was also voted "Press Photo of the Year" in the
World Press Photo competition in Amsterdam. (As a member of that year's
jury, I abstained.) On September 11, 1973, Salvador Allende, Chile's first
Marxist president, died, perhaps a suicide, in the military overthrow of his
regime. Four months later, a *New York Times* correspondent in Latin America
was offered negatives of photos showing Allende, gun in hand, leading the defense of the Presidential Palace in Santiago, shortly before his death. The pic-

An anonymous member of his staff took this picture of Chilean president Salvador Allende Gossens on September 11, 1973—the day he died in a military coup. *The New York Times* published it and distributed it through New York Times Pictures; it would go on to win the grand prize in the World Press Photo contest on March 27, 1974. *Courtesy,* The New York Times

tures had been taken by one of Allende's aides, who was still hiding in Chile and therefore could not claim credit. To this day I do not know his name, but his negatives are unmistakable: a piece of thread in the camera back shows up on the left-hand side of each frame. The *Times* published one picture on January 26, and NYT Pictures distributed it worldwide.

So far we were syndicating only *Times*-produced pictures, a package a day sent by mail or wire. My next move was to develop a weekly international picture service called "Pictures of Our Times," drawing as much or more on free-lance photographers as on those of the *Times* and aimed primarily at foreign markets. The new service started with a bang in April 1975. The *Times*'s roving Asian correspondent Sydney Schanberg, with whom I had a close rapport, was now in besieged Phnom Penh. Sydney went to great lengths to illustrate his stories: either he shot his own pictures or he got the best available photographer. As the Khmer Rouge approached the Cambodian capital, foreign editor James Greenfield ordered Schanberg and Joseph Lelyveld, the other *Times* correspondent there, to get out. Instead Sydney cabled back:

I HAVE MADE JUDGMENT TO STAY. I WOULD APPRECIATE YOUR SUPPORTING THAT JUDGMENT RATHER THAN SENDING ME ALARMIST CABLES WHICH WILL ONLY MAKE A DIFFICULT SITUA-

TION MORE DIFFICULT. DITH PRAN [the *Times*'s Cambodian stringer] IS WITH ME. HE HAS ALSO DECIDED TO STAY ON HIS OWN JUDGMENT. WE EVACUATED HIS WIFE AND FOUR CHILDREN. . . . I NEED YOUR SUPPORT NOT A CONFRONTATION. I MADE MY JUDGMENT SANELY AND I WILL DO MY BEST FOR THE PAPER. I WILL FILE WHATEVER AND WHENEVER I CAN.

Interned in the French embassy with a handful of other journalists for two weeks, Schanberg finally crossed the border into Thailand on May 2. NYT Pictures offered Schanberg's story of the fall of Phnom Penh, with seven pictures by Italian freelance Ennio Iacobucci and five by Dith Pran, who had been taken captive and would not be heard from again for two years. The story of Schanberg's joyful reunion with Dith Pran became the book and movie *The Killing Fields*. Dith Pran is now a *Times* photographer in New York.

No matter how well NYT Pictures did, it wasn't enough for the management. I now had bosses on three levels, and I was working harder than ever. I made no effort to conceal my unhappiness. One day I was invited to lunch at the Harvard Club with Buck and his immediate boss. They told me that if I resigned, they would pay me through the end of the year. That was it. No pension, no benefits beyond that. It was clearly suicidal for me to consider this, at fifty-nine. I decided to go over their heads, to the highest *Times* authority of all, the publisher. I wrote an eight-page history of my entire career at the *Times* and tried it out on Scotty Reston. He agreed to forward it to Punch. The publisher soon replied with a letter that assured me of his sympathy with "the problems you have raised." He arranged that I would not only be paid until the end of that year but would also receive a *Times* pension. I signed off on the deal and went to Amsterdam, for the third year in a row, to be a judge of World Press Photo, and from there to Budapest, to speak at the opening of an exhibition of Robert Capa's pictures, his first ever in his native Hungary.

Andrei Sakharov, the noted Russian physicist and dissident, talks to his wife, Yelena Bonner, who interpreted for us in their Moscow kitchen in February 1977. He had recently won the Nobel Prize for Peace. The first issue of *Quest*, which we presented to him along with *Time* magazine's cover story about him, lies on the table. Ms. Bonner later wrote a message for us to carry back to New York, in defiance of the KGB. JOHN G. MORRIS

30

Various Quests

W hat next? Although I'd experienced joblessness before, I had only vaguely considered what life would be like after the *Times*. But I didn't need to worry. As it had before, work presented itself. For twenty years I had been exhorting photojournalists in one way or another, writing such articles as "Let's Make Honest Pictures," "Photographers Don't Think!," and "The Art of Seeing." I had spoken on platforms in a dozen states. I never addressed questions of technique. I talked about photographers I had known, including some who had given their lives in the pursuit of photojournalism. It was no way to make a living, but I became a sort of ambassador (or gadfly) of the photojournalism community.

In 1961, I was invited to deliver the keynote address of the annual Cross Country Photojournalism Seminar of the National Press Photographers Association, known as the "Flying Short Course." On the trip, which took us to Los Angeles, Kansas City, Atlanta, and Columbus, Ohio, I got to know the NPPA's indefatigable Joseph Costa, "Mr. Press Photographer." The immigrant son of a Sicilian cobbler, Costa had started as an eight-dollar-a-week office boy on the New York *World*. In 1920, at age sixteen, he became a *World* staff photographer, at twenty-five dollars a week, getting so many scoops that the *Daily News* hired him away for eighty dollars—no doubt the highest salary in press photography at that time. It got its money's worth. Costa figured out a way to get a picture of murderess Ruth Snyder as she died in the electric chair at Sing Sing. He imported a *Chicago Tribune* photographer for the job, as he himself would have been recognized. They used a small glass-plate camera strapped to the photographer's left ankle with a cable release running up his leg. When Costa became chief photographer for Hearst's King Features, his exploits continued. In 1937, he slipped a camera under his shirt and photographed a Baltimore man being flogged for beating his wife. In 1953, from a blimp, Costa made a color picture of the night takeoff of a Navy fighter from an aircraft carrier, using hundreds of flashbulbs strung the length of the ship's flight deck. Costa became the NPPA's first president and for years edited the NPPA magazine *National Press Photographer.* He led the organization's campaign for opening courtrooms to cameras.

In 1974, the NPPA's incoming president, Bill Strode of the Louisville *Courier-Journal,* looked around for a new editor. I proposed Midge—I was still on *The New York Times.* By this time, through years of shared association with Magnum, *Post,* and *Times* photographers and after many arduous hours as a photo researcher, Midge had become a picture professional. She had never edited a magazine but got the job. I volunteered my help, and our New York apartment became the magazine's office. Reflecting the growing interest of NPPA members in television, we changed the magazine's name to *News Photographer.* To pack in as much news as possible, and as many names, we created a flexible section called "NewsViews," a title that sticks to this day (as does *News Photographer*). "Pictures of the Month" showed winning photos from NPPA's monthly "clip contest" for published pictures. Long captions explained the circumstances under which they had been made—not just technical data but the feelings of the photographers, their subjects, editors, and readers, and the repercussions. Layouts showed picture play. *News Photographer* thus became a kind of running journalism text—what works, what doesn't.

Recognizing the void between news photographers and their bosses, we tried to create a dialogue. Gene Roberts, then *The Philadelphia Inquirer*'s executive editor, wrote, "If there is any one single thing wrong with photography in American newspapers, it is that photo editors are not given enough voice in the handling, the play and the cropping of pictures." Editor Charles Bailey of the *Minneapolis Tribune* expressed his views on stretching his paper's picture budget to send photographers overseas. The *Chicago Tribune*'s managing editor, Maxwell McCrohon, talked about newspaper design, "a widely misunderstood part of our craft." Gloria Emerson spoke of her despair when editors choose the wrong picture.

I had long been fascinated by the interrelationship of pictures and political power. When the assassination of John Kennedy propelled him into the White House, President Lyndon Johnson asked the United States Information Agency to lend him "that Jap photographer" who had covered one of Johnson's world tours. The "Jap" photographer was the American-educated Yoichi Okamoto, head of USIA's pictorial branch and a U.S. Army lieutenant in World War II.

Johnson gave Okamoto unparalleled access, permitting him to walk into the Oval Office without asking. Richard Nixon gave *his* White House photographer, Ollie Atkins, no such freedom, but President Gerald Ford went Johnson one better, not only appointing a skilled photographer, David Hume Kennerly, but also a professional picture editor, Sandra Eisert of Louisville's *Times*. She and Kennerly broke new ground in candid presidential coverage, even releasing pictures of the president's jovial celebration with Henry Kissinger in the Oval Office when "only" fifteen U.S. Marines (plus twenty-six others) died in the 1975 rescue of forty seamen aboard the merchant ship *Mayaguez* after its seizure by Cambodian Communists in the Gulf of Siam.

Soon after the 1977 inauguration of President Jimmy Carter, I went to see Jody Powell, his press secretary, who received me while getting his hair cut in the White House barbershop. I tried to sell him the idea of adding a picture editor (me) to his staff, but Powell didn't buy it. Ronald Reagan, four years later, hired photographer Michael Evans, whom I had unwittingly helped to train by bringing him from Cleveland to *The New York Times*. Reagan, however, saw visual history only in terms of "photo ops."

In 1976, Robert Shnayerson, a former senior editor of *Time*, then the editor of *Harper's*, asked me to join him and a group of talented journalists in creating an idealistic new magazine called *Quest*—with a slash to celebrate each year of renewal, beginning with *Quest/77*. Dedicated to vivid, often gritty stories about the pursuit of excellence, it had the strange backing of a wealthy California evangelist, Herbert W. Armstrong, a former Chicago advertising executive, who supported prestigious cultural causes in an effort to soften his fundamentalist image. Shnayerson accepted Armstrong's money under an ironclad agreement that Armstrong would keep his hands off the magazine's editorial content; in fact, the two men never met or spoke.

As soon as *Quest's* first issue closed, I took off on a quest of my own, a seven-day tour of Moscow and Leningrad, with Midge and a group of ophthalmologists. At Kennedy Airport I was startled to see, on the cover of *Time*, a color portrait of Andrei Sakharov, leading a story of the Russian dissident movement. I bought three copies, resolving to personally deliver one to the man himself. Sakharov, the physicist who had given Russia the hydrogen bomb, was now in open revolt against the Soviet Communist regime, the intellectual symbol of dissent. One reason he could not be silenced was that his picture had often appeared in *The New York Times*. It's much easier to dispose of a faceless adversary.

From the huge Moskva Hotel I phoned Christopher Wren, Moscow bureau chief of the *Times*. He hustled over to get us. I showed him *Time* and said that I'd like to give Sakharov a copy. Chris phoned him, and half an hour later we were face-to-face with Sakharov and his wife in their kitchen. Sakharov studied the *Time* story, to which he had contributed. Meanwhile, his wife, Yelena Bonner, told us the news: The day before, Sakharov had received a much-appreciated phone call from Jimmy Carter. We sat for almost an hour, while Wren talked to the couple in Russian. When it was time to go, Yelena asked us to take a letter to a prominent New York editor.

Back in our hotel room, Midge wadded up Bonner's note and stuffed it in the casing of a deodorant stick. Perhaps it was the first place an inspector would have looked, but we were amateurs. Upon our departure, we went through emigration and outbound customs without a hitch, but not until the motors of the Boeing 707 revved up on the runway did we feel safe again.

At *Quest*, I participated in making dozens of assignments to photographers on a wide variety of stories, with the lowest failure rate of any publication in my experience. During that time Bob Shnayerson gave me nine bylines. I am proudest of a piece that Shnayerson entitled "Images of Overcoming." It concerned Peter Magubane, an innovative and daring South African photographer. Magubane, son of a Soweto vegetable peddler, had learned photography on *Drum*, the *Life*-size picture monthly that gave voice to black Africa. In 1961, *Drum*'s pictures began to reach the world through Magnum. Peter gave up school to work at *Drum* as a tea boy and messenger, often driving for the editor, Tom Hopkinson—later to become *Sir* Tom for his contributions to journalism, starting with *Picture Post*. Encouraged and disciplined by *Drum*'s Berlin-born picture editor, Jürgen Schadeberg, Peter roamed the streets of Johannesburg with a camera at night and fell asleep in the office after he developed his pictures. For *Drum* he shot stories on the black children who worked long hours in the potato fields, driven by overseers; he also recorded the lives of gold miners living in primitive hostels, forced to line up naked for inspection. He routinely covered demonstrations and riots. Frequently arrested, he spent almost two years in prison—of which 586 days were passed in solitary confinement.

Magubane was not only fearless but also ingenious. Covering a trial, he buried his Leica in a loaf of bread. When he had "eaten" enough in the courtroom, he went out and returned with the camera in a milk carton, shooting more pictures by "sipping" through a straw. He became a staff photographer for Johannesburg's *Rand Daily Mail*, which in 1977 ran on its front page a color photo of Walter Cronkite congratulating Peter for winning South Africa's top prize in journalism, the equivalent of a Pulitzer, for his coverage of the 1976 race riots. Incredibly, this son of a Soweto peddler has published eleven books (they are no longer banned in South Africa). He has had exhibitions in New York, London, Paris, and Berlin and won the Robert Capa and Erich Salomon prizes for dedicated photojournalism. Publishing Magubane was one of *Quest*'s finest moments.

For *Quest*, I profiled Peter Magubane, the remarkable South African photographer whose lifelong talent and dedication have won him a place in the world history of photojournalism. Son of a Soweto vegetable peddler, Peter joined the staff of *Drum*, edited by Sir Tom Hopkinson. Peter was frequently arrested, served 586 days in solitary confinement, and was banned from his profession for five years, only to emerge as the "inside" photographer of Nelson Mandela when the South African leader was released from prison. JURGEN SCHADEBERG/Drum

In 1978, only two years after the start-up, *Quest*'s evangelical backer tired of Shnayerson's provocative liberalism and decided to fire him. I joined the staff in full revolt. Shnayerson's chair was saved, for two more years, but in January 1981 Armstrong violated the original agreement by scheduling an article in which he had particular interest. Shnayerson resigned, taking the key editors with him. *Quest* rapidly declined and died quietly.

In 1975 my wife, Midge, and I persuaded Gene and Aileen Smith, despite their failing marriage, to address the National Press Photographers Association convention in Jackson Hole, Wyoming. Gene lectured with their pictures of Minamata. When he came to this famous picture of Tomoko in the bath, he broke into tears. GARY SETTLE/The New York Times

31

After Gene

he morning of October 16, 1978, I had an appointment at the Arizona
Mortuary on University Boulevard in Tucson. It was there that I looked
into the face of W. Eugene Smith for the last time. It was curiously relaxed,
as if to say, "Now it's up to you." Which it was. Two years before, Gene had
asked me to be the executor of his estate. Now, after consulting his children, I
had to release his neatly dressed corpse to the flames of the crematory. I
thought of all the times that Gene had threatened suicide, in order to get his
way. His father's suicide had made credible this dreadful weapon of the de-
pressed. Gene seemed often to have sufficient cause. Lincoln Kirstein, Gene's
friend and admirer, once said, "A full account of Smith's life would be too
painful to write." Kirstein spoke too soon. In his last decade, W. Eugene Smith
transcended his troubles. He found his manifest destiny despite his despair, em-
bracing defeat in a special kind of triumph.

During his Magnum years Gene had rented a loft on Sixth Avenue, in Manhattan's wholesale flower district. I seldom visited Gene there. I simply found it
too painful. I could not help but think of the family he had abandoned in Croton. Gene's sense of black humor may have kept him going, but it only de-
pressed me. Three remarkable young women sustained him during that time,
when he was virtually an outcast from the profession of photojournalism.
United in their fascination with Gene and sympathy for one another, there
never seemed to be any jealousy among them. First there was Carole Thomas,
a seventeen-year-old art student when she came to him in 1959. They fell in
love and talked of marriage, but Gene was not divorced. In 1960, they had a
sudden, totally unexpected opportunity to escape this dilemma. Gene was in-

vited by Hitachi, makers of everything from turbines to transistors, to spend
nine months in Japan on a huge industrial assignment in twenty-seven loca-
tions. In a repeat of the Pittsburgh performance, Gene took an overabundance
of pictures. Upon their return, he became increasingly dependent on Carole
while continuing to drink and take drugs. When he became impossible, Carole
would leave him, returning when he appeared to straighten out. Gene finally
obtained a divorce from Carmen, but as an actual wedding approached Carole
came to her senses. She fled to California, where she has lived ever since. Gene
was devastated. For months his behavior was erratic. He repeatedly threatened
suicide. Midge and I received more than one such call; Gene's son Patrick and
his wife, Phyllis, would often drive into the city in the middle of the night in response to his pleas.

In the summer of 1969, Gene met Leslie Teicholz at Woodstock. She was
shooting publicity pictures for Channel 13, New York City's public television
station. Gene offered her work at his loft. She knew that he was looking for a replacement for Carole and so declined. But he persisted, and she was finally persuaded to join him in his work—nothing personal. Leslie happened to be at the
loft the afternoon Cornell Capa called Gene to offer him a retrospective show at
the Jewish Museum under the auspices of the Fund for Concerned Photography. Spontaneously, Gene told Cornell that he would do it, but only if "this person Leslie" would help. Originally planned for New York's Museum of Modern
Art as a show of two to three hundred prints, the Smith exhibition grew and
grew at the Jewish Museum, winding up with approximately 542 images, including a tray of continuously projected slides on World War II. Gene called it
"Let Truth Be the Prejudice." Leslie's role was crucial. With tactful persistence,
she kept Gene on track for the year that the show took to prepare but kept re-
sisting his romantic overtures.

Gene lived on love. Occasionally he would go to Philadelphia to see Margery
Lewis, who by now had changed her name to Smith, and their son, Kevin. On
August 2, 1970, returning from such a visit, Gene was surrounded by a gang
of black youths a few blocks from the station in Philadelphia. They stripped
him of his cameras and clothes and threw baseballs at his naked testicles. A
few days later, Gene told Peter Pollock of the Art Institute of Chicago, who had
come to visit, "I realized what they were doing. I was to be 'the nigger' at whom
whites have always thrown baseballs at country fairs and circuses." A few
weeks later, a TV crew came from Japan to do a Fuji film commercial. A twenty-
year-old Japanese-American girl from Stanford University came along as interpreter. Aileen Mioko Sprague knew little about photography and had never
heard of W. Eugene Smith. When they left, Aileen stayed behind. She never returned to Stanford; instead, she became Gene's personal assistant for the "Jewish Museum Show," the name that sticks with it to this day. She soon moved
into the loft. He proposed marriage on numerous occasions.

This photograph of Tomoko in her mother's arms has been called the pietà of modern photography. Invalided from birth by the "Minamata disease," caused by mercury pollution, Tomoko became the inspiration of the Japanese people's crusade for compensation for the ravages of heavy industry, a battle still joined. W. EUGENE SMITH /*Courtesy, Aileen M. Smith*

The exhibition was hailed by most critics, even by the conservative Hilton Kramer of *The New York Times*, who had deplored "The Family of Man." Soon afterward, it was invited to Japan, Gene and Aileen along with it. Thanks to his first visit, Gene was big news in Japan. *Asahi Shimbun* reported that "W. E. Smith (52) will cover fishermen in Minamata who are suffering from water pollution very badly, and report it to the world." The Smiths—Aileen and Gene had married in Tokyo—arrived in Minamata in September 1971, planning to stay three months. They stayed three years. They were determined to tell the story of "Minamata disease," first noticed in the 1950s when house cats of the community had gone berserk and jumped into the sea. Soon it began to affect people, whose lips and limbs would tingle and then become numb; their speech would slur. They lost control of their bodies; many died. Fetuses were affected; women gave birth to deformed children. In 1959, the disease was traced to methyl mercury wastes from the Chisso chemical factory. Upon reaching the sea the sludge poisoned the fish, a staple of the Japanese diet.

For eighteen dollars a month the Smiths rented a house belonging to one of the victimized families, sharing a dirt-floored kitchen and bath, where they developed film. One by one they got to know the sufferers: Shinobu Sakamoto, a lovely teenager who often thought of killing herself; Tomiji Matsuda, a young baseball fan who would never have a chance to play the game—he was blind; Takako Isayama, a child who had to be carried everywhere but had the strength to say "Strawberries—wow!"; and Tomoko Uemura, who was blind and speechless and whose limbs were deformed. Gene Smith's photograph of Tomoko being bathed in her mother's arms became the symbol of Minamata and has been described as the pietà of our industrial age.

On January 7, 1972, the Smiths joined a delegation of patients from Minamata for a demonstration at Chisso's Goi plant, near Tokyo. With clear deceit, Chisso permitted them to enter. Once inside, Gene and several others were seized and beaten. Gene was first kicked, then picked up by six men who "slammed my head against the concrete, the way you would kill a rattlesnake if you had him by the tail." Then he was tossed outside the gate. He would suffer enduring pain from that beating for the rest of his life. The incident made Gene's a familiar face on Japanese TV. A courageous Tokyo department store opened a two-hundred-print show on Minamata. Almost fifty thousand people went through it in twelve days. The Smiths' next objective was a book on Minamata. They had hardly begun work on it when Gene, traveling by train from Tokyo to Minamata, began vomiting blood and had to be rushed to the Shizuoka city hospital. Aileen took an all-night train and arrived the next morning. Two months later there was another emergency. Gene called Jim Hughes, editor of *Camera 35* (and Gene's future biographer), in New York. He had had a relapse, was abusing drugs and drink again, and Aileen was not around. Gene needed medical attention, and he was far from home. Hughes, who had just published twenty-four pages of the Smiths' Minamata pictures (Aileen had wielded the camera as well), called around until he found an angel in the person of Larry Schiller, the Los Angeles–based photographer/editor/movie producer and ingenious fast-talker who had sold me Jack Ruby's story in 1964. Larry admired Smith and agreed not only to put up airfare for Gene's return but to send photographer Paul Fusco from California to help bring him back.

After he had had a chance to recuperate in the States, Gene and Aileen returned to Minamata for the summer and fall of 1974. They wanted the people of Minamata to see their own story in photographs. Gene was ill, but they worked on the book. Gene wrote to me, "If we can finish it, the Minamata book will be its own landmark." Their next year was one of public acclaim and private misery. The book was published, and the International Center of Photography exhibited their photos of Minamata. Thanks to them, this small city became a world symbol of environmental hazards and, as *The New York Times* called it, "a case study in Japanese politics."

Midge and I had talked Gene and Aileen into making a joint appearance at the 1975 NPPA convention at Jackson Hole, and it was there that we learned what was going on in their lives. Their marriage was falling apart, but they played the charade of togetherness. Aileen had reached the breaking point in

Japan. She realized that she would have to assert her independence if she was to survive. To cushion himself, Gene had established a standby relationship with Sherry Suris, a young New York freelance photographer. Back in New York, Aileen found a place of her own.

In 1976, Gene's doctors found that he had diabetes, in addition to his other ailments. They ordered him not to drink under any circumstances. Sherry tried her best to police him, but he simply would not comply. Besides, they were broke—the book advance was long gone—and drink took Gene out of his pain. Few of his honors paid off in cash. Jim Hughes and I, a "rescue committee" of two, got to work. I read in the *Times* that the University of Arizona had established a Center for Creative Photography in Tucson, for the purpose of preserving photographers' archives, and that they had acquired those of Ansel Adams. Knowing Ansel to be one of Gene's longtime friends and admirers, despite their different styles, I called him at his studio in Carmel, California. Ansel put me into touch with John Schaefer, president of the University of Arizona, and on Schaefer's next visit to New York we met in the office of attorney Arthur Soybel, who was negotiating Gene's divorce from Aileen. Schaefer said that he could appoint Smith to the faculty if Gene would donate his archives to the center—negatives, prints, correspondence, all the raw material of his working life—as Ansel had. But he could keep his master prints to benefit his children. In exchange, Gene would be appointed professor, with a darkroom, assistants, and a $30,000 annual salary. In November, the movers left for Tucson with 44,000 pounds—22 tons—of prints, negatives, contact prints, magazines, books, letters, file cabinets (dozens), desks, easy chairs, tapes, and phonograph records (thousands). Gene had saved everything, even old laundry lists and pawn tickets. One book carton, for example, held nothing but lens caps. When Gene arrived in Tucson he found a postcard from Ansel: "Congratulations . . . I think I should come down and learn how to make a photograph." A few days later, feeling dizzy, Gene was advised to check into a hospital for tests. On the day he was due for release, he had a massive cerebral hemorrhage and went into a coma. Sherry immediately flew to Tucson, followed by Gene's children: Juanita from Oregon; Marissa, Shana, Patrick, and Patrick's wife, Phyllis, from New York; and Kevin from Berkeley, where he was finishing law school. It was the first time Kevin had met his siblings. Patrick had not even known of Kevin's existence: his sisters had only recently learned that Patrick was not the only son and had kept that fact from him.

Gene remained in a coma into January. He had agreed to speak to the Copperstate Press Photographers at Arizona State University in Tempe on March 4. In February, it seemed obvious that he could not do it, so I agreed to appear in his place. I flew to Tucson on March 1, visiting him in the hospital that afternoon. To my astonishment I found Gene determined to go to Tempe. By the next day, he had his doctors talked into it, so Sherry and I got him to a hotel in Tempe for the night and sneaked him into the auditorium the next day. We kept him backstage while I showed and discussed Smith's slides with his own taped commentary. Then I said, "I'm sure you all know why Gene couldn't make this talk himself today. He wanted *so* much to be here, but the president of the University of Arizona said no, his doctors said no, all common sense said no . . . but . . . *here he is!*"

With this, Sherry wheeled Gene out from backstage. There was pandemonium as six hundred photographers and students cheered for ten minutes. Gene, unable to speak, could only wave, his eyes flooding tears. Amazingly, by summer Gene was sufficiently recovered to make a trip to New York to talk with a magazine editor about shooting a story on John Travolta. He then returned to Tucson, where he actually taught class for a few days. One Sunday morning he stole out of his house to buy a beer and collapsed on the floor of the neighborhood convenience store. He died soon after.

From the mortuary I went to see John Schaefer and the university's principal attorney, who asked me what I thought the Smith estate was worth. Sherry had told me the night before that Gene had eighteen dollars in the bank and thousands of dollars in past due bills. Without hesitation, I replied, "About a million dollars." They didn't blink. Sherry had also told me that Gene had vastly underestimated the number of his master prints. There were thousands, perhaps six thousand. It was all that Gene had to leave to his children, but I was determined to make them a small fortune. Three of the five children were desperately poor, their needs urgent. Things had changed since Gene's Magnum years, when we had been lucky to sell an occasional print for fifty dollars—not just Gene's but also those of Magnum "contributors" Edward Weston and Ansel Adams. Thanks in large part to Ansel Adams, Adams's business partner, William Turnage, and a few shrewd dealers, a market for photographic prints developed in the seventies. I am glad to say that by now sales of prints from the Smith estate have exceeded my original estimate.

It was the creative side of the Smith legacy, however, that presented the greatest challenge. I soon realized how enormously fortunate Gene had been in making his move to Tucson's Center for Creative Photography. I had to make a dozen or so trips to Tucson, and on most of them I worked with Smith's personal curator, W. S. "Bill" Johnson. An experienced librarian and scholar, Bill dedicated himself to preserving the integrity of Smith's archive. In the spring of 1980, I went to Tucson for two weeks with Midge. She had been operated on for breast cancer, and we thought the change and sunshine would do her good. She had come to know Gene well in his last years—of us she was the one who had usually taken his calls for help. One day Bill Johnson told us over lunch of his dream of publishing a catalogue raisonné of the center's two thousand best Smith images. Midge immediately said, "Bill, just *do* it. Make us a rough dummy and we'll take it back to New York and sell it." He did, and we did. Michael Hoffman of Aperture, in what I termed "an act of faith," took on the project and obtained funding. Johnson's *W. Eugene Smith: Master of the Photo Essay* is a classic, unfortunately now out of print.

In 1980, Howard Chapnick of Black Star spurred several friends of Gene's—the "rescue committee" had grown from two to five (we were joined by Jim Hughes, attorney Arthur Soybel, and acc camera repairman Martin Forscher)—to found the W. Eugene Smith Memorial Fund, meant to encourage "photographers who work in the tradition of W. Eugene Smith" to undertake concrete projects that need noncommercial support. Such grants, of $10,000 to $20,000, have been made every year since; photographers from ten countries have won so far, among them Jane Evelyn Atwood (the first recipient), Eugene Richards, Sebastião Salgado, Gilles Peress, Donna Ferrato, James Nachtwey, and Cristina Garcia Rodero.

In 1980, Midge and I attended the annual Rencontres Internationales de la Photographie in Arles, where I had been invited to speak, in the great old Roman amphitheater, about "You-jenn" Smith. As at Tempe, I showed Cornell Capa's "Images of Man" filmstrip on Gene, brilliantly edited by Sheila Turner Seed for Scholastic, with Gene's own commentary. The problem was to first play Gene's words, in his own voice, and then translate them, phrase by phrase, into French. Fortunately, I was given a translator who understood intuitively. We had time for only one rehearsal, but the show itself, with a thousand people watching in total silence, went perfectly. I added Gene's words, from the back cover of the Minamata book:

> Photography is a small voice, at best, but sometimes—just sometimes—one photograph or a group of them can lure our senses into awareness. . . . Someone—or perhaps many—among us may be influenced to heed reason, to find a way to right that which is wrong. . . . The rest of us may perhaps feel a greater sense of understanding and compassion for those whose lives are alien to our own. . . . Photography is a small voice. . . . It is an important voice in my life, but not the only one. I believe in it.

Midge died of cancer on July 9, 1981. She had lived just long enough to see, and to fully appreciate, the words that Bill Johnson chose to appear on the dedication page of his catalogue raisonné. He had kept it secret from her:

FOR MIDGE MORRIS

One day in 1984, a French doctor named Jean-Louis Etienne knocked on the door of my Paris apartment. He calmly announced that he intended to walk, alone (unaccompanied even by dogs), to the North Pole. Would the *National Geographic* be interested? Two years later the magazine published his story, and with it the story of a much larger American expedition that reached the Pole almost simultaneously—after first encountering Etienne unexpectedly in the Arctic wastes.
JIM BRANDENBURG/National Geographic

32

Geographic Agonistes

Twice now I had been cheated, by premature death, of the woman I loved. Six months after Midge died, I wrote to my friends around the world. Many had known Midge, some had not; some had known Dèle long before Midge. Of necessity it was a form letter, combining a final tribute to Midge with the news that "I am thinking seriously of making a major change of scene toward the end of this year, perhaps relocating to Paris." Each letter carried a personal message. There were scores of replies. One who responded was Tana Hoban, a photographer from Philadelphia whom I had known ever since *Ladies' Home Journal.* Tana was well regarded as a photographer of children, making such soft, sensitive images that Edward Steichen had chosen her as one of six women photographers for a group show at the Museum of Modern Art in 1949. I had been of no great help to her career. I had given her one assignment in my *Journal* years and one for *The New York Times* that had gotten lost in the mail. Tana had moved to New York in 1974 and built a beautiful studio apartment in a loft near Union Square. She now specialized in making photo books for young children, mostly conceptual, such as *Shapes and Things, Look Again!, A. B. See!* Shortly after receiving my "form letter," Tana called. I suggested a movie. We met at the box office, and she invited me home for dinner afterward. From that first date, I was hooked. We began to talk of a move to Paris. I was writing a story for *National Geographic* on the centennial of the Brooklyn Bridge, with pictures by Donal Holway, a former *New York Times* staffer. The *Geographic's* editor, Bill Garrett, and his wife, Lucille, were intrigued by my new relationship and invited us for a weekend. They were immediately charmed by Tana. I told them, in confidence, that we would marry and move to Paris in the spring. Could I be the *Geographic*'s Paris correspondent? Bill seemed to like the idea.

On March 17, 1983, the newlyweds arrived at Charles de Gaulle Airport. We have lived in Paris ever since. After all these years, I should admit to being an expatriate. I prefer the self-depiction of Irwin Shaw, who lived here twenty-five years: "I was never a Parisian. I was always an American, on an extended visit, to be sure."

One evening long ago, in the kitchen of his first Virginia home, modestly tucked into a Washington suburb called Vienna, I said to Wilbur E. Garrett, "Bill, if only your name were Grosvenor, you would be editor of *National Geographic* someday." I was wrong. Twenty years later, Bill Garrett did indeed become the editor of the magazine which, more than any other, is an American institution. Ten years after that, on a few minutes' notice, Garrett was discharged from that exalted post by a Grosvenor, Gilbert Melville, and escorted from the building—never to return. I watched from a short distance the rise and fall of one of the boldest and most powerful editors in the history of magazine publishing.

In August 1989, editor W. E. "Bill" Garrett of *National Geographic* celebrated thirty-five years of steady advancement on the magazine staff. There was a big party, for which this special "cover" was made up in full color. Six months later, on a few minutes' notice, Garrett was fired and escorted from the building.
© DAVID ALAN HARVEY

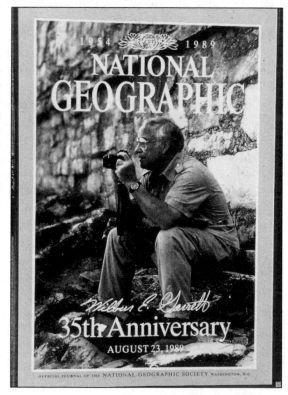

Three generations of the durable Grosvenor family have maintained control of the magazine and its quasi-public publishing "society" for a century. It all began with a meeting of thirty-three distinguished Washingtonians at the Cosmos Club on January 13, 1888. They were there to found "a society for the increase and diffusion of geographical knowledge." For ten years the National Geographic Society floundered, putting out an occasional magazine. In 1897, the inventor Alexander Graham Bell became president of the society "in order to save it." Bell had no intention of running the society himself, but he had a candidate, who would soon become his son-in-law. Bell's choice, and that of his daughter Elsie, was Gilbert Hovey Grosvenor, then twenty-three. Gilbert became the National Geographic Society's first full-time employee on April 1, 1899. His title was assistant editor, but he ran the society's magazine and soon proved that his genius was not confined to editing. He dignified subscribers by calling them "members" of the society, even though they never got to vote on anything. "Dr." Grosvenor—the doctorate was honorary—retired in May 1954. One of his last acts as editor was to accept an award from the University of Missouri. While there, he hired for an assistant editor post one of Cliff Edom's graduate students, Wilbur E. Garrett, whom I had just met at the picture workshop in Mexico, Missouri. It was not exactly a propitious time to join the *Geographic*. Gilbert Hovey Grosvenor, or "GHG"—editors at the *Geographic* are referred to by initials—had turned the editorship over to his assistant of forty-nine years, John Oliver La Gorce. "JOL" was something of a disaster during his three years as editor. An archconservative, he personally put down women—they lunched separately at the *Geographic* for years. He despised blacks and Jews. To the staff's relief, La Gorce retired on January 8, 1957. Melville Bell Grosvenor, GHG's son, took over. He edited the magazine with enormous verve. He spent summers at the Bell estate in Nova Scotia. He sailed his forty-six-foot yawl *White Mist* on long cruises. He was demanding and impulsive, decreeing in August 1959, for example, that the *Geographic* would henceforth have a picture on every cover—color, of course. The decade of his editorship is called the "golden age" of the National Geographic Society for good reason. Membership rose from 2,175,000 to 5,500,000. More important was the esprit that developed in his regime. He hired so many Missourians—products of the School of Journalism and/or the Missouri Workshop—that they became known in house as the "Missouri mafia." He also sought professionals from newspapers, hiring Robert E. Gilka from the *Milwaukee Journal* and creating a new position, director of photography, for James M. Godbold, chief photographer of the *Minneapolis Tribune*.

There was already another Grosvenor in line: Gilbert Melville Grosvenor, one of MBG's two sons. He had intended to go into medicine, but in the summer of 1953, heading into his senior year at Yale, he went to Holland on a dike-building project and took some pictures. They were published the next year. With this smell of the printed page, his *Geographic* career began; he never worked anywhere else. He and Garrett became especially good friends.

In 1967, at sixty-five, MBG kicked himself upstairs, retiring from the editorship and presidency of the society to become chairman of the board and editor in chief. In selecting the next editor he took the easy way out, naming his deputy, Frederick G. "Ted" Vosburgh, a solidly professional text editor who would leave the picture people alone. As I saw it, it would have been too painful for Melville to choose among the younger editors. He had become as fond of Bill Garrett as of his own son Gil.

Gil Grosvenor and Bill Garrett advanced steadily up the masthead, Grosvenor always a step ahead in title and power, Garrett generally a step ahead in influence and popularity. "GMG" was named editor in 1970. He was only thirty-nine. Like his father, Gil Grosvenor edited *National Geographic* for a decade. Garrett became Grosvenor's deputy for illustrations, Joseph Judge the deputy for text. Gil and Bill worked closely together, in a state of constant creative tension. Garrett was gregarious, a "man of the people"; Gil was socially uncomfortable, a loner. A good sailor, Gil preferred the high seas to high society. Garrett was the innovator, always pushing the magazine in new directions. In 1977, alarmed by what they saw as "advocacy journalism," conservatives on the board tried to create an "editorial oversight committee." Their case was strengthened when the South African Tourist Board accused the *Geographic* of "anti-white racism" in an article that frankly examined the problems created by apartheid—they had seen an advance copy. I accidentally became involved because of a lunch date with Garrett. On the shuttle from New York, I was surprised to see Walter Cronkite of CBS—I'd heard him broadcast from South Africa only two nights before. We shared a cab from National Airport. When I mentioned this to Garrett, he jumped: "He's just the man I need." He sent the article to Cronkite, who looked it over and said it was balanced and fair. Bill reported this to Gil; the article ran. Grosvenor won his battle with the trustees: there would be no oversight committee. When Melvin Payne retired from the society's presidency in 1980, Gil was elected president but was denied what his father and grandfather had achieved: to be both editor of *National Geographic* and, simultaneously, president of the society. He was not at all happy about that.

Thus Bill Garrett became editor, with all the perquisites of that position: a full-time limousine and chauffeur, a grand corner office, freedom to travel as he wished. Having fought alongside Gil to maintain the editor's prerogatives, Garrett now sought the same privileges for himself—and found it not so easy with his predecessor next door in the executive suite. They were still friends, but I could detect a difference—even in 1975 when Midge and I joined the Garretts and Grosvenors at the Jackson Hole convention of the NPPA. Together we made a whitewater raft trip on the Snake River. As president, Gil Grosvenor's primary concern was to keep the society in good financial health. His editor, however, had some expensive ideas. When my Paris assignment was agreed upon in 1983, Garrett left it to the last minute to inform Gil. I would be "responsible for coordinating the magazine's editorial activities in Europe," logging my time at forty dollars an hour. I would watch the press and contact journalists, artists, scholars, scientists—and foremost photographers. There was a small advertising office on the Champs-Élysées, headed by the brilliant, glibly multilingual Michel Boutin, but I would be independent.

Soon after I arrived I was handed a big challenge: to organize coverage of the balloon race that would launch from the place de la Concorde on Sunday, June 26, 1983, honoring both the bicentennial of man's first flight, in a balloon designed by France's Montgolfier brothers, in 1783, and James Gordon Bennett, Jr., founder of the newspaper that is now the *International Herald Tribune*. Bennett had sponsored the first such race, also from the place de la Concorde, in 1906. My colleagues in Washington had made a deal with Cynthia Shields, an American balloonist, to write her own story and take *Geographic* staff photographer Otis Imboden along. To win, however, we placed our bets on Maxie Anderson and his copilot, Don Ida. With two other teammates, Maxie had been the first to cross the Atlantic by balloon. The balloon flying farthest would win the race. Maxie was making no predictions but seemed confident when I lunched with him on Friday. On Sunday morning, the sun was shining but the weather forecast was terrible: thunderstorms were predicted. The weather experts met at noon and reluctantly agreed to a launch. The bags were resplendent, in crazy colors, as they rapidly filled with helium. First off was Maxie Anderson, trying to beat the storm. A few minutes later, he radioed, "We're being sucked up in this weather—I'd advise no further launchings until conditions improve." The order to hold was given, but it was already too late for Cynthia Shields. The rain then fell in torrents; we were all drenched. Heading out of Paris under a 1,500-foot overcast, Cynthia decided to land her balloon as soon as possible. At the city line, a forty-story office building loomed ahead, but well below. A sudden downdraft caught the balloon, dropping it a hundred feet or more. "No more ballasting, everybody down!" Cynthia yelled, as the gasbag collided with the building, brushed alongside, and then, miraculously, broke clear without damage. Two hours later, we learned that she had landed safely in the field of an astonished farmer.

Nothing much was heard from Maxie Anderson. On Monday afternoon, photographer Peter Turnley, whom I had assigned to mission control, called: "John, from what I've just overheard, I'm afraid Maxie's crashed—on the border of East Germany." Soon it was confirmed; he and Don Ida were dead. Their balloon's release mechanism had apparently misfired, and their gondola had fallen more than a hundred feet. The *Geographic*'s twenty-page story, which

In threatening weather, the James Gordon Bennett balloon race launched from the Place de la Concorde on June 26, 1983. It was my task to arrange coverage of the complex event for *National Geographic*. I used eight photographers and obtained one picture by advertising in Paris newspapers. The race ended in tragedy as veteran balloonist Maxie Anderson and his co-pilot Don Ida were killed in a crash near the East German border. JAMES A. SUGAR/National Geographic

could run only months later, was tastefully assembled from all these elements, with credits to nine photographers. One of them was an amateur who had photographed Cynthia's balloon as it brushed against the office building. I had obtained it by placing a "photo wanted" ad in two Paris newspapers.

I thought I had covered the most difficult balloon story of all time, but no. One Friday night in September, a year later, a call came from Bob Gilka, who had succeeded Jim Godbold as the *Geographic*'s director of photography. Bob never wasted words: "John, there's a guy named Joe Kittinger who's about to launch a balloon from Caribou, Maine. He's going to try to solo across the Atlantic. His balloon is carrying the National Geographic Society flag. Need I say more?" A retired colonel in the U.S. Air Force, Kittinger was the holder of the world's high-altitude parachute jump record—102,800 feet. Now he was about to make my life impossible.

By early Monday it looked as though Kittinger would cross the French coast between Nantes and Bordeaux. I called photographers Peter Turnley and Jean-Guy Jules in the middle of the night, sending Turnley to Nantes and Jules to Bordeaux on the first morning flights. I told each to reserve a helicopter upon arrival. It soon became clear that Turnley, in Nantes, was too far north. Turnley's pilot agreed to take him to Biarritz.

About midnight, calling from the Biarritz tower, Turnley told me he had voice contact with Kittinger. "Want to talk to him?" We spoke, on a relay through the tower, for several minutes. Kittinger was evasive when asked about his plans. A night landing would be dangerous. The winds were picking up. Just after midnight he crossed the French coast and, skirting the Pyrenees, headed straight across southern France for the Mediterranean. It had never occurred to me that he would *overfly* France. The next morning I had two helicopters at the Toulouse airport, an important passenger in one of them. Jean-Guy Jules, ever the gallant Frenchman, had offered a ride to Sherry Reed, Joe Kittinger's girlfriend. Both photographers took off in hot pursuit. Jules finally spotted the balloon off the Riviera coast, but flying so high that pursuit would require oxygen. His pilot, his ears bleeding from the altitude, refused to fly further. When Turnley stopped for fuel at Saint-Tropez, I told him to pick up Jean-Guy and Sherry at the Cannes airport. The chase continued. AP told me that Kittinger was apparently heading for Corsica. I worried that he would go on to Italy. It was "absolutely forbidden" to make aerial pictures in Italy without military permission, and it would take days to obtain such permission.

For hours, silence. I figured all was lost. But in midafternoon Turnley called from a hospital in Nice. He had just taken Kittinger there by helicopter from Italy! Kittinger had landed in a forest near Cairo Montenotte, to the astonishment of some woodcutters. He had suffered a broken ankle but was otherwise okay. The *Geographic* helicopter had landed several hundred meters away, and Sherry had rushed into the arms of her hero. We all celebrated, a few nights later, at Maxim's.

One day in early 1984, a stranger knocked on the door of my apartment at 15 quai de Bourbon. He introduced himself as Dr. Jean-Louis Étienne, a specialist in sports medicine and nutrition. He told me he was planning to walk alone, pulling a sled, to the North Pole. Would *National Geographic* be interested in his story? I was immediately attracted by the simplicity of Étienne's approach. We offered him a contract. The following spring Étienne set out from Canada but fell into a crevasse and severely injured his shoulder sixteen days into his journey. Undaunted, he returned in the spring of 1986, with renewed support from the *Geographic*, though the magazine was also backing a dogsled expedition of seven men and one woman led by Will Steger. On April 8, in the trackless arctic wastes, the Steger dogs bolted at the sound of another human. It was Étienne, on the thirtieth day of his sixty-four-day solo to the Pole. In September, the *Geographic* published thirty pages by Steger, six by Étienne. Seldom have men competed so hard for space in a magazine. Through the *Geographic* they became such good friends that they later joined forces to traverse the Antarctic.

In December 1987, I proposed an issue on "France Today," to be published in

1989, coinciding with the bicentennial celebration of the French Revolution. In December 1988, Garrett came to Paris to interview President François Mitterrand for the special issue. Bill and I both knew that the time had come for me to move on—my contract would end in March. We celebrated with lunch at Maxim's. Garrett and Grosvenor came to Paris in June 1989 to promote the special issue on France. They stayed in separate hotels; I noticed that they hardly spoke to each other. A year went by, and I was absorbed in my files, planning this book. On April 17, a friend called from Washington to read me a headline on page one of *The Washington Post:* EDITOR FIRED AT NATIONAL GEOGRAPHIC. I was not surprised, but I was stunned by the abruptness of the act. There had been a routine meeting of the full board of trustees the previous Thursday, with Garrett present. A change of editors had not been discussed, but Gil had assembled a seven-man "executive committee" immediately afterward. They had approved his secret plan: to replace Garrett with William Graves, the sixty-one-year-old senior assistant editor for expeditions, jumping over Garrett's three deputies: Joseph Judge, Charles McCarry, and Thomas R. Smith.

On Monday, April 16, Grosvenor called a 3:30 meeting of senior editors in the *Geographic*'s editorial "control center." A few minutes after three, Grosvenor summoned Garrett to his office and told him they could no longer work together. He then introduced Garrett to a "facilitator," a total stranger, who would see him out of the building. En route to the staff meeting, Grosvenor and Graves stopped to see Judge, the senior associate editor. They told him of the change, that he too was being dismissed but would have an opportunity to write for the magazine. Judge refused the arrangement. Grosvenor then announced to the other assembled editors that Garrett had resigned and Bill Graves would be his replacement. Garrett has never returned to the magazine's offices. Nor did Judge return before his death from cancer in 1996. On May 7, Charles Trueheart gave further details in the *Post*'s Style section. By then the other two Garrett deputies were gone. McCarry, the very talented editor-at-large who handled freelance writers, announced at a staff meeting that there was no point in his hanging around. Tom Smith, after first being assured that he would be sorely needed, was told to go. The slate was clean.

After reading the *Post* story, I wrote to Gil Grosvenor, recalling our vacation together in Jackson Hole: "I have just read, with immense sadness, Charles Trueheart's long piece in the *Post*. It breaks my heart. I recall the time, fifteen years ago, when three men rode a raft down the Snake. . . . I could never have believed that one of us would wind up throwing his friend out of the raft, without a rope. . . . It gives me some comfort to think that Bill will continue swimming against the stream. I'll be right in there with him." Not surprisingly, I received no answer. I resolved never to set foot again in the *Geographic*'s offices—at least not until Garrett himself was invited back. But in 1994, in Washington for the preparation of this book, I decided to see if Gil Grosvenor wished to tell me his side of the story. He gave me half an hour. He said that Bill had been clearly insubordinate and had been warned many times. There simply could not be two top executives in the society. He had sought advice from lawyers and from "people who deal with such situations," and they counseled him to take such action.

I replied that I felt he had consulted the wrong people and that the way in which Garrett had been terminated was inexcusable. I told him that I hoped for reconciliation. That hope has proved forlorn. Instead, many more of my cherished colleagues have left *National Geographic.*

The ill-fated French photographer Michel Laurent runs down the Champs-Élysées in pursuit of a picture for AP. He wrote about it: "Paris photographers have become a bunch of sheep. It's not funny that we have so little liberty, yet I continue to pass the barriers." His efforts won him a Pulitzer Prize, shared with Horst Faas. Later, as a photographer with Gamma on assignment for *Newsweek*, Laurent became the last photographer killed while covering the war in Vietnam—two days before it ended.

33

Paris, Capital of Photojournalism

My move to Paris with Tana in 1983 represented more than a personal preference, a desire for a more amiable lifestyle. It meant relocating to the world's capital of photojournalism. Unfortunately, this well-earned reputation has been sullied, perhaps for a long time to come, by the death of Diana, Princess of Wales, in a horrendous car crash in the tunnel under Place de l'Alma on August 31, 1997. She was fleeing the paparazzi (the term originates from the relentless street photographer Paparazzo in Fellini's *La Dolce Vita*). The public perception that Paris is infested with such celebrity hounds developed within hours of Diana's death. The truth is somewhat different.

The independent press photo agencies of France have led the way in global news coverage since the weekly *Life*'s demise. Agency freelancers, not magazine staffers, now supply most magazine needs. The godfather of the French picture agency business was Louis Dalmas, a well-connected cousin of Prince Rainier of Monaco. In 1958, Dalmas opened what he called "the world's first agency of photo reportage" in Paris. Like the Garai brothers, the founders of Keystone, Dalmas would do anything to get a picture. Once he parachuted a photographer into the ocean off Brazil in order to have pictures of the hostage crisis on board the liner *Santa María*, which had been seized by Portuguese rebels. The audacious young photographers hired by Dalmas scored scoop after scoop—until they got a look at the books and decided they could do better on their own.

In 1967, an agency was founded that would change the course of photojournalism, as Magnum had changed it twenty years earlier. It was the cre-

With photographer (and wife) Tana Hoban at our Paris apartment, 1990. © GAIL H. ALEXANDER

ation of four quite different partners: Hubert Henrotte, a photographer of the newspaper *Le Figaro*; Hugues Vassal and Léonard de Raemy, two veteran photographers of celebrities; and Raymond Depardon, a scoop artist from the Dalmas agency. They called the new agency Gamma. As at Magnum, they shared the revenues—and the risks—with the photographers. They were soon joined by a twenty-seven-year-old photographer named Gilles Caron. He and Depardon fast established the journalistic reputation of the young agency. Caron seemed to be everywhere. In 1970, he spent a month in captivity in Chad with Depardon and an Anglo-French journalist named Robert Pledge. Then he was off to Cambodia. On the fifth of April, on the highway that runs from Phnom Penh to Vietnam, he disappeared. In four years as a journalist he had covered 387 stories. Much as the death of Robert Capa had compelled Magnum to persevere against all odds, the loss of Gilles Caron inspired Gamma. By 1973, there were thirty-six people working in Paris, and a New York office had been opened in the West Seventy-second Street apartment of photographer Jean-Pierre Laffont and his wife, Éliane. Then the young agency almost died. Hubert Henrotte, who had been running the business as *gérant* (legal director), abruptly split with the other founders. For three days there was turmoil as photographers came in the night to remove their archives from the Paris office. Henrotte took most of the photographers with him. A new agency was born. Most of the staff stayed with Gamma, but in New York Éliane Laffont changed the name on her doorbell to SYGMA.

Raymond Depardon was left to run Gamma, with Floris de Bonneville as editor and Jean Monteux as salesman. Depardon asked Pledge, his fellow hostage in Chad, then an editor of *Zoom*, to establish a New York office. They recruited new photographers. Pledge signed up David Burnett, Douglas Kirkland, and Rick Smolan. In Paris, Depardon signed an Iranian named Abbas, a Brazilian named Sebastião Salgado, and another Frenchman, Jean Gaumy. All four later joined Magnum.

In May 1972, a baby-faced AP photographer from Paris named Michel Laurent joined Midge and me for dinner in our New York apartment. He had just won the Pulitzer Prize, with Horst Faas of AP, for the controversial series of pictures the two had taken the previous December in Dacca, at the end of the war between India and Pakistan that had given birth to Bangladesh. The pictures showed four Bihari prisoners who had been taken by Bengali soldiers to the Dacca racetrack for exhibition to the press and the angry populace. Among the dozen or so photographers gathered round were Marc Riboud of Magnum, Australian photographer Penny Tweedie, the two men from AP, and some young Asians. What began as interrogation of the prisoners soon became bullying. The photographers began recording the scene. One soldier poked a bayonet at one prisoner and then another, drawing blood. Riboud turned away in disgust, feeling that the photographers' presence was inciting the soldiers. Perhaps it was. The situation rapidly got out of control, with no one in command. The stabbing continued until all four prisoners were dead. Faas and Laurent recorded the gruesome scene. Their next problem was to get their pictures past the Indian censors. They handed their films over to a London-bound courier, and the images were distributed to the world over the AP wire. We ran one picture on the front page of *The New York Times*. I was disturbed by the ethics of the situation. A few weeks later, Marc Riboud came to New York and told me his own version of the incident and why he had left the scene. Late that night, Michel Laurent and I discussed it in my apartment. He understood Marc's point of view but convinced me that the photographers had been powerless to stop the slaughter. Some years later, Riboud was told by Prime Minister Indira Gandhi that the publication of those pictures around the world had so shocked and embarrassed the Indian authorities that severe orders had been issued: there must be no further such incidents (or at least none with photographers around). Faas and Laurent performed a public service. They well deserved their Pulitzer.

Michel Laurent returned to Paris and joined the Gamma agency. On April 28, 1975, on a Gamma assignment for *Newsweek*, he was covering the chaotic defense of Saigon as the North Vietnamese approached. On the road just ahead of him, Christian Hoche of *Le Figaro* was wounded. Michel went to his aid and was killed in cross fire; he was the forty-sixth, and last, correspondent to die in the long war in Vietnam. It ended two days later.

Knowing how difficult it had been for Magnum, I could not believe that both Gamma and Sygma would long survive. Not only do they persist, but they have been joined by others. In 1968, a hustling Turkish journalist named Goksin Sipahioglu started his own agency in an office over a candy shop on the Champs-Élysées, assisted by a bright young journalist from Kansas named Phyllis Springer. He called it "Sipa"—nobody can pronounce Goksin's entire surname. The most adventurous of agents, Goksin's door is always open. Paris is full of photographers, editors, and agents who have worked for Sipa at one time or another.

The most eccentric French picture agency, Vu, grew out of the tabloid *Libération*, which is almost a way of life for its readers. At 350,000, it is third in daily circulation to its intellectual rivals, the conservative *Le Figaro* (700,000) and the liberal *Le Monde* (400,000), which uses photographs only in feature sections. "*Libé*," as *Libération* is affectionately known, could well be called *The Daily Surprise*. At *Libé*, visual content is taken as seriously as words. Page one is never stylistically the same two days in a row. Occasionally the results are odd, but they are never dull. *Libé* was first published at the liberation of Paris in 1944 but did not last long. In 1973 the title was taken over by a group of intellectuals headed by an iconoclastic Maoist, Serge July. Jean-Paul Sartre was a director. The paper, idealistic but irresponsible, stopped publication for four months in 1981 while July looked for money, assembled a new team, and created a new format. As picture editor he hired a young philosopher named Christian Caujolle, who had never worked on a newspaper. In 1986 Caujolle sold July on the creation of a house photo agency, called Vu. Today Vu is independent. It makes assignments far afield and brings in the work of foreign photographers. During the 1989 revolt in Beijing's Tiananmen Square, Caujolle obtained exclusive pictures from Chinese dissidents whose identities he still protects.

In 1990, another agency came to Paris. Robert Pledge parted company with Gamma in 1975 to found Contact Press Images. In 1990, he opened a Paris branch and became a transatlantic commuter. Contact is the smallest and most exclusive of the independent agencies. Its dozen full-time photographers include three top winners of World Press Photo: David Burnett, Frank Fournier, and Alon Reininger. Close to a quarter of Contact's revenue is generated by Annie Liebovitz, a contributing photographer since the start.

World Press Photo began as the 1955 brainchild of three press photographers, in a smoke-filled meeting of the Dutch Society of Photo Reporters. Realizing that the annual contest for Holland's Press Photo of the Year was unlikely ever to attract much attention, they decided to start a contest for all the world, inviting an international jury. The organization floundered through its first decade and probably would have folded but for the vision and organizing ability of the Dutch magazine editor Joop Swart, who took on its leadership in 1966. Swart carefully chose members of each year's nine-man jury to straddle the realpolitik of the Cold War. He balanced the professionalism of Western jurors, always a majority but not a solid one, with representation from East Bloc and Third World countries. Thus it was not possible for a Russian juror to veto a picture of the 1968 "Prague spring," but neither could an American veto a harsh image from Vietnam. World Press Photo thus became a meeting point for East and West. In 1974, on my first visit to Amsterdam as a jury member, Swart himself came to Schiphol Airport at dawn to meet the flight from New York. Volunteers did all the work. Swart's vision has now been rewarded. There is a budget of around $2 million a year and a full-time staff of fourteen headed by Marloes Krijnen, one of Holland's leading women executives. Close to four thousand photographers, from more than a hundred countries, now participate. The exhibition of prizewinning pictures goes to thirty-eight countries. The World Press Photo yearbook is published in six languages, and the magazine-style *World Press Photo Newsletter* is mailed twice a year to five thousand world leaders in photojournalism. The Dutch government, recognizing that World Press Photo pays diplomatic dividends, is supportive but not interfering. Foreign Minister Hans van den Broek hailed the organization as "the United Nations of photography," crediting press photographers with putting pressure on violators of human rights and calling the camera a "nonviolent weapon which can inform and mercilessly expose abuses, with a lasting impact upon millions of people."

In 1989, Swart invited me back to chair the jury judging the 1988 photos. It was exhausting but exhilarating trying to achieve consensus from the views of a Russian, an Italian, a Brit, an editor from China, a German, a Chilean, and two Hollanders. Fortunately, there were no major wars to photograph in 1988, although the year had seen the birth of *intifada* in Gaza. The most tragic single event had been a major earthquake in Soviet Armenia. When it came to select the World Press Photo of the Year, the choice seemed to lie between two photos, one vertical, one horizontal, of virtually the same moment: a grieving father surrounded by mourners, burying his son in a snowy grave. We did not know whose pictures we were judging. Mostly on the basis of composition, we finally chose the vertical. It turned out to be by David Turnley of the *Detroit Free Press*. The horizontal? It was by his twin brother, Peter Turnley, working for *Newsweek*.

After the judging, I commented, "A new class of photojournalist has arisen, the world-class photographer. He or she may work in Asia one day, in Europe the next, in Africa a week later." The redheaded Turnley brothers are perhaps the most remarkable example of this "world class" of photographers who "network" the world in pursuit of stories. They were born in Fort Wayne, Indiana, on June 22, 1955—David three minutes ahead of Peter. Both enrolled at the University of Michigan. It was their decision to major in French literature that had the biggest effect on their future. First David, then Peter, took a term off to study at the Sorbonne. After graduation from Ann Arbor their paths split. David joined the *Detroit Free Press.* Peter went to Paris and enrolled in the Institut d'Études Sciences Politiques. The twins looked so much alike and their careers were so parallel that for years I distinguished them by saying "P for Peter for Paris; D for David for Detroit."

In 1985, David persuaded the *Free Press* to send him to South Africa to report on apartheid, a subject of great interest to the Detroit paper's racially mixed audience. He stayed almost three years—and found himself a fiancée in Cape Town. He also produced a powerful book, *Why Are They Weeping?: South Africans Under Apartheid.* While sympathetic to Nelson Mandela, who was then in prison, David moved between the two worlds, black and white, making friends in both. This illustrates the Turnleys' philosophy. Consummate politicians, they never take *anyone,* no matter how humble, for granted. As one editor put it, "The Turnleys are out to charm the world." Reared in a close and caring family, they treat the Family of Man as an extension of theirs.

Howard Chapnick of Black Star was honored at the 1990 photojournalism festival in Perpignan, in the south of France. With him stand the Turnley twins, David and Peter, also honored. This annual September event has become the meeting point for the world's photojournalists. Chapnick, beloved by photographers for his devotion to them and their work, died in 1996. PHILIPPE BONSIGNOUR/*Courtesy, Visa Pour l'Image*

Peter Turnley did not have it easy for the first few years in Paris. He worked as a printer in the Picto lab and also assisted Robert Doisneau. He lived on the Ile de la Cité, a few steps from Notre Dame, in a sixth-floor *chambre de bonne*. His big break came in 1984, with a cover story for *Newsweek* on the fortieth anniversary of D-Day. He has worked for *Newsweek* on contract ever since, in every continent except South America. In 1986, Peter obtained long-term press accreditation to the USSR, which brought him an unexpected prize: a girlfriend, Amy Roth, an American member of the Moscow TV press corps. They are now married and live in Paris. In 1988, the *Free Press* quickly agreed when David Turnley asked to establish his base in Paris. Despite being neighbors, the twins are apt to meet even more often in distant places. The work of the two is almost indistinguishable in journalistic quality—as difficult to tell apart as the brothers themselves. When the Paris opera opened on place de la Bastille in Paris to celebrate the bicentennial of the French Revolution, Mikhail Gorbachev spotted David Turnley in the crowd. Thinking him Peter, he rushed over to extend his hand. But when both Turnleys were in South Africa, awaiting the release of Nelson Mandela, Winnie Mandela threw her arms around Peter, whom she was seeing for the first time.

If there is a crisis in world photojournalism today, it is a crisis of editing and publishing, not of photography. We have thousands of magazines, some of them excellent and a few very profitable, but most are edited by their readers. Nowhere is this clearer than in France, where *Paris Match*, currently the world's most sophisticated popular picture magazine, is also one of the most shameless. The August 21, 1997, *Match* cover was headlined: *"Diana: Le Baiser"* ("Diana: The Kiss"), with a sequence of color pictures devoted to the princess and her Egyptian playboy boyfriend, Dodi Al Fayed, in their bathing suits, billed as *"Exclusif: le reportage qui bouleverse la famille royale"* ("the reportage that deeply distresses the royal family"). Three weeks later *Match* ran a chaste black-and-white portrait by Patrick Demarchelier on its cover, "courtesy of *Harper's Bazaar.*" Inside, fifty unbroken picture pages told Diana's life story—with substantial assistance from the detested paparazzi. Perhaps this one issue of *Match* best demonstrates the clear editorial and public ambivalence concerning the ethics of photojournalism. Had photographers not so covered her, people throughout the world would never have come to know, love, and—ultimately—mourn their princess.

On that fateful night of August 30, 1997, photographers from Gamma, Sygma, and Sipa joined the paparazzi in pursuit of Princess Diana. In the soul-searching that followed her death, Gamma's cofounder Raymond Depardon said he could not help but feel ashamed of the course taken by his former colleagues, although he blamed today's relentless commercial pressures. "It is up

Paris Match is currently the world's most sophisticated popular picture magazine. It is also one of the most shameless, as witness these two covers, separated by three weeks and by an event—the death of Princess Diana—that would create a raging global debate about the taking of celebrity images and their consumption. *Courtesy,* Paris Match/RIGHT: PATRICK DEMARCHELIER/*Camera Press/Imapress*

to each [journalist] to determine his own conduct," he said, adding that he himself had abandoned long-lens photography. Nevertheless, he warned that candid, unposed pictures should remain the goal of photojournalists: "These are the images that permit us to understand our times. . . . All the great [photographers] have worked this way, photographing in the street, without asking permissions."

Unlike Henry R. Luce, who had the courage of his convictions, today's editors watch to see what sells, just as today's politicians adapt their policies to the polls. The line between journalism and entertainment is blurred. Most—thankfully, not all—American newspapers are more and more insular, ignoring the world. Fewer than half the pages in most publications *inform* the reader; the majority are there to *sell* something. Only *National Geographic,* among major magazines, runs picture stories unbroken by advertising. No wonder serious photographers have turned to producing books and exhibitions.

I cannot help but admire the courage and dedication of today's roving photojournalists. It's not just the Turnleys. Look at the pictures by James Nachtwey and Susan Meiselas of Magnum, Anthony Suau and Stanley Greene of Vu, and Christopher Morris of Black Star—to name only some Americans. They are an endangered species, as a report of the New York–based Committee to Protect

Journalists makes clear. In 1996, 27 journalists were killed and 185 were imprisoned in the pursuit of their duties throughout the world.

Since 1989, a remarkable annual convention has been held in the sunny Catalan city of Perpignan, in southern France. Called Visa Pour l'Image, it is the annual festival for the world's photojournalists, with exhibitions, projections, press conferences, and debates. In 1990, a young photographer named Gad Gross attended the festival, having just graduated from Harvard. He had been inspired by Robert Capa and Don McCullin to cover postrevolutionary Romania. He found, to his disillusionment, "how quickly the people are forgotten in their misery, once that misery has stopped being sensational." Early in 1991, a Kurdish rebel soldier offered to take Gross and two other journalists into Iraq to cover the Kurds' struggle for independence. They ran into an Iraqi patrol. Gross and his escort were killed; the other two journalists escaped. At the Harvard memorial service, one of Gross's teachers said, "I think he felt that his actions mattered, that his photographs could change people's views." That epitaph speaks for many, if not most, of the young photographers who roam the world today.

The 1997 Perpignan photojournalism festival happened to begin on the day of Diana's death. As usual I attended. Unfortunately, also as usual, virtually all the pictures on serious subjects that were shown there—stories on the causes of war, disease, famine, crime, poverty—are seldom seen in the press. The world does not seem to wish to face its problems. It is ironic that Diana's death momentarily focused attention on a world conference in Oslo devoted to the elimination of land mines, a favorite and worthy cause of hers. Photojournalists have done their part to record this horror. It's up to editors to publish such pictures, and it's up to the public to acknowledge this important work.

This picture was shot in Kuwait in the aftermath of the Gulf War by the Brazilian photographer Sebastião Salgado. I have chosen it to open the last chapter of this book for two reasons: it dramatizes to me the futility of war, a scourge of humanity and the environment; and it demonstrates the power of still photography to compress a lasting message into one image, the special power that is photojournalism's. SEBASTIÃO SALGADO/*Contact Press Images*

34

The Gulf

In his book *Second Front*, a powerful indictment of press coverage of the 1991 war in the Persian Gulf, John R. MacArthur writes, "The press has never prevented a war from starting and has never forced the government to terminate one." Perhaps. In the case of the Gulf War, it could even be said that the American mainstream press actually promoted war. This led me for a time, in the winter of 1990–1991 in Paris, to become a political activist. I had hoped that America had learned a lesson from Vietnam, that our country would never again go recklessly to war to fight for unclear and undebated objectives. But in the 1980s the Cold War was still with us, a war mercifully unfought, but one with long-lasting psychological consequences. It left us with unreasoned fears. It also brought us a massive "defense" establishment, an establishment always eager to prove its worth.

In 1983 a situation developed in the tiny Caribbean island republic of Grenada. The nine-year-old nation of 90,000, known mostly for nutmeg, was in a state of acute unrest. Its Marxist prime minister had been assassinated, and the six-member Organization of Eastern Caribbean States, all former British colonies, called upon the United States to restore "peace and stability." The Reagan administration was more than happy to respond. The president saw little Grenada, where six hundred Cubans were building an airfield, as "a Communist beachhead." The "lovely little war," in the words of one correspondent, lasted about forty-eight hours. Its contribution to military history is insignificant, except for one important innovation: Grenada allowed the Pentagon to test a new system of press coverage, or rather *non*-coverage. The White House at first lied, saying that the invasion was not under way, when in fact it was. Only the picture agency Sygma, which had had the foresight to get a film crew to Grenada before the invasion, obtained significant pictures. *National Geographic* reviewed the situation one year later, publishing no combat pictures at all. The island has not been heard from since.

George Bush, Ronald Reagan's heir, actually benefited from photojournalism in his 1989 rout of Panamanian "strongman" General Manuel Antonio Noriega. On May 7, 1989, the general set aside the results of the presidential election, holding on to power for himself. Three days later, the men who had been elected protested in the streets of Panama City and were beaten up by Noriega's paramilitary "Dignity Battalions." Vice president–elect Guillermo Ford was beaten repeatedly. As he staggered down the street, covered with blood, he was photographed by a television cameraman and by Les Stone of Reuters and Ron Haviv of AFP. George Bush saw the film on television and held an emergency meeting that night in the White House. Bush told the meeting that such an attack on *Americans* would be intolerable, requiring immediate action. The Pentagon was ordered to prepare plans for a U.S. military coup, under the code name Blue Spoon, later changed to Just Cause.

Seven months later the trigger came along. An off-duty Marine lieutenant ran a Panama Defense Force roadblock and was shot dead. A Navy lieutenant, who had witnessed the shooting, was held four hours and roughed up. That was enough for the Joint Chiefs of Staff and the president. Twenty-four thousand men and women went into action, along with weapons of high sophistication, including the first use of the F-117A Stealth fighter-bomber. U.S. casualties included 24 dead, 324 wounded. The Panamanian casualties can only be estimated, but it seems probable that for every American killed there were at least ten dead Panamanians—the majority *civilians.*

The American press, although complaining about the lack of journalistic "opportunity," was almost universally supportive of Just Cause. A hastily organized press pool was flown in after. Only one picture of the Panama invasion turned up in NPPA's annual *Best of Photojournalism*. It showed a camouflage-clad soldier using hand signals to order an orange soda at a lunch counter in Panama City. The other customers were paying no attention.

Richard Cheney, George Bush's secretary of defense, and Colin Powell, the new chairman of the Joint Chiefs of Staff, were elated with their successful application of the doctrine of "overwhelming force"—and presumably with how they had put one over on the press. They would soon have a chance to apply their discoveries on a much broader scale. When news reached Washington on the evening of Wednesday, August 1, 1990, that Iraqi tanks were rolling down a six-lane superhighway into Kuwait City, Defense Secretary Dick Cheney and General Colin Powell stayed home. Powell told *The Washington Post,* "This ain't our show." The president arose early and signed an executive order freezing Iraqi assets in the United States and shutting off trade. He then left for Aspen,

Colorado, first telling the press that military intervention was not under consideration. Unfortunately for future world tranquillity, George Bush shared the platform of the Aspen Institute later that day with Margaret Thatcher, who well recalled her triumph in the Falkland Islands in 1982. Reminding Bush of Neville Chamberlain's capitulation to Hitler in Munich, she said, Saddam Hussein "must be stopped." Bush returned from Aspen Thursday night a changed man. General Norman Schwarzkopf, commander in chief of the portable "Central" Command, based at MacDill Air Force Base, Florida, was asked to come up with a plan for "defending" Saudi Arabia. Troop deployment began.

I followed the situation in a state of alarm and, with seventeen expatriate friends, organized Americans for Peace. Our aim was to discourage combat and to find other means of punishing Saddam Hussein. We petitioned the White House and Congress. We marched twice to the American embassy, the second time more than a hundred strong. We joined the protest marches of other Parisians, which drew up to 100,000 people. Our AMERICANS FOR PEACE banner was applauded the length of the route. Through paid announcements in the *International Herald Tribune,* our movement spread to London, Geneva, Rome, Stockholm, Tokyo, and Washington, involving about a thousand people worldwide. Not one picture appeared in the American press. I reflected, cynically, that if only Jane Fonda had joined our first march—she and husband Ted Turner had visited Paris the week before—we would have made the U.S. papers.

It astonished me how uncritically the media went along with the military buildup. As in the Tonkin Gulf, so it was in the Persian. On November 1, George Bush gave a secret order: double the force in Saudi Arabia, but don't tell anybody until after the congressional election of November 6. On January 17, at precisely the time secretly planned, the one-way aerial war began. Not only did the worldwide public receive pictures—LIVE!—of bombing with "pinpoint precision," the public also saw—LIVE!—for the first time ever, pictures that gave a small idea of what it was like to be under aerial bombardment. They were taken from the comparative comfort of the ninth-floor hotel room of CNN's Peter Arnett. Arnett also managed to go into the streets to inspect damage, interview bomb victims, and, eventually, interview Saddam Hussein. From the Pentagon's viewpoint this was a disturbing development. It was hinted that Arnett was a traitor.

For the ground war to come, the Pentagon announced rules that represented a throwback to the censorship and pooling of World War II—as updated by Ronald Reagan's policy of noncoverage in Grenada. Nothing could be published that the Department of Defense wanted kept secret. Journalists covering combat would be required to join pools, and "minders" would accompany them to avoid giving offense to "Arab sensibilities." There was to be no freedom of movement, as there had been in Vietnam. Copy, pictures, and tapes would have to be cleared. The picture pool consisted of five members: Associated Press, Reuters, *Time, Newsweek,* and *U.S. News & World Report.* They agreed to the restrictions. Fortunately, though, the system soon broke down. Journalists, led by the foreign press, went off on their own. Some, such as the French agency Sygma, had their own direct satellite links, and thus could avoid the censorship. Thus Sygma, as a group, managed to produce a fairly comprehensive visual record of the war. The Sygma book *In the Eye of Desert Storm* was even supported by Kodak. David Turnley of the *Detroit Free Press* managed to dodge his "minder" by joining a medical evacuation unit. Aboard a helicopter, he took a remarkable picture of an American sergeant crying when he learned that the body bag next to him contained his buddy—killed by "friendly" fire. Even so, Turnley found his photo on a censor's desk, unsent. Rescued from oblivion, it became the World Press Photo of the year.

The Gulf War was a manifestation of Pentagon *Impact* once again, the enemy shown not as human beings but as impersonal targets. Televised press conferences showed bombs striking home, but not the women and children who were annihilated by "accident" when a "smart" bomb went berserk. Nor did TV show the faces of the unknown hundreds or thousands of Iraqi soldiers who became corpses in the desert. Americans for Peace continued to protest right through the final Senate debate in January 1991. The margin for war, as opposed to sanctions, was narrow, but the administration said the vote would not matter anyhow. When the ground war actually started, Americans for Peace dissolved. As overseas Americans, we did not wish to be charged with deserting our country, even though we thought it in the wrong.

The Gulf War did much to remind us what photojournalists can and can't do, and also what they can do and don't. They are not very good at reporting on the root causes of conflict and war. It is so much easier to wait for the action. Journalists constantly miss the early warnings. The world would profit if as much attention were paid to forecasting crisis as to forecasting the weather. Most Americans had little idea of what Iraq and Kuwait even looked like. Neither were most aware that Iraq had for years been waging a deadly war with Iran, with American aid. Had they been faithful readers of *National Geographic,* they would at least have had some idea of this. In 1988, the *Geographic* published an informative twenty-four-page article on the Gulf, opening with a dramatic color picture of a Singaporean tanker ablaze from an attack by Iranian gunboats and including a picture of a U.S. helicopter carrier escorting a convoy of Kuwaiti tankers through the Gulf. The article pointed out that Iran had been given $19.5 billion of U.S. military aid under the shah and that eight years of war had already cost half a million lives, including thirty-seven crewmen of the U.S.S. *Stark.* This *National Geographic* article was published more than two years before Saddam Hussein's tanks rolled into Kuwait. It had been twenty-

David Turnley took this picture, arguably the best-remembered image of the Gulf War. Like Salgado's picture, it makes hollow that great sanitized "victory." In war, as in life, it ultimately comes down to the individual: here a soldier who cries when he discovers that the body bag next to him contains the remains of his close friend. DAVID TURNLEY/Detroit Free Press/*Black Star*

one years since the *Geographic* had published a piece just on Kuwait—with the charming title "Aladdin's Lamp of the Middle East." That's why the weekly *Life*, with its world picture coverage and speedy distribution, is sorely missed.

It is fashionable to blame television for the problems of print journalism, but I refuse to play that game. Television and print should not be journalistic adversaries. They complement each other. When it comes to a breaking story of worldwide significance, television is now the indispensable medium. In 1989 we watched breathlessly the protests in Tiananmen Square and the breakup of the Berlin Wall; the next year it was Boris Yeltsin standing on a tank in Moscow to confront a Russian coup. The world's statesmen now routinely form judgments based on such images. Perhaps someday world standards of photojournalism will reach the point where international conflicts will be covered evenhandedly by journalists from competing sides. This has happened to a small extent in Bosnia, in Chechnya, and in Palestine following the birth of *intifada*. It is one of the hopeful aspects of the growing outreach of World Press Photo. As of now, the goal of evenhanded world coverage is attained regularly only at the Olympics—and rarely at the United Nations. Once the photojournalists of *all* nations become equally well equipped—not just with cameras, lenses, and film but with visas and credit cards—new dimensions will emerge in the coverage of conflicts.

Revealing root causes takes a little imagination and more than a little courage. There is an international trade fair in Paris every two years called the Salon International de l'Aéronautique et de l'Espace. Some of the businessmen who attend it sell airplanes and related items. Many others are in the weapons business. Here one can buy "combat-tested" missiles, all kinds of "deterrents," and "kill mechanisms"—not to mention fighters, attack bombers, and helicopter gunships. The customers are ministers of "defense" and congressmen who deal with "procurement." They are wined and dined lavishly. They do not wish to be photographed, but there is no hiding the fact that this is the marketplace for what we used to call the Merchants of Death. During the Iraq-Iran conflict, buyers came to Paris from both sides. For years I proposed the subject of arms—and this trade show—to *National Geographic* as one of its "commodity" series, which normally feature such things as wool, silk, pearls, even trash.

One thing photojournalists can do very well is attract attention. There are plenty of things that need it: the shameful condition of schools and hospitals, defective products, threats to the environment. There are new inventions and good ideas, and not just in our own country. Photojournalism, by focusing the world's attention on one individual, personalizes history as never before, making it comprehensible to everyone. In Vietnam, it was Nick Ut's picture of a little girl running from napalm; in Colombia, it was Frank Fournier's picture of a girl slowly being engulfed in volcanic mud; it was David Turnley's picture of the crying sergeant and the body bag. Too often attention is instead focused on the same old celebrities.

To view transient images is not enough. To truly comprehend takes time, and studied comparison. Fortunately, the world now has some assurance that visual records will be preserved electronically and made available to all—first on screen and then, selectively, *in print*. We stand to gain an astounding museum without walls. The child of the future can become a picture editor by simply choosing from a daily menu. It will be the task of tomorrow's teachers to whet, and refine, that appetite.

In 1969 Midge and I attended the formal dinner at which Edward Steichen celebrated his ninetieth birthday at the Plaza Hotel. As he stood there, frail as a twig but still full of sap, he said, "When I first became interested in photography, I thought it was the whole cheese. My idea was to have it recognized as one of the fine arts. Today I don't give a hoot in hell about that. The mission of photography is to explain man to man and each man to himself. And that is no mean function." That indeed is the profound function of photojournalism. War represents failure, a failure to bridge the gulf of human misunderstanding. But war is not the only gulf. The gulf between rich and poor is perhaps the greatest, and the key to many others. In 1993, in São Paulo, I decided it would be appropriate to pay tribute to Sebastião Salgado before a group of Latin American journalists. Salgado is Brazilian, a quiet man whose pictures speak loudly. He had just completed a worldwide study of "workers"—men, women, and children who work with their hands, often under brutal conditions. In what is perhaps the most ambitious photographic project ever undertaken by one man, Salgado traveled to nineteen countries in six years. He photographed steelworkers in France and Ukraine, dam builders in India, slaughterhouse workers in the American Midwest, tea harvesters in Rwanda, sugarcane cutters in Cuba, "sandhogs" at work under the English Channel, ship salvagers in Bangladesh, oil workers taming the wild wells of Kuwait, and miners scrambling for gold in Brazil. His work is a bitter commentary on the Industrial Revolution. One of the most thoughtful of all photographers, Salgado writes, "The planet remains divided, the first world in a crisis of excess, the third world in a crisis of need, and, at the end of the century, the second world—that built on socialism—[is] in ruins. The destiny of men and women is to create a new world." A "Workers" exhibition is touring the world in three editions, and an oversize book has been published in seven languages.

Photojournalism provides a tool to bridge the gulfs of modern society. Photojournalism can be directed at introducing one man to another with respect and compassion. Call it "People Are People" journalism. Call it "Family of Man" journalism. Call it Salgado journalism. But that is not sufficient. John Steinbeck once said, "It is in the things not mentioned that the untruth lies." I would add: Untruth lies in the things *unphotographed*. The world is full of them. Those unmentionable words *and* pictures, working together, can reestablish truth in our time.

When Edward Steichen waved good-bye to me at his home in Connecticut one summer day in 1972, I knew instinctively that I would never see him again. I thought of what he had said, in celebrating his ninetieth birthday at the Plaza Hotel three years earlier: "The mission of photography is to explain man to man and each man to himself. And that is no mean function." © OLIVER MORRIS

Acknowledgments

Many persons are responsible for this book, perhaps most of all those who will never read it: my parents and teachers, notably Robert M. Hutchins and Norman Maclean, more famous for *A River Runs Through It* than for teaching me Freshman English at the University of Chicago. Some are people I never met, such as Lincoln Steffens, whose *Autobiography* inspired me to be a journalist. There was my brilliant classmate Tom Stauffer, with whom I sailed from New Orleans to London in 1935. Fortunately, some early friends (albeit questionable influences) survive: my fraternity brothers in Alpha Delta Phi, Jay Berwanger—first winner of football's Heisman Trophy—and Myron Davis, the kid from Kimbark Avenue who became one of *Life*'s star photographers. I am seriously indebted to another contemporary University of Chicagoan, historian William Hardy McNeill, who saw the potential in my first draft.

I was trained at *Life* in World War II. I saved my files of that period, but to refresh my memory I have sought out those with whom I worked in New York and in the *Life* bureaus in Chicago, Los Angeles, Washington, London, and Paris. The first was Hansel Mieth Hagel, whom I visited at Jackass Flats, the ranch that she and Otto Hagel lovingly created near Santa Rosa, California. Hansel and her companion, Georgia Brown, read every word and urged me on. Another Californian who generously gave me time was Sidney L. James, my great boss in the Los Angeles bureau. In Santa Barbara Richard Pollard shared his memories of *Life*'s halcyon Hollywood days. In addition to having lengthy conversations with Myron Davis and Hansel Mieth, I shared reminiscenses with *Life* photographers Horace Bristol, Ed Clark, John Dominis, David Douglas Duncan, Alfred Eisenstaedt, Andreas Feininger, Johnny Florea, Fritz Goro, Yale Joel, Mark Kauffman, Dmitri Kessel, Ralph Morse, Carl Mydans, Gordon Parks, John Phillips, George Rodger, David Scherman, George Silk, Peter Stackpole, and Charles Steinheimer. In addition to Sid James and Pollard, I have talked with the following *Life* writers and editors: Joseph Kastner, Shelley Smith Mydans, Gerard Piel, Wilmott Ragsdale, and Andrew Heiskell, Time Inc.'s ex-CEO—from whom I once collected Newspaper Guild dues. Whenever I could, I visited Edward K. Thompson, *Life*'s great managing editor, in Westchester. I have also drawn on three exhaustive biographies of *Life* photographers: *Margaret Bourke-White*, by Vicki Goldberg; *Robert Capa*, by Richard Whelan; and *W. Eugene Smith, Shadow & Substance*, by Jim Hughes. I owe much to all three, and also to Vicki for her *The Power of Photography*. I have also drawn on autobiographical works by Alfred Eisenstaedt, Philippe Halsman, Dmitri Kessel, Gjon Mili, Carl Mydans, John Phillips, and Peter Stackpole. I thank Kenneth Schlesinger and Bill Hooper of the Time Inc. Archives; Oliver Gramling, whose *AP, The Story of News* provides background on Wilson Hicks; Antony Penrose, for *The Lives of Lee Miller*; and William L. Shirer, for *The Rise and Fall of the Third Reich*.

When it comes to *Ladies' Home Journal* there's a different cast of characters. I kept in touch by mail with Bruce and Beatrice Gould long after their retirement to Hopewell, New Jersey, and in person with Mary Bass Newlin at her homes on Park Avenue and in Amagansett, Long Island. The Goulds' daughter, Mrs. Frederic B. Krafft, kindly lent photographs. Dee Knapp, my last *Journal* assistant, gave invaluable help. I also thank Tina Fredericks, who succeeded me as the *Journal*'s picture editor and later made the layouts for the *Journal*'s three-part biography of Jacqueline Kennedy. Two of the *Journal*'s staff writers, Joan Younger Dickinson and Maureen Daly McGivern, gave friendly criticism. "Vi" Edom, widow of the University of Missouri's Cliff Edom, refreshed my memories of the Missouri workshops.

I wish to express my thanks to Katharine Graham, Herblock, Russell Wiggins, and Ben Gilbert of *The Washington Post* for continued friendship after my abrupt departure from the *Post*. I thank Ben Bradlee for giving me access to *Post* pictures, and for tipping me off to the best microfilm of *Post* pages—at the Library of Congress. Thomas N. Schroth, former editor of *Congressional Quarterly*, and his wife, Patricia, helped me sort out the trauma of 1964–65. For the record of what actually happened in the Tonkin Gulf I have relied on many recent books, but particularly on Stanley Karnow's *Vietnam: A History*.

At *The New York Times* I should like to thank Clifton Daniel, who hired me, and Gene Roberts, who reviewed portions of my manuscript several weeks before he learned that he would return to the *Times* as managing editor. Of all other *Times* people, past and present, space permits singling out only my soul mates Gloria Emerson and Sydney Schanberg and four photographers who are practically members of my family: Joyce Dopkeen, Donal Holway, Paul Hosefros, and Librado "Lee" Romero.

In between my magazine and newspaper careers came Magnum, the most curious organization of all. Magnum's photographers generally get the credit, and they deserve it, but I should also like to thank the staff members who worked such long hours: Seemah Battat, Inge Bondi, Olga Brodsky, Allen Brown, Nicole Clarence, Trudy Feliu, Sally Goodman, Bessie Grunwald, Sam

Holmes, Lee Jones, Kate Lewin, Gedeon de Margitay, Susie Marquis, Mireille Presle, Margot Shore, Natalie Smith, attorney Howard Squadron, and Michelle Vignes. Also those married to Magnum: Rosellina Bischof, Edith Capa, Yvonne Halsman, Traudl Lessing, Jinx Rodger, and Tess Taconis. Without them, and their successors, there would be no Magnum to celebrate today. I thank Magnum photographers Cornell Capa, Henri Cartier-Bresson, George Rodger, Eve Arnold, and Marc Riboud for critiquing the Magnum chapters, but do not hold them responsible. Magnum's "fortieth anniversary" volume, *In Our Time*, has an excellent historical essay by Fred Ritchin and useful biographies of Magnum photographers by Stuart Alexander.

My move to Paris in 1983 was supported by *National Geographic*, whose alumni W. E. Garrett and Robert E. Gilka have been most helpful. C.D.B. Bryan's *The National Geographic Society: 100 Years of Adventure and Discovery* is the best reference on the *Geographic*'s history. For information on the Paris photojournalism scene I am indebted to Robert Pledge of Contact, Jimmy Fox of Magnum, Phyllis Springer of Sipa, Christian Caujolle of Vu, and to Thomas Gunther, Russ Melcher, Max Scheler, and Warren Trabant. I also drew on John Faber's *Great Moments in News Photography* and on *Profession Photoreporter* by Michel Guerrin of *Le Monde*. For editorial assistance in Paris, I thank Gail Alexander, Stuart Alexander, and Sheldon Heitner.

I should like to pay special tribute to the fifty-three photographers whose work enlivens these pages. Some have given their lives in pursuit of our profession. To call the roll, with the pages where their work appears: Eddie Adams, *238*; Gail H. Alexander, *292*; Rus Arnold, *122*; Peter Bally, *152*; Werner Bischof, *157*; Ron Bennett (UPI), *244*; Neal Boenzi, *235*; Philippe Bonsignour, *296*; Jim Brandenburg, *280*; Esther Bubley, *110*; Cornell Capa, *188*; Robert Capa, *2, 75, 77, 83, 117, 118, 158, 159*; Henri Cartier-Bresson, *86, 140, 162*; Eileen Darby, *38*; Myron Davis, *10, 96*; Patrick Demarchelier, *298*; Joseph Di Pietro, *104*; Alfred Eisenstaedt, *24, 168*; Eliot Elisofon, *52, 57, 59*; Elliott Erwitt, *146, 192* (3); Burt Glinn, *179, 198*; Yvonne Halsman, *34*; Dirck Halstead, *160, 161*; David Alan Harvey, *282*; Bob Henriques, *188*; Tana Hoban, *jacket*; Jack D. Hubbard, *254*; Bob Landry, *48*; Michel Laurent, *262*; Leo Lönnbrink, *205*; Fred W. McDarrah, *246*; Lee Miller, *frontispiece*; Oliver Morris, *307*; Charlie Nye, *127*; Ruth Orkin, *100, 152*; Man Ray, *67*; George Rodger, *139*; Jack Rottier, *202*; Sebastião Salgado, *300*; Jurgen Schadeberg, *271*; David E. Scherman, *66*; Frank Scherschel, *64*; Gary Settle, *253, 272*; David Seymour, *170, 177*; George Silk, *42*; Ernest Sisto, *237*; W. Eugene Smith, *back cover, 26, 180, 183, 275*; Peter Stackpole, *10, 39, 49*; James A. Sugar, *286*; David Turnley, *front cover, 305*; Paul Wagner, *12*; Alex Webb, *194*; Yosuke Yamahata, *98*.

This is also the place to thank, for permission to use unpublished letters, the estates of Ansel Adams, Werner Bischof, Robert Capa, Marlene Dietrich, Ernst

Haas, George Rodger, David Seymour, W. Eugene Smith, and Edward K. Thompson.

Finally, I thank my agent, Robert Lescher, and the veteran editor Gene Young, who critiqued my first draft. I thank Harold Evans, who accepted the second one for Random House. I also thank Sean Abbott, editor; Sybil Pincus, production editor; Lynn Anderson, copy editor; Evan Stone and Kevin Sweeney, proofreaders; Deborah Foley for handling permissions; and designer Tanya Pérez-Rock. For help in rounding up illustrations, I thank Linda Amster, Margaret Beall, Debra Cohen, Mary Engel, Bruce Garvey, Marie-Pierre Giffey, Jane Halsman, Elaine Hart, Michele Laurent, Barbara Mancuso, Doreen Landry Millichip, Shogo Yamahata, and Antony Penrose, keeper of the Lee Miller Archives in Chiddingly, East Sussex.

Unfortunately, my generation of photojournalists—by which I mean the generation with which I started—is fast "disappearing," as the French say. No less than thirteen of my *Life* colleagues mentioned above have left us since I began work on this memoir in 1989. Thus it is with great pride and pleasure that I confirm that the University of Chicago Library has created a "John G. Morris Special Collection" that will house my papers.

Index

Page numbers in *italics* refer to photographs.

ABOUT THE AUTHOR

JOHN G. MORRIS grew up in Chicago and was educated at the University of Chicago. He was a Hollywood correspondent for *Life*, picture editor for *Life*'s London bureau during the war years, picture editor at *Ladies' Home Journal*, the first executive editor of Magnum Photos, picture editor for both *The Washington Post* and *The New York Times*, and a correspondent and editor for *National Geographic*. Morris lives in Paris with his wife, photographer Tana Hoban.

ABOUT THE TYPE

This book was set in Photina, a typeface designed by
José Mendoza in 1971. It is a very elegant design
with high legibility, and its close character fit has
made it a popular choice for use in quality magazines and art gallery publications.